Lecture Notes in Computer Sci

Edited by G. Goos, J. Hartmanis, and J. va

T0250601

Springer
Berlin
Heidelberg
New York
Barcelona
Hong Kong
London
Milan
Paris
Tokyo

Ákos Frohner (Ed.)

Object-Oriented Technology

ECOOP 2001 Workshop Reader

ECOOP 2001 Workshops, Panel, and Posters
Budapest, Hungary, June 18-22, 2001
Proceedings

 Springer

Series Editors

Gerhard Goos, Karlsruhe University, Germany
Juris Hartmanis, Cornell University, NY, USA
Jan van Leeuwen, Utrecht University, The Netherlands

Volume Editor

Ákos Frohner
CERN, 31R-015
1211 Genève, Switzerland
E-mail: Akos.Frohner@cern.ch

Cataloging-in-Publication Data applied for

Die Deutsche Bibliothek - CIP-Einheitsaufnahme

Object oriented technology : ECOOP 2001 workshop reader ; ECOOP 2001
workshops, panels, and posters, Budapest, Hungary, June 18 - 22, 2001 /
Ákos Frohner (ed.). - Berlin ; Heidelberg ; New York ; Barcelona ; Hong Kong ;
London ; Milan ; Paris ; Tokyo : Springer, 2002
    (Lecture notes in computer science ; Vol. 2323)
    ISBN 3-540-43675-8

CR Subject Classification (1998): D.1-3, H.2, F.3, C.2, K.4, J.1

ISSN 0302-9743
ISBN 3-540-43675-8 Springer-Verlag Berlin Heidelberg New York

Springer-Verlag Berlin Heidelberg New York
a member of BertelsmannSpringer Science+Business Media GmbH

http://www.springer.de

© Springer-Verlag Berlin Heidelberg 2002
Printed in Germany

Typesetting: Camera-ready by author, data conversion by PTP-Berlin, Stefan Sossna e.K.
Printed on acid-free paper   SPIN 10846694   06/3142   5 4 3 2 1 0

Preface

For the fifth time in its history, in cooperation with Springer-Verlag, the European Conference on Object-Oriented Programming (ECOOP) conference series is glad to offer the object-oriented research community the ECOOP 2001 Workshop Reader, a compendium of workshop reports, panel transcripts, and poster abstracts pertaining to the ECOOP 2001 conference, held in Budapest from 18 to 22 June, 2001.

ECOOP 2001 hosted 19 high-quality workshops covering a large spectrum of research topics. The workshops attracted 460 participants on the first two days of the conference.

Originally 22 workshops were chosen from 26 proposals by a workshop selection committee, following a peer review process. Due to the overlaps in the areas of interest and the suggestions made by the committee six of the groups decided to merge their topics into three workshops. This book contains information on the panel, poster session, and 17 workshop reports, for which we have to thank our workshop organizers, who did a great job in preparing and formatting them.

The reports are organized around the main line of discussion, comparing the various approaches and giving a summary on the debates. They also include the list of participants, affiliations, contact information, and the list of contributed position papers. Although they usually do not include abstracts or excerpts of the position papers, they do give useful references to other publications and websites, where more information may be found.

Most of the reports are less than 20 pages long, but there are two exceptions: *Quality of Service in Distributed Object Systems and Distributed Multimedia Object/Component Systems* and *Advanced Separation of Concerns*. We respected the need here for a larger number of pages, since both workshops attracted a high number of participants and lasted for two days.

This book was only possible due to the help of the respective workshop organizers and the panel, poster, and workshop organizers in general.

February 2002   Ákos Frohner

Organization

ECOOP 2001 was organized by the Informatics Department of the Eötvös Loránd University under the auspices of AITO (Association Internationale pour les Technologies Objets) in cooperation with ACM/SIGPLAN.

The proceedings of the main conference were published as LNCS 2323.

Workshop Co-chairs: Ákos Frohner (Eötvös Loránd University)
Jacques Malefant (Université de Bretagne Sud)
Erzsébet Angster (Dennis Gábor College)

Panel Chair: Tamás Kozsik (Eötvös Loránd University)

Poster Co-chairs: Viktória Zsók (Eötvös Loránd University)
István Juhász (University of Debrecen)

Workshop Selection Committee

Ákos Frohner (Eötvös Loránd University, Budapest, Hungary)
Jacques Malefant (Université de Bretagne Sud, Vannes, France)
Erzsébet Angster (Dennis Gábor College, Budapest, Hungary)
Sabine Moisan (INRIA Sophia Antipolis, France)

Table of Contents

11th Workshop for PhD Students in Object-Oriented Systems

Gilles Ardourel[1], Michael Haupt[2], José Luis Herrero Agustín[3]**,
Rainer Ruggaber[4], and Charles Suscheck[5]

[1] LIRMM, University of Montpellier, France
ardourel@lirmm.fr
[2] Institute for Software Technology, Darmstadt University of Technology, Germany
haupt@informatik.tu-darmstadt.de
[3] University of Extremadura, Spain
jherrero@unex.es
[4] Institute of Telematics, University of Karlsruhe, Germany
ruggaber@tm.uka.de
[5] TurboPower Software Company, USA
charless@turbopower.com

Abstract. At its 11th edition, the PhDOOS workshop has become an established annual meeting of PhD students in object-orientation. The main objective of the workshop is to offer an opportunity for PhD students to meet and share their research experiences, to discover commonalities in research and studentship, and to foster a collaborative environment for joint problem-solving. PhD students from both industry and academia are encouraged to attend in order to ensure a broad, unconfined discussion. Senior researchers are also welcomed during the plenary sessions, as they may provide insightful viewpoints and advices to the PhD participants. The workshop also aims at strengthening the international Network of PhD Students in Object-Oriented Systems (PhDOOS). Initiated during the 1st edition of this workshop series at ECOOP'91, this network counts approximately 125 members from all over the world. There is a mailing list and a WWW site, used mainly for information and discussion on OO-related topics.

1 Workshop Aims

This report is on the 11th PhDOOS workshop, held over two days (June 18–19, 2001) in conjunction with ECOOP2001 in Budapest, Hungary. PhDOOS is an unusual workshop in that it does not aim to bring together researchers sharing a particular common research goal. Rather, all attendees are Ph.D. students researching topics with a major emphasis on object orientation. PhDOOS is essentially a regular workshop in that papers are submitted and reviewed, accepted papers are presented formally, a proceedings is published and a series of workshops is held.

The intent of the workshop to give participants exposure to presenting and interacting at conferences, to the organizers exposure to running conferences, and to stimulate the cultivation of a research community. Besides technical goals, the workshop also aims at

** supported by CICYT under contract TIC99-1083-C02-02

Á. Frohner (Ed.): ECOOP 2001 Workshops, LNCS 2323, pp. 1–6, 2002.
© Springer-Verlag Berlin Heidelberg 2002

bringing Ph. D. students together for the exchange of experiences in all areas of research and social life.

The acceptance rate of submitted papers is deliberately high. The aim here is to be inclusive rather than exclusive, providing encouragement to Ph. D. students to remain involved in conference-based exchange throughout and subsequent to the completion of their Ph. D. studies.

2   The Conference Program

Like every year the workshop received papers covering a wide range of topics. These ranged from theoretical aspects of object-oriented systems to engineering aspects of object-oriented systems. The accepted papers were to our best knowledge grouped to sessions and presented together. It was not always easy to find a suitable grouping for the papers. The papers and the discussions following the presentations are organized following this grouping. The accepted papers can be found on the workshop homepage at

`http://www.st.informatik.tu-darmstadt.de/phdws`

2.1   Aspect Orientation

Currently aspect orientation receives a lot of attention in research. This can also be seen by the large number of papers that were accepted for presentation. There was a lot of good discussion on the presentations and afterwards during breaks, as people looking at aspect orientation from very different angles were able to contribute to the discussions.

Michael Haupt [1] had the honour of starting the workshop with his presentation. He identified a lack of support for component-based software development in existing programming languages. Even though the object-oriented approach was meant to solve the problem, it did not. Integration-oriented extensions are needed. As a solution he presented JADE (Java Adapter Extension), a tool for the integration of components made available as object-oriented frameworks. Michael was expecting reduced development time and cost as the benefits.

In his presentation Miguel Pérez [2] looked at the relationship between aspect-oriented programming and component based development. He identified the problem that the appearance of aspect-oriented programming has created different models that are incompatible and thus prohibit a cross-model reuse. His idea was to reuse the aspect code obtained from different AOP models and use them as components (so-called aspect components). Furthermore he tried to describe the semantic behaviour so that aspect components can be selected and retrieved from component repositories. In the discussion he pointed out that he used modified sequence diagrams to describe the semantics of AOP and that this methodology applies for new components only.

Paniti Netinant [3] was focusing on aspect orientation in operating system design. As two-dimensional models are not sufficient, he presented a framework that enables a clear separation of concerns. New aspects can be easily added to systems using this framework. The interaction of aspects is specified by a contract, that binds a new aspect to the rest of the system. In response to audience feedback, Paniti described pre and post-conditions useful to verify the aspect properties. The framework itself is language independent and can be implemented in any language. In his prototype the weaving of aspects is done at runtime by the aspect moderator.

The talks of Pierre Crescenzo [4] and Adeline Capouliez [5] were both concerned with different aspects of the OFL (Open Flexible Languages). The OFL defines a meta model for object-oriented programming languages based on classes and is based on the three basic concepts of describing the generalization of the notion of class, relationships such as inheritance or aggregation and the languages themselves. The OFL is a model which enables the description object-oriented programming languages in order to adapt them to the needs of the programmer. In the discussion, Pierre pointed out that OFL is able to create a new language, e.g. it is possible to add multiple inheritance to Java. The resulting language will be executable on any JVM by using a meta-compiler.

In her work [5], Adelines goal was to extend object-oriented languages by orthogonal features like persistence or distribution of data. These features are described using the OFL, that in order to accomplish the given goal has to be extended by techniques from the aspect-oriented programming area.

2.2 Distributed Systems

Object-orientation in distributed systems is an area of research for many years that receives continuous attention. In this years workshop three papers on research in distributed systems were presented.

Attila Ulbert [6] was starting this session. In his work, he tried to overcome the limitations of frameworks for distributed programming regarding their adaptability as they offer only a fixed set of functionality. Especially with mobile computing in mind he described an extensible architecture that tries to overcome these limitations by making semantic elements first class entities. These semantic elements govern the process of remote method invocation, define the message encoding and decoding and determine the communication mechanism. One of the questions from the auditorium was concerned with transparency. Attila responded, that an integration of new features into IDL require a modification of the IDL compiler.

Cyril Ray [7] presented his solution to the scalability problem occurring during object migration in large distributed systems with a lot of objects involved. Instead of having dedicated connections between all the nodes and a single object migration, he proposes the RTB (Round Trip Bus Protocol), that realizes the analogue of a public transport bus to object-oriented distributed systems. He pointed out that further work is needed on the migration policy. Updating the references of migrated objects has to be done by a special service that is not implemented in the current prototype.

Hermes Senger [8] is working on a generic architecture for load balancing in distributed object computing systems. The system was designed for networks of non-dedicated and heterogeneous workstations and enables system and application monitoring. Both, requests and objects can be distributed. The systems realizes features like initial placement, replication and migration of objects. In the discussion Hermes pointed out that replication-safe objects can not be migrated but only be replicated because it is cheaper.

2.3   Design Patterns

In his presentation Yann-Gaël Guéhéneuc [9] used a meta-model to describe design patterns. Based on this meta-model a source-to-source transformation engine was developed that is able to modify the source code to comply with design patterns descriptions. He is also able to detect design patterns in the source code using the meta-model.

2.4   Agents

Ezzeddin Hattab [10] observed that due to the lack of specialized content management systems for web applications, web applications have problems with corrupted, outdated and inconsistent content. He gives an in-depth analysis of additional requirements that have to be met by a web change management. Ezzeddin proposed an agent oriented-approach to solve the problems, in which he maps roles to agents and organizes them in an hierarchical manner.

2.5   User Interface Design

Harald Stöttner [11] described a new approach to the design of platform-independent user interfaces. Based on the description of the user interface, the actual instantiation of a user interface is done by generic visualization components. The key idea in his approach are the so-called base elements, that are identical in each view. The base elements can be extended to customize semantic differences. Based on this description user interface elements unavailable on certain platforms can be emulated.

2.6   Theoretical Issues and Formal Approaches

Hung Ledang [12] addressed the problem of formalizing object-oriented specifications in B. This enables the formal verification of the object-oriented specification with tools supporting B. He emphasized on the modelling of the behavioural aspects of object-oriented specifications. Furthermore, he proposed a rigorous software development process based on the integration of object-oriented specifications and B.

Péter Csontos [13] added to a work presented at PhD-Workshop 2000. In that work the complexity of OO programs was measured. In the current talk, Péter presented an extension which provides a complexity measure for the complexity of exception-handling code. An exception is represented by an edge going from the function call either to the node representing the exception handling part inside the function or to the terminating node if the exception is not handled locally.

2.7   Invited Talks

This year's workshop was very happy and proud to welcome two invited speakers. The first one was Mira Mezini from the Darmstadt University of Technology. She presented her current work that deals with integrating aspect oriented programming with component-based software development. Her very interesting talk was entitled *Advanced Software Composition Techniques used in the Scope of Component-based Software*

Development. One of the main topics of the talk was the need for specifying very fine-grained join points to allow for detailed composition of independently developed software components.

The second invited talk was given by Ivar Jacobson from Rational Corp. He provided an interesting insight in upcoming topics of object-oriented software design. In his talk, entitled *Four Major Trends in Software Development* Ivar Jacobson identified the following trends: reusing components, quality assurance from the beginning, the need for a transparent software platform and using UML all the way down to the specification and even the execution of UML.

3 Concluding Remarks

First of all we the organizers would like to thank all the participants to let the 11th PhD-Workshop happen. Without their initial submission, the presentation and the discussions this would not have been possible. All participants belong to the student network of Ph.D. Students in Object-Oriented systems (`http://www.ecoop.org/phdoos`) and encourage potential future participants to join. Another interesting tradition about the PhD-workshop is, that the organization of the following years workshop is done by this years participants. We are very happy that a big group of participants volunteered for the organization of the already scheduled 12th PhD-Workshop in Malaga, Spain. We wish the organizers all the best and a successful workshop.

Many more thanks are due. Firstly, we would like to thank all the reviewers whose task was the quality-control of the submitted papers and the selection of those finally presented. A big thank you to our keynote speakers, Mira Mezini and Ivar Jacobson. And last but not least we would like thank AITO - without their generous financial support several participants would have been unable to attend.

List of Position Papers

1. Michael Haupt, `haupt@informatik.tu-darmstadt.de`
   (Institute for Software Technology, Darmstadt University of Technology, Germany),
   Concern Integration with JADE
2. Miguel A. Pérez and Amparo Navasa and Juan M. Murillo,
   `{toledano,amparonm,juanmamu}@unex.es` (Department of Computer Science,
   University of Extremadura, Cáceres, Spain), *Searching and recovering non-functional components*
3. Paniti Netinant, `netipan@iit.edu` (Computer Science Department, Illinois Institute of Technology, USA), *Supporting the Adaptable Operating System Design using Aspect-Oriented Framework*
4. Pierre Crescenzo, `Pierre.Crescenzo@unice.fr` (Laboratoire I3S, Sophia Antipolis, France), *The OFL Model to Customize Operational Semantics of Object-Oriented Languages: Application to Inter-Classes Relationships*
5. Adeline Capouillez, `Adeline.Capouillez@unice.fr` (Laboratoire I3S, Sophia Antipolis, France), *Improving the OFL Model Extendibility using Aspect-Oriented Programming Techniques*

6. Attila Ulbert, `mormota@elte.hu` (Department of General Computer Science, Etövös Loránd University, Budapest, Hungary), *Pluggable semantic elements and invocation semantics*

7. Cyril Ray, `ray@ecole-naval.fr` (MaGIS Project - IRENav, France), *Round Trip Bus: A protocol for migrating groups of objects*

8. Hermes Senger, `hermes.senger@cei.sp.senac.br` (SENAC College of Computer Science and Technology, Sao Paulo, Brazil), *Load Distribution for Distributed Object Computing Systems*

9. Yann-Gaël Guéhéneuc and Hervé Albin-Amiot, `guehene@emn.fr`, `albin@emn.fr` (Ecole des Mines de Nantes, Nantes, France), *Design Patterns: A Round-trip*

10. Ezzeddin Hattab and Foto Afrati, `ezz@softlab.ece.ntua.gr` (Electrical and Computer Engineering Dept, National Technical University of Athens, Athens, Greece), *Web Content Change Management using Agent-Oriented Approach*

11. Harald Stöttner, `harald.stoettner@ssw.uni-linz.ac.at` (Institut für Praktische Informatik, Johannes Kepler Universität, Linz, Austria) *A Platform-Independent User Interface Description Language*

12. Hung Le Dang, `ledang@loria.fr` (LORIA, University Nancy, Nancy, France), *Formal techniques in object-oriented software development: an approach based on the B method*

13. Péter Csontos and Zoltán Porkoláb, `csonti@elte.hu`, `gsd@elte.hu` (Department of General Computer Science, Etövös Loránd University, Budapest, Hungary), *On the Complexity of Exception Handling*

Quality of Service in Distributed Object Systems and Distributed Multimedia Object/Component Systems

László Böszörményi[1], Christian Stary[2], Harald Kosch[1], and Christian Becker[3]

[1] Institute of Information Technology, University Klagenfurt, Austria
{laszlo.boeszoermenyi, harald.kosch}@itec.uni-klu.ac.at
http://www-itec.uni-klu.ac.at/
[2] Department of Business Information Systems
University Linz, Austria
christian.stary@ce.uni-linz.ac.at
http://www.ce.uni-linz.ac.at/
[3] Institute of Parallel and Distributed High-Performance Systems
University Stuttgart, Germany
christian.becker@informatik.uni-stuttgart.de
http://www.informatik.uni-stuttgart.de/ipvr/vs/

Abstract. The workshop investigated, to what extent can component technology help to enhance the quality of distributed multimedia systems. Especially, to what extent can we achieve better reuse of multimedia content, reuse of code, interoperability, portability and performance. All authors agreed upon the necessity of building distributed multimedia systems of components as opposed to monolithic systems. The granularity of the components is an open issue, it can be stated, however, that most contributors presented solutions with rather heavy-weight components. Some of the presentations required explicitly standardization of multimedia formats, both for content and meta data. Most presenters touched the topic of multimedia-aware standardized middleware. Available middleware standards still do not support to a sufficient extent techniques to provide a guaranteed quality of service, and fit thus not well to be used for distributed multimedia.
Multimedia system providers are often not interested to publish their interfaces. Thus, even if the internal design is component-oriented, the rest of the world has not much gain from this. Academic research can push openness and have a positive influence on industry.

Keywords. distributed multimedia systems, quality of service, middleware, component based distributed multimedia systems, adaptivity

1 Introduction

1.1 Motivation for DMMOS

The design and implementation of distributed multimedia systems (especially multimedia infrastructure) show a high divergence among proprietary systems - multimedia standards being the only glue keeping them working together. If distributed multimedia is to become a key technology for the next decade then it must adopt object and

Á. Frohner (Ed.): ECOOP 2001 Workshops, LNCS 2323, pp. 7–29, 2002.
© Springer-Verlag Berlin Heidelberg 2002

component-based philosophies. Nowadays, multimedia systems are implemented partly in an ancient, monolithic style, which is acceptable for the childhood of a new technology, but which will not work in its mature phase. Much effort has been invested in developing frameworks to support the client-side of multimedia applications (such as Java Media Framework). Modern middleware approaches also incorporate both component-oriented and quality-of-service aspects (such as Corba 3.0 and Enterprise Java Beans). Object-relational databases provide progressively better support for storing and streaming multimedia data (such as Oracle Video Server). Multimedia standards, more and more, are covering the structuring of multimedia data (such as video-objects in MPEG-4) and are adding semantic information (such as MPEG-7). Nevertheless, relatively little attention has been paid so far to the software technology of entire, large-scale distributed multimedia systems (including applications and infrastructure). It is urgently needed to build fully connected bridges between the three still more or less independent areas: distributed, multimedia and object-oriented systems. These bridges might either stem from modelling approaches for designing or from implementation techniques for distributed multimedia systems. The aim of the workshop is to explore the potential of object and/or component technology in building complex distributed multimedia systems.

1.2 Motivation for QoSDOS

The suitability of the object model for the modelling and implementation of distributed systems has lead to middleware platforms, such as e.g. CORBA, DCOM, Java/RMI, and recently .Net and SOAP. Originally, these middleware systems aim at distribution transparency for application programmers.

However, distributed systems are exposed to system issues, like dynamic performance changes or partial errors, that prevent a complete distribution transparency. Quality of Service (QoS) management addresses these issues. The goal is to add QoS management to the interactions between clients and services.

Support for QoS management in distributed object systems is a hot topic of current research which poses a number of open questions: How is QoS integrated with the object model that emphasizes encapsulation and information hiding? Can one build generic support frameworks for multiple QoS categories, in contrast to specialized, single category systems, such as TAO, Electra, Eternal, DOORS among others? Can QoS be viewed as an aspect in the sense of Aspect Oriented Programming (AOP) or are other classifications more appropriate?

Based on nowadays object-oriented middleware platforms component based systems emerge. The necessity for QoS provision upholds for components as well. The integration of QoS specifications in component models as well as the mapping to underlying QoS provision of object systems is a challenge of the near future.

1.3 A Successful Merge

Realizing the commonality of our motivations and based on the content and the number of the submitted papers, we decided to merge the two workshops. This proved to become a successful merge. 12 papers were presented (from almost as many countries) in 4 sessions. The paper is organized as following: after the general introduction the main issues of the individual sessions are presented. These presentations are centered around the session chair person's introduction and questions, which try to express the essence of the contributions. The authors of the individual presentations had the possibility, beside answering the chair person's questions, to give a very compressed abstract of their work, and a corresponding URL pointing to more detailed technical descriptions. The session's chapters are concluded by the corresponding chair persons. The paper ends with a general conclusion and a common reference list.

In the following we give an overview of the most relevant issues of this double-workshop.

1.4   What Are the Aims and What Are the Problems?

If we build a component based distributed multimedia system, then – above basic functionality – we would like to incorporate the following, let say "compositional" features:

1. Reuse of multimedia content
2. Reuse of code
3. Interoperability
4. Portability
5. Performance

An orthogonal requirement is to provide the necessary *Quality of Service*. Portability, interoperability, reuse of code and content make only sense, if the entire system can provide exactly that QoS that is needed – regardless of the decomposition technology we use. For example, components of a distributed multimedia system can be called interoperable only then, when they are not only able to cooperate, but they can do that with the required QoS. If e.g. we want to deliver streamed video over interoperable middleware products, then it is not enough, if the connected middleware just delivers the video from one point to the other, it has also to preserve the required streaming quality all the time.

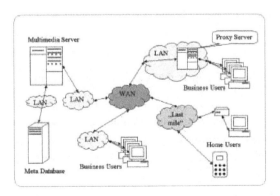

Fig. 1. A typical distributed multimedia system

If we take a look at Fig. 1, we can see the main components of a distributed multimedia system on a coarse granularity level. The arrows stay for communication paths. For most of these paths standardized communication protocols exist, enabling a certain level of interoperability. This is, however, only the smaller part of the story. If we would like to reach a certain level of most of the goodies on the list above, then we have to take a closer look at the elements of the list and their mapping to the components on Fig. 1.

Reuse of Multimedia Content. Multimedia (especially audio/visual) content is typically stored in multimedia storage servers, with a specialized architecture, which prefers striped storage and continuous delivery. Moreover, data describing the multimedia content is often stored in additional, so-called meta-databases. There are a number of de jure and de facto standards for both storing and delivering multimedia– and corresponding meta–data. However, there are a great number of open questions in this area, such as data management in collaborative hypermedia applications or dynamic extensions of databases by user-provided code, e.g. for efficient similarity search. These questions were addressed mainly by the first session, especially in 2.2 and 2.3.

Reuse of Code. The necessary preconditions for efficient reuse of code are that

1. We find the proper granularity of components
2. We take the effort to specify the interfaces

These questions were addressed mainly in the last session, especially in 5.1 in the context of an adaptable virtual video server, and in 5.2 and 5.4 in the context of reusable application code. It was also an important issue of the presentation in 4.1.

Interoperability. The emphasis at the discussion of this question lied mainly on the proper relation between middleware – as the key technology for interoperability – and Quality of Service. There were partly contradictory opinions about the proper placement of QoS management in layered architectures. There are good arguments to put most of the QoS management functionality into the middleware. This approach has, however, also some drawbacks. Related topics were discussed especially in 2.1, 2.2, 3.2, 4.1, 4.2 and 5.3

Portability. Surprisingly, no paper addressed this topic explicitly. This might have several reasons, the most relevant of these might be:

1. Java-based code is considered to be portable anyway – the truth of this statement should be left open at this place.
2. Building of multimedia systems is still in its very childhood, and therefore, portability is not yet a really urgent issue – it may become soon.

Performance. In this context, code mobility is a special issue, which was discussed by a surprisingly great number of presentations. As multimedia often needs high processing capacity, mobile code seems to be a very promising technology. It has the potential to provide solutions that are highly dynamic and efficient at the same time, as shown in 2.1, 2.2 and 3.2.

Quite another view of the performance problem is QoS optimization, e.g. by efficient caching techniques. A very interesting theoretical investigation of this issue was given in 3.3.

Presentation 3.1 introduced a simulation environment to figure out the real advantages of the differentiated services, especially as opposed to the integrated services. The simulation provides beside performance data also a basis for a real implementation.

2 Mobile Agents and Applications

Session Chair: Christian Stary

Distributed multimedia applications are designed to be or at least become highly flexible and reliable network-mediated environments. They require a thorough understanding of Quality of Service and higher level concepts in terms of

- worldwide availability of services, enabling location-independent access to utilities and features;
- asynchronous communication, enabling access and interaction that are coupled loosely over time;
- many-to-many communication and interaction, supporting networks of agents and communities of users as well as individual users and agents, respectively;
- multiple codalities of information, namely embedding time-independent (text, image etc.) as well as time-dependent information (audio, video etc.) into distributed data management.

At the level of usage, achieving high QoS will lead to

1. a high degree of interactivity, i.e. active user or agent support rather than reactive behavior of users or agents;
2. the accumulation of group knowledge, such as organizational memories or shared repositories distributed over sites, however, timely updated and kept consistent;
3. supportive systems with respect to social or networked processes through real-time collaboration, making the status of engagement of users and agents available to communities.

The participants have been asked to provide answers to the following questions with respect to the application track:

1. The contributions were heterogeneous in the sense they do not tackle the same level of abstraction. However, each of them is related to another in terms of service provision. Please provide information about your developed or proposed services you consider to be relevant to be provided for applications built on top of your system / concept.

2. The concept of mobile agents is one that indicates the crucial role of virtuality in distributed multimedia systems. Please state, what, at the conceptual level, you consider essential for the structure of material (data), the manipulation facilities and navigation paths to be supported through mobile agents and virtual information spaces.

2.1 Vagabond: A CORBA-Based Mobile Agent System
by L. Zoltan and B. Goldschmidt (email: laszlo@iit.bme.hu)

Abstract. Although there is already a multitude of mobile agent systems around, we were curious how they worked, and how difficult it is to create one. On the workshop we have introduced our *Vagabond* mobile agent system.

The system uses CORBA as a networking middleware, and consists of *inns* (agencies) that are able to receive and run *vagabonds* (agents). The inns are simple CORBA object. The vagabonds are simple Java objects that implement the *Vagabond* interface. They can take any serializable object with them during migration.

The migration is simple. The client has to create the vagabond, and create two CORBA objects, *XNotibed* and *Itinerary*. The former gets the results from the agent, the latter has the information what agencies are to be visited.

The agent (its byte code and serialized state) is sent to the agency (*Inn*), which dynamically loads it, and calls its execute() method. After completion the agency sends the results to the *XNotibed*, gets the name of the next agency from *Itinerary* and sends the agent (with modified state) to it.

On the server side there is a security class: Watchman, which is an extension of java.lang.SecurityManager. The agents are started inside a thread (VagabondThread), and each thread has an own threadgroup. The number of threads per threadgroup can be set, and Watchman checks at every thread-modifying method call if the number of threads are exhausted or not. If yes, it throws a security exception, and thus prevents the agent to create a new thread. Furthermore it does not allow the agents to access threads outside their threadgroup.

In order to test the efficiency of our system, we compared it to two other available agent systems: Voyager and Grasshopper [1,2]. The results have shown that all the three had very similar round-trip-times, which suggests that our initial simple strategy is good enough in comparison.

We intend to improve to system to use SSL for network communications, and to incorporate XML to describe the agents' semantics to the agencies, thus enabling our system to communicate with other, arbitrary agencies that only have to implement a simple wrapper gate-keeper.

Answers

1. *Vagabond*'s most important feature is its simplicity and that is CORBA-based. These two aspects provide to users the opportunity to easily modify and tune the system to their specific needs, e.g. run it inside a multimedia database, while the system is fast and reliable enough for serious usage as well.

2. Creating our agent system we faced the problem of having no real and working standards available for interactions of mobile agent systems. We consider interoperability and heterogeneity the most important features of a distributed environment. Agent systems should have a common interface, agents should have standard semantics so that any agent could visit any agency without code-rewrite.

The Web page of *Vagabond* is:
`http://www.inf.bme.hu/~balage`.

2.2 Mobile Agents in a Distributed Multimedia Database System
by M. Döller and H. Kosch (email: {harald,mdoeller}@itec.uni-klu.ac.at)

Abstract. Distributed multimedia database systems are actually in use for many different applications (e.g. content-based retrieval (CBR)). These applications are mostly implemented as a client/server solution. This implicates main disadvantages (e.g. waste of bandwidth, waste of time, etc.). In this context, we introduced a new mobile agent technology, the so called M^3 system (**M**ulti**M**edia Database **M**obile agents) where the agency may reside inside an Oracle database. The advantage of this approach is the combination of advantages of mobile agent technologies (e.g. autonomy, mobility, enhancement of functionality) and database services such as recovery, transaction handling, concurrency and security. The M^3 agency system is implemented on top of the Oracle 8i JServer environment and realizes mobility with the embedded Visibroker Corba ORB. More technical information on our system can be found in [3].

Our M^3 agency system might lead to a new generation of distributed multimedia database systems. For instance, consider a distributed nearest-neighbor search for images. Instead of downloading the best matches from all involved image databases, as required in a client/server solution, the mobile agent incorporates the result of the first visit as internal state and uses it for further search. This has a double gain: (1) The agent can gather the, let's say, best three results from an arbitrary number of databases. (2) The database system can be advanced with any additional functionality (e.g. different image search algorithms, information filtering algorithms, data transforming algorithms, and so on.). Currently used agency systems residing in a database system focused only on simple database functionality (e.g. insert items into a datawarehouse [4]).

Answers In answer to the session chair's questions we can state the following:

1. Due to the fact that our M^3 agency system may run inside a database system it has direct access to its data through server-side JDBC. Moreover, the former server-side JDBC coupled with the *inter*Media Java classes allows the agency to propose direct and fast retrieval functionality of multimedia data. This is used by the agent's logic to provide more complicated and not yet available multimedia services. Such services could be for instance an image agent which implements a nearest-neighbor search or a information filtering algorithm.
2. The multimedia object types of Oracle's *inter*Media (i.e. ORDImage, ORDAudio and ORDVideo) provide methods for the access to the multimedia data as entire object or to their components (e.g. pixels, frames). Thus, the agent designer has to

supply only the algorithmic logic for the desired manipulation function, but not the access logic.

See for more information:
`http://www-itec.uni-klu.ac.at/~mdoeller.`

2.3 Data Management of Collaborative Hypermedia in Tele-education
by A. Auinger (email: andreas.auinger@ce.uni-linz.ac.at)

Abstract. The work being presented has been performed within the SCHOLION project, aiming at scalable technology for teleteaching and telelearning. SCHOLION is an application that couples hypermedia technology and Computer-Supported Work features for distributed learning. It is implemented as a client/server system, storing the learning material in a database on the server side. This database does not only contain the content of the material that may of any codality (text, image, video etc.) but also the context of usage, namely in terms of individual views on the material and the discussions of content among teachers and students.

The client as well as the server are designed platform-independent. At the client side the modules of the system are kept: the editor, the browser, and the discussion board that is linked to the content of the material stored in the database. The Oracle enterprise edition 8.1.5 data management is linked to Java 2 (JDK 1.3) applications via a an Oracle JDBC Thin Driver Type 4 connection. The conceptual structure of the learning material as well as that of the navigation and interaction minimizes data transmission required in the course of teaching and learning. Context-sensitivity is provided through the profile concept that keeps the material separated from the collaborative and individual actions, since they are stored with links to the material in the profiles, but apart from the multimedia data.

In the ambition to generate a higher degree of openness an XML version is currently developed, leading to two different markup languages, according to the separation of the material from the interaction part. The SCHOLION Markup Language SchoML will capture course material through general information, educational guidance, meta information, and content modules, whereas the Profile Markup Language ProML will structure course independent and course dependent knowledge, such as keywords and course history, respectively.

Answers In answer to the session chair's questions we can state the following:

1. SCHOLION requires high level services in terms of communication facilities, storage of material as well as content provision. Communication facilities are enablers for transmitting content, navigation and collaboration information in real time. As soon as two users collaborate a reliable communication has to be established.

   For the storage of material, information of different codalities has to be stored and be accessible for designing courses as well as improving the knowledge transfer process (e.g., through assigning a video to an answer in the discussion board). The material has to be accessible over the Internet in a consistent and timely way. Finally, the material's context of use has to be kept throughout interaction, in order to empower users to refer to content at any time of collaboration.

What the system delivers, are high level services in terms of a semantic structure and a set of collaboration features for context-sensitive navigation and interaction based on a consistent set of data and a context-sensitive, traceable history of collaboration among learners and teachers. It is a specific domain solution at a meta-layer, both at the structure and the behavior level.

2. The concept of mobile agents is one that indicates the crucial role of virtuality in distributed multimedia systems. Please state, what, at the conceptual level, you consider essential for the structure of material (data), the manipulation facilities and navigations paths to be supported through mobile agents and virtual information spaces.

Mobility in the domain of tele-teaching is a topic that has to be considered in the context of user needs as well as the different settings when and where knowledge transfer occurs. In case knowledge transfer might occur at remote locations it makes sense to provide a virtual terminal in form of PDA. However, not all users will be satisfied due to the limitations of such kind of terminals. The display might be too small, the processing power might be too low etc. As such mobile agents might be useful as complimentary device for interaction and collaboration, however with restricted capabilities for users to all respects - presentation and structure of material, features for interaction and navigation.

2.4 Session Chairs' Conclusions

Application development in the field of highly flexible distributed development embedding mobile agents, introducing personalized content-retrieval and context-sensitive collaboration features, highly depends on the availability of dependable and efficient services. As the contributions have revealed, according to the fact they were addressing different layers of distributed systems, not only at the level of request brokerage but also at the level of data management and human-computer interaction meeting both requirements, high performance, and reliability, require compromises, if not novel concepts.

In the Vagabond approach, networking has been based on CORBA instead of RMI or raw sockets for creating a mobile agent platform. In the M^3 approach, at the level of data management, mobility has been enabled through an agency on top of the database server concept with the embedded Visibroker Corba ORB leading to an efficient and effective for search procedures in image databases. In the tele-education solution, navigation and interaction information has been de-coupled from the content, in order to minimize network traffic with respect to transmit content. Context-sensitive interaction, in addition, requires a domain-oriented structure of the data.

Future development clearly point into abstract representation of middleware and data, in terms of XML. For instance, the Vagabond approach will be improved through using SSL for network communication. In the SCHOLION approach dedicated markup languages, one for the material, and one for interaction profiles, are going to be developed. Moving into that direction, developers expect a higher degree of interoperability as well as high-level descriptions of the semantics of services, software agents, and data structures. Both should lead to more efficient and effective distributed multimedia solutions.

3 Algorithms for Quality of Service (QoS)

Session Chair: László Böszörményi

In this session two presentations about QoS-aware middleware and one about optimization of QoS-aware resource management were given. It is still an open discussion whether or not it makes sense at all to invest great effort in QoS-aware resource management, instead of concentrating on enhancing raw power. It is not clear either, what is the proper place to implement such a resource management. Quality adaptation was also touched several times. Quality adaptation gives us a lot of freedom in maintaining multimedia, it is, however, not for free.

The participants have been asked to provide answers to the following questions:

1. Is QoS based resource management worth its value?
2. Is middleware the proper place for QoS support in distributed multimedia systems?
3. Is quality adaptation a viable technique for multimedia communication?

3.1 A Java-RMI Implementation of the Differentiated Services Architecture by S. Terrasa, S. Sáez, and J. Vila (email: ssaez@disca.upv.es)

Abstract. The paper presents a distributed object oriented simulator of the *Diffserv* [5, 6] architecture that is being implemented in Java. This simulator can be a useful tool to study different network configurations and to perform experiments to measure transmission rates, packet delays, jitter, required buffer sizes, and packet loss rates for different network configurations. The tool is also aimed to develop Diffserv components in a progressive way, thus providing a virtual environment where real components interact with simulated ones, that have not developed yet. The idea is providing a simulated environment where real components can be tested.

Answers

1. Is QoS based resource management worth its value?
   Yes. Particularly in Real-Time Systems this approach is now very promising since it provides a new way to specify requirements in a more flexible and comprehensive way. It allows to deal with a wider range of systems, specially a class of "soft" real-time systems (multimedia systems) with a wider range of applications than typical "hard" real-time systems whose specifications could only be expressed in terms of "deadlines" (deterministic maximum delays)
2. Is middleware the proper place for QoS support in distributed multimedia systems?
   It is not very clear yet. It strongly depends on the approach followed by QoS at network level and *IETF* decisions and the standards. Several models are still under discussion (integrated services, differentiated services...) Although complementary,

none of them has been consolidated or widely implemented. However, it seems to me that the *IntServ* model would fit better for placing QoS support in middleware. *DiffServ* is more a "network level" approach.

3. Is quality adaptation a viable technique for multimedia communication?
   Similar answer to the previous one. Although it seems the more logical approach it strongly depends on the future of networks. With nowadays networks, it seems clear that a compromise between quality and available bandwidth is the only way to support multimedia communication. Most multimedia servers (Real Server etc...) provide this feature, and they also use some kind of feedback from the network to estimate some connection parameters, for example the needed buffering for a particular connection. However, how multimedia connections will be integrated into Internet is not clear yet: although bandwidth reservation has been advocated by most approaches, the Internet philosophy (free access, no restrictions,...) does not match this approach.

3.2   Proposal for a QoS-Aware Middleware for Adaptive Multimedia Data Transfer
by B. Csizmazia (email: csb@itec.uni-klu.ac.at)

Abstract. At the workshop the design of a novel middleware supporting adaptive transfer of discrete and continuous multimedia data was presented. The presented system allows building QoS-based adaptive multimedia protocol frameworks from pre-defined and user-defined QoS-aware service objects, supported by the ANTS active network system. One of the main advantages of the system is that the framework allows building of multimedia communication systems where applications invoke only the services they really need.

The proposal is destined to eventually support quality-adaptive MPEG-4 video transport over networks where active network nodes change video flows during transport in that they perform media scaling (and thus, quality variation) operations when required (for example, in congestion situations or for delivery of video flows to end systems with different playout capabilities).

The key components of the system are the ANTS layer [7], an object-based active network infrastructure that sits below the layer supporting various QoS policies, the network load monitoring layer. The purpose of this layer is to provide the necessary information and control mechanisms with respect to QoS for the protocol and service components of the upper layers.

Our implementation is a pure Java solution thus providing the portability and safety common to these systems.

For our purposes – the transfer of MPEG-1 or MPEG-4 multimedia data – the following protocol objects are necessary (they were presented at the workshop): *MPEG-1 encoder and decoder, MPEG-4 encoder and decoder, still images display, packetizer, NAK/PAR object with a client-side object providing FIFO delivery, ANTS datagram communication object, unicast reliable communication object, layered multicast streaming object.*

Answers Relating our work to the session chair´s questions we can state the following answers:

1. In our opinion, QoS-based resource management makes it possible for applications to use and pay only for services they really need and use.
2. In distributed multimedia systems, many of the above mentioned circumstances (network congestion, heterogeneity in the network) can cause the network service's quality to change. The network and the middleware abstracting from it, are best positioned to react to such situations.
3. Because of the above mentioned heterogeneity of network nodes and end-user devices, storing every multimedia data on the server in every format is infeasible and impossible. People invest lots in portable computers and in mobile phones, but the capabilities of these systems are very restricted. People need a solution that makes it possible to use this equipment. That's why quality adaptation is a viable technique for multimedia communication.

Project URL:
`http://www.ifi.uni-klu.ac.at/ITEC/Staff/Balazs.Csizmazia!.`

3.3   Simple Algorithms for QoS Optimization with Discrete QoS Options
by S. Podlipnig (email: spodlipn@itec.uni-klu.ac.at)

Abstract. Quality of Service (QoS) control is an important topic in multimedia system research. Multimedia applications can differ greatly in their requirements for service quality and the resources available to them at the time of use. Adaptive multimedia applications can work with different amounts of resources resulting in different quality levels. To maximize the offered quality of a multimedia system, one has to allocate shared resources to competing applications according to these quality-resource trade-offs. Our work is based on a problem formulation given in [8]. The problem classification is based on the criteria whether the system deals just with a single resource or with any number, and on whether there is a single QoS dimension or multiple. This leads to four problem classes. In this paper we deal with the SRMD (Single Resource and Multiple QoS Dimension) problem. Three different algorithms are presented in [8] for the SRMD. A practical performance evaluation shows that a simple approximation algorithm yields the biggest benefit for the limited computational time it consumes.

Our paper[1] shows that the SRMD can be reformulated as a MCKP(Multiple Choice Knapsack Problem) with dummy items. This simple mapping gives us the opportunity to reuse algorithms that were originally proposed for the MCKP [9]. We show that the approximation algorithm given in [8] is a practical implementation of the greedy algorithm for the MCKP. These algorithms run in $O(n \log n)$ time, where n is the number of competing applications. For small n this is sufficient. For larger n an $O(n)$ algorithm can be reused from the MCKP. Furthermore we discuss possible applications of the MCKP in networks and distributed systems.

---

[1] see the technical report TR/ITEC/01/2.02

Answers Relating our work to the session chair´s questions we can state the following answers:

1. QoS based resource management is an important topic as long as raw power can not guarantee QoS sufficiently. It is questionable if enhancing raw power will be a solution in the next few years, as new increasing application demands and increasing number of users overload systems.
2. Middleware should include some sort of QoS support as it constitutes one link in the end-to-end QoS chain of many modern applications.
3. Quality adaptation is necessary in modern multimedia applications. As reservation based mechanisms can not be used efficiently in large distributed systems and as heterogenity of end devices increases through mobile devices, adaptive applications are an interesting alternative to non-adaptive ones.

A technical report TR/ITEC/01/2.02 can be found at:
`http://www.itec.uni-klu.ac.at/~spodlipn/`.

3.4 Session Chairs' Conclusions

The session discussed algorithmic and performance issues of Quality of Service. The three presentations showed a surprisingly heterogeneous picture, and illuminated the topic from quite different point of views.

Presentation 3.2 discussed the advantages of mobile code, based on the ANTS technology. The investigation is based on a real prototype implementation. Paper 3.1 is based on a simulation environment, aiming, however, at a real implementation. The contribution in 3.3 presents a theoretical approach, supported by simulation results. A general consensus could be achieved in the following issues:

1. QoS-aware resource management (as opposed to best-effort) is inevitable for distributed multimedia systems. Even if raw computer and communication power would grow exponentially in the future, without a QoS-aware resource management no high-quality multimedia systems can be built.
2. This needs QoS-aware middleware – even if this does not suffice to solve all problems of a multimedia oriented resource management.
3. Quality adaptation is a quite new, but very promising approach, as it takes advantage of the relatively high degree of freedom we have at the storage, delivery and presentation of multimedia data.

4 QoS in Distributed Object Systems

Session Chair: Christian Becker

After last year's successful Quality in Distributed Object Systems workshop at ECOOP 2000 this year's call for papers did not receive the same attention. However, since the topics are close to these of DMMOS the organizers decided to merge the workshops. Due to a sudden illness of a participant only two papers were presented. John Zinky presented new features in QuO (Quality Objects) and Gina Fábián presented the QoS Provision Service (QPS). Both of the presentations addressed generic QoS integration in CORBA. Because of the very much different approaches the presenters were asked the following questions.

The source code of QPS and further information can be found at the following webpage: `http://quamj.sourceforge.net`

1. Which QoS characteristics should be addressed by QoS capable middleware in order to provide interoperability for a distinct set of QoS?
2. Which extensions in addition to portable interceptors and pluggable protocols are needed for QoS management in CORBA as an example for middleware platforms?
3. Should QoS management be separated from client and service implementations and will this lead to a lack of QoS adaption?

Since both approaches rely on QoS provision in the underlying middleware these questions are thought to provide a summarization of the experience made in the individual approaches as well as the follow up to the summarization of discussions. Interesting right now is the potentially open engineered precautions for QoS in recent CORBA specifications. Although the OMG QoS effort has been pushed by the realtime community the mechanisms integration hooks, i.e. interceptors and pluggable protocols, are suitable for other QoS characteristics as well. Both presented approaches provide QoS support on the same layers with similar means - at least at the middleware layer. This indicates that there are some agreed integration points of QoS mechanisms in middleware architectures.

The Quality Objects project provides QoS specification as contracts similar to IDL as interface contracts. The QoS specification is translated into configuration of mechanisms in the underlying middleware platform. In the QoS Provision Service (QPS) the QoS specification and negotiation is done via a the service. Hence the specification and provision is more tightly coupled in terms of the architecture than in QuO where explicit translation is needed. In contrast to QuO binding of a QoS to a client server relationship is done for a single application and server object.

4.1 Quality Objects (QuO)
by John A. Zinky (email: jzinky@bbn.com)

Abstract. The Quality Objects (QuO) Framework enables applications built on distributed object middleware to adapt to changes in Quality of Service (QoS) at runtime. In distributed systems the interaction between clients and remote objects is not a sample method call but a complex infrastructure to move the request from the client to the server. Managing QoS for this interaction involves inserting monitoring and control code throughout the infrastructure. The QuO Framework opens up and organizes this infrastructure to allow easy insertion and reuse of adaptive behavior for managing QoS. QuO uses several techniques for inserting code into different parts of the middleware, including traditional techniques, such as libraries, distributed services, and reflectivity. QuO also uses a code generator to generate smart proxies and stubs. Quality Description Languages (QDL) are used to describe the adaptive code at a high-level. The QDL is woven together with the Interface Description Language (IDL) used by traditional middleware to generate the smart proxies and stubs. QDL is a group of Aspect Oriented Programming Languages which exploit knowledge specific to the domain of distributed object middleware. QDL is independent of programming language (Java or C++) and middleware (CORBA or RMI). QuO 3.0 introduces a new architectural component called a Qosket, which bundles adaptive behavior into a reusable specification.

Answers

1. QoS management is still too immature a technology to achieve interoperability amongst components. No consensus exists for how to describe different QoS facets, such as performance, realtime, dependability, or security, let alone how to compose them. Also to be effective, application-domain knowledge needs to be factored into any QoS adaptive code. QuO takes the pragmatic approach of offering a toolkit for constructing adaptive code out of reusable pieces. QuO allows reusable QoS adaptive functionality to be defined in terms of Qoskets. Application developers can extend their existing remote objects by combining the Qosket with their specific application-level adaptive behavior. For example, an application may call different remote methods depending on which remote resource is the bottleneck.

2. CORBA's open implementation extensions are extremely helpful for implementing QoS management at the middleware layer. Other middleware environment, such as RMI, DCOM and SOAP, do not have these features, hence will lag behind CORBA in their evolution towards QoS management. But all these middleware systems can be extended from both the top and bottom. QuO uses a CORBA Gateway to added extensions below the ORB at the networking layer. A CORBA Gateway proxies a remote object and allows code to be inserted which changes and routes underlying GIOP messages as they are forwarded to the remote object. A CORBA Gateway acts as an interceptor, because it can manipulate the raw request and reply messages. Also, it acts as pluggable protocol, because the GIOP messages can be encapsulated in any new inter-gateway protocol. But more important, the Gateway can add QoS management to new Locations in the network topology, hence a mesh of Gateways act as an application-level active network. QuO use delegation to extend the remote objects stubs and skeletons, above the ORB. QuO has extensive code generation support for creating QoS adaptive delegates and plans to use the CORBA smart-proxy as the standards emerge.

3. QoS Management is a difficult job that application programmers need to deal with as their applications become distributed. The trick is to separate out the QoS Management role, so that it can be done by more experienced programmers and its results can reused by the vast majority of application programmers. We hope that the development of Qoskets will be a first step in this separation.

QuO Version 3.0 is available with binary versions of the code generators for Linux, Solaris and NT operating systems. QuO and its manuals can be downloaded from the QuO webpage:
`http://www.dist-systems.bbn.com/tech/QuO.`

4.2 The QOS Provisioning Service (QPS)
by G. Fábián and A.T. van Halteren
(email: {g.fabian,a.t.vanhalteren}@kpn.com)

Abstract. To support the growing number of QoS sensitive applications, next- generation middleware has to control system-specific QoS mechanisms such as OS scheduling and network bandwidth reservation. The challenge for future object middleware is to provide application level QoS provisioning, through a high-level language in a way that maintains distribution transparency. The QoS Provisioning Service (QPS) presented here is a CORBA ORB service that establishes QoS for a single binding between a client application and a server object. It uses the QoS Modeling Language (QML) [10] for high-level QoS specifications, and performs QoS negotiation between client application, server object and the Distributed Resource Platform (DRP). Low-level QoS mechanisms can be plugged into QPS through a generic interface. QPS is designed as a CORBA ORB service and it uses standardized ORB extension hooks, therefore it can run as a service on any ORB implementation that provides these extension hooks.

Answers

1. QoS interoperability can be defined at system level. To achieve this, a standardized interface is necessary to express the QoS capabilities of the middleware and a standardized interaction mechanism to be able to guarantee end-to-end QoS behavior. In our approach, the QoS characteristics supported by the middleware is determined by plug-ins that have been inserted into the QoS Provisioning Service (QPS). These plug-ins provide resource management mechanisms in the network or end-systems. As a result, the middleware can offer guarantees for the delay and rate of method invocations.

2. Pluggable protocols offer a good extension mechanism, but unfortunately they are not standardized by the OMG, which has resulted in different interfaces for pluggable protocols for various ORB implementations. Standardization of pluggable protocols is therefore necessary. Along the same lines, a standardized interface that enables the control of the scheduling of messages on the POA would be a good way forward. This allows a QoS-capable ORB to give priority to QoS-enabled method invocations over non-QoS enabled invocations.

3. Separation of service implementations and the use of system level QoS management is conceptually a good way forward, however a number of difficulties have to be dealt with. Separation through standardized interfaces should unify the great variety of mechanisms that can be used to manage QoS, and the different levels and sophistication of these mechanisms need to be defined. Also, the way a service interacts with QoS mechanisms may require sophisticated programming techniques (e.g. querying available QoS mechanisms, event handling, reactiveness, etc.) therefore, these mechanisms need to be standardized as well.

4.3 Session Chairs' Conclusions

Although QoS support in middleware is crucial for applications and frameworks based upon, there is still little understanding of some fundamental aspects of QoS provision.

While the middleware community seems to agree on similar layers for QoS mechanisms in the ORB there are important questions yet unanswered. Binding client, service, and QoS can be done in manifold ways. However, choices made here influence the QoS mechanisms heavily - imagine binding two QoS characteristics at a time to a client service relation. The resulting requirements on the QoS mechanisms can be hard to solve depending on the QoS characteristics. Furthermore, application specific knowledge has to be incorporated into some QoS mechanisms. This is already understood and QoS is characterized by many researchers as an aspect in the sense of the aspect oriented programming (AOP). Beside some research projects there is little support from products as well as from specifications to handle the integration of QoS provision and the application.

With the growing importance of component based software the component frameworks will have to become QoS aware. However, if the middleware is not QoS aware will prevent many QoS characteristics from being implementable. Therefore QoS integration in distributed object systems still offers enough questions justifying research.

5   Component-Based Architectures

Session Chair: Harald Kosch

This session was surely the most homogenous session which concerns the contents of the papers. All four papers and respective talks argued for the use of a component-based architecture for distributed multimedia systems. Further common agreement was achieved on the fact that broadly used component-based architectures lack means for distribution, i.e. they concentrate mainly on client or server architecture (e.g. the Java Media Framework). Moreover, it was common sense that related middleware technologies, such as CORBA proposed by the OMG, offer only limited solutions to a component-based multimedia architecture. Although interesting multimedia delivery specific interfaces exit in these standards, yet good implementations are rarely available. This is mostly due to the complexity of the interface definitions proposed.

In this scope, all talks suggested novel ideas to introduce distribution in a component-based architecture for multimedia systems. The way they do it and where they do it, differed very much from approach to approach. This was also the main point of discussion after and during the various talks. For instance, A. Beugnard propose to encapsulate the distribution in so called 'Mediums', special communication components, whereas, E. Santos considers the communication platform as a special programmable component. The question of the 'where to integrate distribution' was also a hot topic, for instance, R. Tusch consider a virtual adaptive video server architecture, where components might migrate to nodes on the delivery path to the client depending on the real-time requirements of the multimedia data and resource availabilities. Contrarily to this, the other authors suppose that client, server, communication network have its own components which fit statically together in order to build a complete system.

A final interesting point was the question of reuse of available middleware components. Although all authors commented on the drawbacks of existing middleware solutions, all presented implementations finally relied for low-level functionality on a certain middleware. Thus components where considered only for high-level application oriented functionality.

The questions which arise in this context are the following :

1. What are your components?
2. Are your components reusable and generic?

In the following the authors describe briefly their approaches and identify answers to these questions.

5.1 Modules of an Adaptive Virtual Video Server Architecture
by Roland Tusch (email: roland@itec.uni-klu.ac.at)

Abstract. The unique characteristics of digital video streams concerning huge storage, high-bandwidth and real-time delivery requirements impose challenges in designing video server architectures. Efficient means for storing, retrieving, manipulating and sending video data are required, both concerning the server's hardware and software. In this paper, a design of a modular video server architecture for use in a virtual environment is presented. The main goal of the architecture is to provide *server-level* adaptivity to improve load-balancing and scalability by reducing network traffic. This is mainly achieved by using a virtual server environment for migrating and replicating critical services in situations of high load and bottlenecks. However, the modularity and adaptivity of the proposed architecture may impose some disadvantageous impacts on the performance behavior of the system, which is still an open issue.

In existing architectures the term *adaptivity* mostly belongs to their ability to deliver different qualities of video streams concerning color-depth and resolution. However, this kind of adaptation only belongs to streams (*stream-level* adaptivity) and does not take into account runtime constraints concerning the server's topology. If e.g. a number of closely aligned clients is requesting at least parts of the same video stream, it would be of advantage to migrate or replicate the buffering component somewhere in the neighborhood of those clients. This kind of *server-level* adaptation results in shorter startup delays, improved scalability and reduced network traffic. To enable server-level adaptivity, the server's topology has to follow a component-based architecture.

Answers

1. The basic components of an adaptive video server architecture, regardless whether it follows the single or distributed server model, are represented by mainly four modules: *request processing*, *data repository*, *server configuration* and *monitoring*. The request processing module covers all the required functionality for processing data-query or data-acquisition requests. It consists of the interacting submodules *contact management*, *admission control*, *service control*, *resource management* and *proxy*. The proxy module e. g. is responsible for re-sequencing and merging data from multiple servers into one coherent stream for delivery to the client. Implementing this module as a service, its components could be migrated from one host to another using *Symphony* [11], a management infrastructure for virtual servers in Internet settings.

2. The functionality of each module is described by interfaces, where different implementations for the interfaces allow the server to behave generic. Moreover, components like e. g. the *federative resource manager* [12] in module *request processing*,
providing a combination of resource reservation and adaptation for an arbitrary
server resource, are even reusable for other server architectures.

For more information see:
http://www.ifi.uni-klu.ac.at/Publications/pubfiles/
pdffiles/2001-0028-RT.pdf.

5.2 A Component-Based Architecture for Distributed Multimedia Applications by Antoine Beugnard (email: Antoine.Beugnard@enst-bretagne.fr)

Abstract. Applications development relies more and more on the use of components.
Database, real-time micro-kernels, standard libraries of data types or of GUI components
are frequently reused. Smalltalk parts, and more recently Java beans or ActiveX components have popularized this approach, but for centralized application only. On one hand,
some technologies such as CORBA proposed by the OMG offer some pieces of solutions. Criticized [13], they usually reduce the interaction to a predefined communication
model (a kind of remote procedure call) resulting in a unique layer of communication
(middleware) that compels components that want to use it to adopt it. On the other hand
so many protocols are dedicated to multimedia-streaming transportation that it is hard
to select one in this jungle.

We propose a different approach [14] that encapsulates communication services
(such as method calls or Real-Time Protocol) in reusable components. This leads to an
architecture for distributed applications where "the communication" is considered as a
reified component.

Architecture Description. An application is an assembly of many components. We
distinguish two kinds of components: classical components and communication components called Mediums. Communication components offer:

1. A specific interface (contract) to this communication mean,
2. Actual transportation services,
3. Specific services (configuration, quality of service, viewers, . . .)

This leads to a three entities software architecture: two of them are reused (components and mediums) and the third, adapters that adapt and connect components together,
ensures all specific features of the application.

Answers

1. In order to build a complete system, mediums and classical components are linked
- locally, since distributed features are encapsulated into mediums - either directly,
when interfaces (contracts) match, either via adapters that are dedicated parts of
code.

2. Mediums are reusable since they encapsulate any level of communication abstraction. From an asynchronous point-to-point channel to a real-time video broadcasting protocol. These abstractions can be reused in any system where they are required. Mediums are generic since the same communication abstraction can be implemented different ways. For instance a shared memory medium could have a centralized or a distributed - with or without caching and coherency controls - versions. Dealing with scalability could be simplified by mediums substitution.
   We do believe that communication reification allows to better reuse protocols and to better handle distributed system complexity.

For more information consider:
`http://www-info.enst-bretagne.fr/medium/`.

5.3   Middleware for the Broadcast Environment
by E. Santos (email: ernesto.santos@inescporto.pt)

Abstract. TV Broadcasters are becoming increasingly aware of the advantages of using IT technology in their production systems: lower costs, vendor independence through the use of open technologies, integration of the many disparate systems in the organizatio... The ORBIT project is introducing MBE (Middleware for the Broadcast Environment), an IT component based architecture to accommodate handling of several different kinds of concepts in the production environment.

Answers

1. What are your components and how do they fit together to build a complete system? MBE Components are realizations of Business Objects, which are the central concepts in the production environment, as the user perceives it. Examples of Business Objects are devices, processes or units of work being produced. To build a complete system, user requirements are analysed to identify the central concepts, and CORBA Components [15] implementing their logic are deployed. In the CCM (CORBA Components Model), it is possible to declare in a standard way details such as the dependencies between Components, their persistent state or deployment information. These tools provide the basic framework to build a complete system by connecting MBE Components.
2. Are your components reusable and generic?
   Since the CCM is followed, MBE Components provide the necessary interfaces that allow their location and manipulation even by generic management applications from different vendors. The exposed custom functionality is clearly defined at the interface level in OMG IDL, which is language independent, therefore allowing reuse of Components over a wide range of applications. As for the knowledge managed by a Component, it is represented using multimedia standards (such as MPEG for audiovisual data). However, when required, Components may be built flexible and generic enough to accommodate even for proprietary data representations. Examples of this are Components holding descriptive data represented using XML [16]. These use lower level services capable of applying generic data model

independent operations on XML data such as search or transformation. Finally, the realized Business Objects encapsulate rules that are common in production and may therefore be reused in different deployment scenarios.

URL for further information:
`http://mog.inescporto.pt`.

5.4 Compositional and Architectural Evolution Issues: A Comparison between JMF and MultiTEL
by M. Pinto, M. Amor, C. Canal, and L. Fuentes
(email: {pinto,pinilla,canal,lff}@lcc.uma.es)

Abstract. The growing complexity of Web-based services in general, and multimedia services in particular, makes it necessary to apply engineering methods to their development. In particular, Multimedia Engineering may be considered as the field in Software Engineering which deals with the development of open, reusable and quality multimedia and Web-based software [17]. In this work we apply current trends in Software Engineering, such as component and framework technologies, to the development of multimedia services over the Web, and we present a comparison between two different solutions in use today: Java Media Frameworks (JMF) [18], Sun's platform for capturing and storing media data, and MultiTEL, a non-commercial compositional framework developed by the authors of this work.

Answers

1. The MultiTEL compositional model provides the separation of concerns between computation and coordination by encapsulating them into two different entities. The compositional units of the model are Components, that encapsulate computation, and Connectors, that encapsulate the coordination protocols. The set of connections between the components and connectors of an application defines the architecture of the application. The connection between components and connectors is dynamically established in MultiTEL at run time, providing a powerful mechanism for late binding among them. This is very useful for implementing applications in open systems, in which components evolve over time, or applications with dynamic topologies, such as multimedia applications.
2. MultiTEL defines an application framework that first, describes a generic software architecture, in terms of abstract components and connectors. Secondly, it provides the implementation of some of those abstract components and connectors. In this sense, multimedia application builders could have access to a set of reusable software components, which greatly facilitate the services implementation, while hiding from the service designer the details of underlying technologies and the complexity of interaction patterns.

The Web page of MultiTEL can be found at:
`http://www.lcc.uma.es/~lff/MultiTEL`

5.5 Session Chairs' Conclusions

Although being the final session, and already late in the afternoon, the session was highly animated. This was due to the different point-of-views on the architectural design, also to the engagement of the authors and the audience. We could identify common points which concern the need for components for the design of distributed multimedia systems, and identify open questions.

Finally, it shall be noticed that the applications studied for validation of fitted of course to the specifics of the model proposed. So, to my opinion, it would be of great interest, to take all applications used in the different papers and talks and to allow the authors to apply their view of a component to the applications used by other authors. One could learn if his/her approach is really a general-purpose one (all papers claim this)?

6 General Conclusions

The workshop investigated, to what extent can component technology help to enhance the quality of distributed multimedia systems. Especially, to what extent can we achieve better reuse of multimedia content, reuse of code, interoperability, portability and performance. We can summarize the results of the presentations and discussions as following:

1. Component based architectures:
   All authors agreed upon the necessity of building distributed multimedia systems of components as opposed to monolithic systems. The granularity of the components is an open issue, it can be stated, however, that most contributors presented solutions with rather heavy-weight components. This suggests that too fine granular decomposition is not regarded as relevant by most workshop participants.
2. Standardization of multimedia content formats:
   Some of the presentations required explicitly standardization of multimedia formats, both for content and meta data. There are lot of open issues in this field.
3. Multimedia-aware standardized middleware:
   Most presenters touched this topic. Available middleware standards still do not support to a sufficient extent techniques to provide a guaranteed quality of service, and fit thus not well to be used for distributed multimedia.
4. Important role of academic research:
   Multimedia system providers are often not interested to publish their interfaces. Thus, even if the internal design is component-oriented, the rest of the world has not much gain from this. Academic research can push openness and have a positive influence on industry.

The full-day double-workshop had an inspiring impact on the participants. We left Budapest with a lot of new insights and still more new questions.

References

1. Objectspace. Voyager. `http://www.objectspace.com/products/voyager`.
2. IKV++. Grasshopper 2, the agent platform. `http://www.grasshopper.de`.
3. H. Kosch, M. Döller, and L. Böszörményi. Content-based indexing and retrieval supported by mobile agent technology. In *Accepted at the 2nd International Workshop on Multimedia Databases and Image Communications (MDIC 2001)*, Amalfi, Italy, September 2001.
4. E. Weippl, J. Altmann, and W. Essmayer. Mobile database agents for building data warehouses. In *In Proceedings of the Eleventh International Workshop on Database and Expert System Applications (DEXA)*, pages 477–481, Greenwich, UK, September 2001. IEEE Computer Society.
5. E. Davies Z. Wang D. Black, M. Carlson and W. Weiss. Architecture for Differentiated Services. 1998.
6. D. Clark R. Braden and S. Shenker. Integrated Services in the Internet Architecture: an overview. 1997.
7. D. Wetherall, J.V. Guttag, and D.L. Tennenhouse. Ants: A toolkit for building and dynamically deploying network protocols. In *In Proceedings of the IEEE OPENARCH'98*, San Francisco, CA, USA, April 1998.
8. C. Lee. *On Quality of Service Management*. PhD thesis, Carnegie Mellon University, August 1999.
9. D.-Z. Du and P. M. Pardalos. *Handbook of Combinatorial Optimization (Vol. 1)*. Kluwer Academic Press, Boston, 1998.
10. S. Frolund and J. Koistinen. Quality of service specification in distributed object systems design. In *Proceedings of the 4th USENIX Conference on Object- Oriented Technologies and Systems (COOTS)*, Santa Fe, New Mexico, April 1998.
11. R. Friedman, E. Biham, A. Itzkovitz, and A. Schuster. Symphony: Managing Virtual Servers in the Global Village. Technical Report CS0939-1998, Department of Computer Science, The Technion, Haifa, Israel, 1998.
12. G. Hölzl and L. Böszörményi. Distributed Federative QoS Resource Management. In *Future Generation Computer Systems*, number 16, pages 717–725, 2000.
13. C. Thompson. Workshop on compositional software architectures, 1998. Workshop Report, Monterey, California, January 6-8, `http://www.objs.com/workshops/ws9801/report.html`.
14. A. Beugnard and R. Ogor. Encapsulation of protocols and services in medium components to build distributed applications. In *Engineering Distributed Objects (EDO'99), Workshop, ICSE 99 , Los Angeles*, May 17-18, 1999.
15. Object Management Group. CORBA Components - Volume I. 1999.
16. W3C. Extensible Markup Language (XML). 2000.
17. A. Ginige and S. Murugesan. Special issue on Web Engineering. *IEEE Multimedia*, 18(1 & 2), 2001.
18. Sun Microsystems Inc. Java Media Framework Guide. 1999.

Formal Techniques for Java Programs

Gary T. Leavens[1], Sophia Drossopoulou[2], Susan Eisenbach[2], Arnd Poetzsch-Heffter[3], and Erik Poll[3]

[1] Department of Computer Science, Iowa State University, USA
leavens@cs.iastate.edu
[2] Department of Computing, Imperial College London, Great Britain
{scd,se}@doc.ic.ac.uk
[3] Fachbereich Informatik, FernUniversitaet Hagen, Germany
Arnd.Poetzsch-Heffter@Fernuni-Hagen.de
[4] Department of Computer Science, University of Nijmegen, The Netherlands
erikpoll@cs.kun.nl

Abstract. This report gives an overview of the third ECOOP Workshop on Formal Techniques for Java Programs. It explains the motivation for such a workshop and summarizes the presentations and discussions.

1 Introduction

The ECOOP 2001 workshop on Formal Techniques for Java Programs was held in Budapest, Hungary. It was a follow-up for last year's ECOOP workshop on the same topic [DEJ+00a] [DEJ+00b], the first ECOOP workshop on this topic [JLMPH99], and the Formal Underpinnings of the Java Paradigm workshop held at OOPSLA '98 [Eis98]. The workshop was organized by Susan Eisenbach (Imperial College, Great Britain), Gary T. Leavens (Iowa State University, USA), Peter Müller (FernUniversität Hagen, Germany), Arnd Poetzsch-Heffter (FernUniversität Hagen, Germany), and Erik Poll (University of Nijmegen, The Netherlands). Besides the organizers the program committee of the workshop included Gilad Bracha (Sun Microsystems, USA), Sophia Drossopoulou (Imperial College, Great Britain), Doug Lea (State University of New York at Oswego, USA), and Rustan Leino (Compaq Computer Corporation, USA). The program committee was chaired by Sophia Drossopoulou.

There was lively interest in the workshop. Out of many submissions, the organizers selected 13 papers for longer presentations, and three for short presentations. There was one invited talk, given by Gilad Bracha of Sun Microsystems. Overall, 36 people from 30 universities, research labs, and industries attended the workshop.

Motivation. Formal techniques can help to analyze programs, to precisely describe program behavior, and to verify program properties. Applying such techniques to object-oriented technology is especially interesting because:

- the OO-paradigm forms the basis for the software component industry with their need for certification techniques.
- it is widely used for distributed and network programming.

Á. Frohner (Ed.): ECOOP 2001 Workshops, LNCS 2323, pp. 30–40, 2002.
© Springer-Verlag Berlin Heidelberg 2002

- the potential for reuse in OO-programming carries over to reusing specifications and proofs.

Such formal techniques are sound, only if based on a formalization of the language itself.

Java is a good platform to bridge the gap between formal techniques and practical program development. It plays an important role in these areas and is becoming a de facto standard because of its reasonably clear semantics and its standardized library.

However, Java contains novel language features, which are not fully understood yet. More importantly, Java supports a novel paradigm for program deployment, and improves interactivity, portability and manageability. This paradigm opens new possibilities for abuse and causes concern about security.

Thus, work on formal techniques and tools for Java programming and formal underpinnings of Java complement each other. This workshop aims to bring together people working in these areas, in particular on the following topics:

- specification techniques and interface specification languages
- specification of software components and library packages
- automated checking and verification of program properties
- verification technology and logics
- Java language semantics
- dynamic linking and loading, security

Structure of Workshop and Report. The one-day workshop consisted of a technical part during the day and a workshop dinner in the evening. While the food in Budapest was delightful, this report deals only with the technical aspects of the workshop.

The presentations at the workshop were structured as follows.

- 9:00–10:00 Opening Session, and Invited Talk by Gilad Bracha: "Adventures in Computational Theology: Selected Experiences with the Java(tm) Programming Language "
- 10:15–11:15 Language Semantics I
    - Alessandro Coglio: "Improving the Official Specification of Java Bytecode Verification"
    - Kees Huizing and Ruurd Kuiper: "Reinforcing Fragile Base Classes"
- 11:25–12:25 Language Semantics II
    - Davide Ancona, Giovanni Lagorio, and Elena Zucca: "Java Separate Type Checking is not Safe"
    - Mirko Viroli: "From FGJ to Java according to LM translator"
    - Mats Skoglund and Tobias Wrigstad: "A mode system for read-only references in Java"
- 13:45–15:45 Specification and Verification I (Java Card)
    - Pierre Boury and Nabil Elkhadi: "Static Analysis of Java Cryptographic Applets"
    - Peter Müller and Arnd Poetzsch-Heffter: "A Type System for Checking Applet Isolation in Java Card"

- Gilles Barthe, Dilian Gurov, and Marieke Huisman "Compositional specification and verification of control flow based security properties of multi-application programs"
- 16:00–17:30 Specification and Verification II
  - Peter Müller, Arnd Poetzsch-Heffter, Gary T. Leavens: "Modular Specification of Frame Properties in JML"
  - John Boyland: "The Interdependence of Effects and Uniqueness"
  - Ana Cavalcanti and David Naumann: "Class Refinement for Sequential Java"
  - Joachim van den Berg, Cees-Bart Breunesse, Bart Jacobs, and Erik Poll: "On the Role of Invariants in Reasoning about Object-Oriented Languages"
- 17:45–18:30 Short presentations and closing session
  - Claus Pahl: "Formalising Dynamic Composition and Evolution in Java Systems"
  - M. Carbone, M. Coccia, G. Ferrari and S. Maffeis: "Process Algebra-Guided Design of Java Mobile Network Applications"
  - Peep Küngas, Vahur Kotkas, and Enn Tyugu: "Introducing Meta-Interfaces into Java"

The rest of this report is structured as follows: Sections 2 to 6 summarize the presentations and discussions of the technical sessions of the workshop. The conclusions are contained in Section 7. A list of participants with email addresses can be found in the Appendix. The workshop proceedings are contained in [DEL+01].

2   Language Semantics I

Because Java security is based on type safety, correct implementation of bytecode verification is of paramount importance to the security of an implementation of the Java Virtual Machine (JVM). In his contribution [Cog01a], Alessandro Coglio provided a comprehensive analysis of the official specification of bytecode verification and explained techniques to overcome the shortcomings. The insight underlying the analysis was gained during a complete formalization of Java bytecode verification [Cog01b]. The critique on the official specification lists places of redundancy, unclear terminology (e.g., static and structural constraints are both static in nature which might lead to confusion), lack of explanation, contradictions (e.g., the specification says that uninitialized objects cannot be accessed as well as that a constructor can store values into some fields of the object that is being initialized), and errors that were reported elsewhere.

Based on this critique, Coglio suggested improvements to the JVM specification. He discussed the merging of reference types and suggested that sets of type names should be used to express the merged types. This is an improvement over solutions that are based on existing common supertypes, because it avoids premature loading. For checking the subtype relation, he also proposed a solution that does not need premature loading. The basic idea is to generate subtype constraints at verification time. These constraints are checked when additional classes are loaded.

Furthermore, Coglio suggested that Java should make a clear distinction between *acceptable* code, i.e., code that does not lead to runtime type errors, and *accepted* code, i.e., code that satisfies declarative and decidable conditions guaranteeing type safety.

Since it is, in general, undecidable whether a bytecode sequence is acceptable, the bytecode specification should define what accepted code is and compilers should be constraint to generate only accepted code.

The second presentation of this session given by K. Huizing is discussed in section "Specification and Verification II", because its topic is closer related to the other papers of that session.

3   Language Semantics II

Davide Ancona, Giovanni Lagorio, and Elena Zucca [ALZ01] looked at the problem of ensuring type safety for separately-compiled language fragments. They showed that with current Java development systems it is possible to compile fragments, alter and recompile some of them and in the process introduce type errors that are only caught at link time. They believe that these errors should have been caught earlier, in the compilation process.

Ancona, Lagorio, and Zucca went on to propose a formal framework for expressing separate compilation. They defined a small subset of Java and conjecture that within their framework, type errors would be caught at compilation rather than linking time. Their scheme would mean that a programmer could always have a single set of source fragments, that could be recompiled together to produce the current executable, a property not held by actual Java programs.

Mirko Virolli [Vir01] described work he is doing on adding parametric polymorphism to Java starting with Featherweight Generic Java [IPW99]. Parametric polymorphism is added via a translator called LM and the translation process is complex. To understand the complexity, a formalization of LM has been done so reasoning about its properties is possible. The LM translator is modeled as a compilation of FGJ into full Java. The model should help with the implementation of a correct translator.

Skoglund and Tobias Wrigstad [SW01] proposed an extension of Java syntax (with type rules) to include modes that will restrict some mutations of shared objects. There are four proposed modes, which include **read**, **write**, **any** and **context**. Objects in **read** mode cannot be altered, although objects in **write** mode can be. Objects in **any** and **context** mode are readable or writable depending on the context. The system is statically checkable. In addition to the modes, there is a dynamic construct called **caseModeOf** which enables the programmer to write code depending on the mode of an object. Java's lack of a construct (unlike C++) to restrict the altering of objects has been tackled by others, but the authors believe earlier attempts to solve this problem are too restrictive.

4   Specification and Verification I (Java Card)

Three of the papers presented at the workshop were about Java Card, a simplified version of Java designed for programming smart cards, which has been attracting a lot of attention in the formal methods community. The small size of Java Card programs, which have to run on the extremely limited hardware available on a smart card, and the vital importance of correctness of typical smart card applications, notably for bank cards and mobile phone SIMs, make Java Card an ideal application area for formal techniques. Indeed, both the smart card industry and their customers have recognized the important role that formal methods can play in ensuring that the (very high) security requirements for smart card applications are satisfied.

The paper by Pierre Boury and Nabil Elkhadi [BE01] was about a technique for static analysis of confidentiality properties of Java Card programs (also called "applets").

Java Card programs typically rely on cryptography to ensure security properties, such as authentication (e.g., of a mobile phone SIM to the mobile phone network) and confidentiality (by the creation of secure channels). Even though standard cryptographic algorithms are used for this, ensuring that these are used correctly in a program, so that no confidential data is ever disclosed (leaked) to unauthorized parties, is notoriously difficult. The approach taken by the authors has been to adapt formal models that have been proposed for the analysis of cryptographic protocols to the verification of confidentiality properties of Java Card applets, using the technique of abstract interpretation. The outcome of this work is an tool, called "StuPa", which can automatically verify confidentiality properties of Java Card class files.

The paper by Gilles Barthe, Dilian Gurov, and Marieke Huisman [BGH01] considered another class of security properties for Java Card programs, namely properties about control flow.

Global properties about a collection of interacting Java Card applets on a single smart card are expressed in temporal logic. The idea is then that "local" properties about the individual applets are found, and it is then formally proved that these local properties together imply the required global properties. The proof system used to prove that the local properties imply the required global ones is based on the modal μ-calculus. To verify the local properties an existing technique, which uses an essentially language independent program model, is instantiated to Java Card. The local properties of the individual applets are verified automatically, using model checking.

The paper by Peter Müller and Arnd Poetzsch-Heffter [MPH01] is an application of type system ideas to the Java Card language. In Java Card, applets are isolated in the sense that they are "not allowed to access fields and methods of other applets on the same smart-card." (If this happens anyway, a `SecurityException` is supposed to be thrown by the smart-card's virtual machine.) The problem addressed is how to statically check applet isolation in Java Card programs, which would avoid the problem of producing lots of Java smart-cards that have code that could cause `SecurityExceptions`. The type system in the paper prevents such errors, using mostly static checks.

The approach taken to this problem is to adopt the author's previous work on type systems for alias control [MPH00]. The type system tracks what context owns each reference in a conservative manner, and thus can prohibit accesses to other contexts that would otherwise cause a `SecurityException`. The checking is not completely static, because in some cases one must use Java-style downcasts to recover exact information about the context to which a reference belongs. Besides easing debugging, this type system could also lead to improvements in the runtime overhead experienced by Java Card programs, provided the execution engine takes the previous work of the type checker into account.

5   Specification and Verification II

The paper by Kees Huizing and Ruurd Kuiper [HK01] contained a new analysis of the fragile base class problem. The fragile base class problem arises when one has a correct base class (i.e., a superclass), a correct derived class (i.e., a subclass), and then changes the base class in such a way that it is still correct, but the derived class is no longer correct [MS98]. One difficulty is that the programmers working on the base class may have no idea of what derived classes exist, so they have no way of ensuring the correctness of the derived classes. This points to a weakness of the specification of the base class.

The analysis by Huizing and Kuiper focuses in particular on the specification of class invariants. The problem, they say, is that the derived class may have a stronger invariant than the base class (as permitted by standard definitions of behavioral subtyping), but that this stronger invariant is not preserved by methods of the base class. They describe a specification formalism, called "cooperative contracts" to avoid this problem, as well as a stronger notion of behavioral subtyping. This stronger notion of behavioral subtyping (called "reinforced behavioral subtyping"), requires that every non-private method inherited from the base class (i.e., which is not not overridden in the derived class), does, in fact, preserve the derived class's possibly stronger invariant. The programmer of the derived class can use the source code of the base class in this proof, and can override base class methods to meet this proof obligation as well. However, in some cases, to allow reasonable derived classes and the use of method inheritance, the authors further propose stronger forms of method specification. In particular, a "cooperative contract" allows the postcondition of a method to refer to the postconditions of other methods it calls. The developer of the base class can plan ahead for future derived classes by referring to the postconditions of other methods in its method specifications. These parameterized postconditions change their meaning in the context of a derived class, since the specifications of the methods of a derived class will refer to the overriding method.

The extended abstract by Cavalcanti and Naumann [CN01], describes "ongoing" work "on refinement calculus for sequential Java." The refinement calculus is a formalism for systematic development of correct programs [Mor90]. Refinements can involve both algorithmic and data refinements. A data refinement replaces a data structures and the methods that manipulate them with different data structures and methods. The paper extends these ideas to classes, by allowing one to replace the implementation of a class (including its fields and methods) with another implementation. In the refinement calculus, such a refinement step must be proved correct by exhibiting a forward simulation relation, which relates the states of the original (abstract) class to those of the replacement (concrete) class. The paper states a soundness theorem for this form of data refinement.

The work contains two "surprises." The first is that the forward simulation must be surjective in the sense that there cannot be any concrete values that do not represent some abstract values. This requirement is needed in a language that can have uninitialized variables, or call-by value-result or result. The second surprise was that the simulation relation has to be total if the language has angelic variables (or an equally powerful construct, such as specification statements). Another interesting aspect discussed is that, apparently, the results show that an equality test that tests the identity of objects does not preserve data refinement.

The paper by Peter Müller, Arnd Poetzsch-Heffter, and Gary Leavens [MPHL01] tackles the notorious problem of modular verification of frame properties. Frame properties specify which locations (i.e., fields) may be modified by a method. For an object oriented language it should be possible to specify such properties in an abstract way, so that subclasses have the freedom to introduce additional fields that can be modified. Clearly one wants to reason about these properties in a modular way, so that frame properties can be specified and verified of an individual class irrespective of the context in which it is used, and irrespective of additional (sub)classes that may exists in this context. Finding a proof system that allows modular verification of frame properties has been recognized as an important open problem, and has attracted a lot of attention in the past few years.

This paper presents a concrete proposal to extend the behavioral interface specification language JML (Java Modeling Language [LBR01]) for Java with constructs to specify frame properties in a modular way, and a sound proof system allowing modular verification of these frame properties. The technique is based on a more general framework for the modular verification of Java programs introduced in the recent PhD thesis of Peter Müller [Mül01], which in turn builds on work by Rustan Leino [Lei95]. Key to the whole approach is an ownership model, in which the object store (i.e., the heap) is partitioned into a hierarchy of so-called "universes" and which imposes restrictions on references between different universes. This alias control type system allows frame properties of a method to only refer to "relevant" locations, so that the frame properties are effectively underspecified. A client calling a method can use the methods specification to reason about the called method's relevant locations, and can reason directly about abstract locations that may depend on them.

The paper by John Boyland [Boy01] described interdependence between effects and uniqueness of references. The *effects* of a method are the locations that the method reads and writes. As in the work described above and Leino's work, effects should be described abstractly, without mention of implementation details such as protected or private fields of objects. To enforce this abstraction, for example, to prevent representation exposure, one must prevent representation exposure, by confining subobjects used in the implementation of an abstract object. One way to accomplish this without copying is by having unique references. A *unique* reference is the only reference to an object in a program. The enforcement of uniqueness and optimization techniques such as alias burying, depend on knowing the effects of methods. For example, alias burying requires that when a unique variable is read, all aliases to it must be dead; hence this technique requires knowledge of what locations a method will read.

Since checking both effects and uniqueness annotations requires the semantics of the other, one can check them modularly by using specifications for each method. That is, when checking a method's annotations for effects and uniqueness, one assumes the annotations for all called methods.

The paper by Joachim van den Berg, Cees-Bart Breunesse, Bart Jacobs, and Erik Poll [vdBBJP01] discussed problems relating to the semantics and modular verification of class invariants. This presentation used JML to illustrate the issues. Invariants can cause significant problems for modular verification, because the class invariants of all objects are supposed to hold at all calls and returns from all public methods. Aliasing, if not controlled, can cause methods to break invariants of objects other than the method's receiver. Call-backs also cause difficulties, because a method that might call back may find the receiver object in an inconsistent state. This suggests that the official semantics in JML [LBR01] is unworkable for verification, because it requires that before a method is called on an object o, one must establish not only the calling class's invariant, but also the invariant for o's class. This touched off a lively discussion among the participants, with Boyland suggesting that read clauses could help [Boy01], and Poetzsch-Heffter suggesting that alias control could allow the invariant to be checked modularly [Mül01, MPHL01].

6   Coordination, Scripting, and Specification

The last session consisted of three short presentations.

Claus Pahl [Pah01] developed a process calculus to capture the establishment and release of contracts. This calculus, which is a variant of the π-calculus, formalizes dynamic composition and evolution in Java systems.

Marco Carbone, Matteo Coccia , Gianluigi Ferrari and Sergio Maffeis [CCFM01] proposed ED_-, a coordination and scripting language. This language is based on Hennessy and Riely's Distributed π-calculus [HR99], which they implemented in Java, using the class loader, reflection, and sockets. They are now working on a type system for security.

Peep Küngas, Vahur Kotkas and Enn Tyugu in [KKT01] suggested "meta-interfaces" as a means to specify classes, and defined their composition. Meta-interfaces define which interface variables are computable from others, and under what conditions. The techniques used are similar to those used in constraint logic programming.

7   Conclusions

The interest in the workshop, and the lively discussions at the workshop itself show that many researchers are applying their techniques to either the Java language or to programs written in Java.

Java provides interesting language features, which need to be explored further. Their precise description is both scientifically interesting, and practically relevant.

Although Java is a rather complex language, having a common programming language makes it significantly easier to compare and discuss different approaches and techniques, and stimulates cooperations. This synergy was evident at the workshop, which helped make it a highly successful event that was appreciated by the participants.

The interests of the participants were very wide: source language semantics, source language extensions, bytecode verification, specification languages, reasoning about program correctness, security, applets, Java card, effects, refinement, coordination. Nevertheless, the common language provided enough common ground to allow for many interactions. In future workshops, it has been suggested that papers could be distributed in advance, and the program committee could assign to smaller working groups the task of reading these papers and addressing specific questions.

Several of the participants have come to that workshop for the third time, and expressed the intention of coming again.

List of Participants

Last Name	First Name	Email
Ancona	Davide	davide@disi.unige.it
Boury	Pierre	Pierre.Boury@dyade.fr
Boyland	John	boyland@cs.uwm.edu
Bracha	Gilad	gilad.bracha@sun.com
Breunesse	Cees-Bart	ceesb@cs.kun.nl
Clarke	David	dave@cs.uu.nl
Coglio	Alessandro	coglio@kestrel.edu
David	Alexandre	adavid@docs.uu.se
Drossopoulou	Sophia	sd@doc.ic.ac.uk
Eisenbach	Susan	sue@doc.ic.ac.uk
El Kadhi	Nabil	nelkadhi@club-internet.fr
Hamie	Ali	a.a.hamie@brighton.ac.uk
Huisman	Marieke	Marieke.Huisman@sophia.inria.fr
Huizing	Kees	keesh@win.tue.nl
Josko	Bernhard	josko@offis.de
Kotkas	Vahur	vahur@cs.ioc.ee
Kuiper	Ruurd	wsinruur@win.tue.nl
Kungas	Peep	peep@cs.ioc.ee
Lea	Doug	dl@cs.oswego.edu
Leavens	Gary	leavens@cs.iastate.edu
Maffeis	Sergio	maffeis@di.unipi.it
Markova	Gergana	gvm@cs.purdue.edu
Mughal	Khalid	khalid@ii.uib.no
Naumann	David	naumann@cs.stevens-tech.edu
Pahl	Claus	cpahl@compapp.dcu.ie
Poetzsch-Heffter	Arnd	poetzsch@fernuni-hagen.de
Poll	Erik	erikpoll@cs.kun.nl
Pollet	Isabelle	ipo@info.fundp.ac.be
Rensink	Arend	rensink@cs.utwente.nl
Retert	William	williamr@pabst.cs.uwm.edu
Skoglund	Mats	matte@dsv.su.se
Teschke	Thorsten	thorsten.teschke@offis.de
Viroli	Mirko	mviroli@deis.unibo.it
Vu Le	Hanh	Hanh.Vu_Le@irisa.fr
Wrigstad	Tobias	tobias@dsv.su.se
Zucca	Elena	zucca@disi.unige.it

References

[ALZ01]   D. Ancona, G. Lagorio, and E. Zucca. Java separate type checking is not safe. Available in [DEL$^+$01], 2001.

[BE01]   P. Boury and N. Elkhadi. Static analysis of Java cryptographic applets. Available in [DEL$^+$01], 2001.

[BGH01]   G. Barthe, D. Gurov, and M. Huisman. Compositional specification and verification of control flow based security properties of multi-application programs. Available in [DEL$^+$01], 2001.

[Boy01]   J. Boyland. The interdependence of effects and uniqueness. Available in [DEL$^+$01], 2001.

[CCFM01] M. Carbone, M. Coccia, G. Ferrari, and S. Maffeis. Process algebra-guided design of Java mobile network applications. Available in [DEL$^+$01], 2001.

[CN01]   A. Cavalcanti and D. Naumann. Class refinement for sequential Java. Available in [DEL$^+$01], 2001.

[Cog01a] A. Coglio. Improving the official specification of Java bytecode verification. Available in [DEL$^+$01], 2001.

[Cog01b] A. Coglio. Java bytecode verification: A complete formalization. Technical report, Kestrel Institute, Palo Alto, 2001. Forthcoming at www.kestrel.edu/java

[DEJ$^+$00a] S. Drossopoulou, S. Eisenbach, B. Jacobs, G. T. Leavens, P. Müller, and A. Poetzsch-Heffter. Formal techniques for Java programs. In Jacques Malenfant, Sabine Moisan, and Ana Moreira, editors, *Object-Oriented Technology. ECOOP 2000 Workshop Reader*, volume 1964 of *Lecture Notes in Computer Science*, pages 41–54. Springer-Verlag, 2000.

[DEJ$^+$00b] S. Drossopoulou, S. Eisenbach, B. Jacobs, G. T. Leavens, P. Müller, and A. Poetzsch-Heffter, editors. *Formal Techniques for Java Programs*. Technical Report 269, Fernuniversität Hagen, 2000. Available from www.informatik.fernuni-hagen.de/pi5/publications.html.

[DEL$^+$01] S. Drossopoulou, S. Eisenbach, G. T. Leavens, P. Müller, A. Poetzsch-Heffter, and E. Poll. Formal techniques for Java programs. Available from http://www.informatik.fernuni-hagen.de/import/pi5/workshops/ecoop2001_papers.html, 2001.

[Eis98]   S. Eisenbach. Formal underpinnings of Java. Workshop report, 1998. Available from www-dse.doc.ic.ac.uk/~sue/oopsla/cfp.html.

[HK01]   K. Huizing and R. Kuiper. Reinforcing fragile base classes. Available in [DEL$^+$01], 2001.

[HR99]   M. Hennessy and J. Riely. Type-safe execution of mobile agents in anonymous networks. In Jan Vitek and Thomas Jensen, editors, *Secure Internet Programming: Security Issues for Distributed and Mobile Objects*, volume 1603 of *Lecture Notes in Computer Science*. Springer-Verlag, 1999.

[IPW99]   A. Igarashi, B. Pierce, and P. Wadler. Featherweight Java, a minimal core calculus for Java and GJ. *OOPSLA '99 Conference Proceedings*, pages 132–146, October 1999.

[JLMPH99] B. Jacobs, G. T. Leavens, P. Müller, and A. Poetzsch-Heffter. Formal techniques for Java programs. In A. Moreira and D. Demeyer, editors, *Object-Oriented Technology. ECOOP'99 Workshop Reader*, volume 1743 of *Lecture Notes in Computer Science*. Springer-Verlag, 1999.

[KKT01]   P. Küngas, V. Kotkas, and Enn Tyugu. Introducing meta-interfaces into Java. Available in [DEL$^+$01], 2001.

[LBR01]   G. T. Leavens, A. L. Baker, and C. Ruby. Preliminary design of JML: A be-havioral interface specification language for Java. Technical Report 98-06p, Iowa State University, Department of Computer Science, August 2001. See `www.cs.iastate.edu/~leavens/JML.html`.

[Lei95]   K. R. M. Leino. *Toward Reliable Modular Programs*. PhD thesis, California Institute of Technology, 1995. Available as Technical Report Caltech-CS-TR-95-03.

[Mor90]   C. Morgan. *Programming from Specifications*. Prentice Hall International, Hempstead, UK, 1990.

[MPH00]   P. Müller and A. Poetzsch-Heffter. A type system for controlling representation exposure in Java. Published in [DEJ$^+$00b], 2000.

[MPH01]   P. Müller and A. Poetzsch-Heffter. A type system for checking applet isolation in Java Card. Available in [DEL$^+$01], 2001.

[MPHL01]   P. Müller, A. Poetzsch-Heffter, and G. T. Leavens. Modular specification of frame properties in JML. Available in [DEL$^+$01], 2001.

[MS98]   L. Mikhajlov and E. Sekerinski. A study of the fragile base class problem. In Eric Jul, editor, *ECOOP '98 — Object-Oriented Programming, 12th European Conference , Brussels, Proceedings*, volume 1445 of *Lecture Notes in Computer Science*, pages 355–382. Springer-Verlag, July 1998.

[Mül01]   P. Müller. *Modular Specification and Verification of Object-Oriented Programs*. PhD thesis, FernUniversität Hagen, 2001.

[Pah01]   C. Pahl. Formalising dynamic composition and evolution in Java systems. Available in [DEL$^+$01], 2001.

[SW01]   M. Skoglund and T. Wrigstad. A mode system for read-only references in Java. Available in [DEL$^+$01], 2001.

[vdBBJP01] J. van den Berg, C.-B. Breunesse, B. Jacobs, and E. Poll. On the role of invariants in reasoning about object-oriented languages. Available in [DEL$^+$01], 2001.

[Vir01]   M. Viroli. From FGJ to Java according to LM translator. Available in [DEL$^+$01], 2001.

Automating Object-Oriented Software Development Methods

Bedir Tekinerdoğan[1], Motoshi Saeki[2], Gerson Sunyé[3], Pim van den Broek[1], and Pavel Hruby[4]

[1] University of Twente, Department of Computer Science, TRESE group, P.O. Box 217, 7500 AE Enschede, The Netherlands
{bedir,pimvdb}@cs.utwente.nl, http://wwwtrese.cs.utwente.nl
[2] Tokyo Institute of Technology, Department of Computer Science, Tokyo 152-8552, Japan
saeki@se.cs.titech.ac.jp, http://www.se.cs.titech.ac.jp
[3] IRISA, Triskell Research Group, Campus de Beaulieu, 35 042 Rennes
http://gerson.sunye.free.fr
[4] Navision Software a/s, Frydenlunds Alle 6, 2950 Vedbaek,
ph@navision.com, http://www.navision.com

Abstract. Current software projects have generally to deal with producing and managing large and complex software products. It is generally believed that applying software development methods are useful in coping with this complexity and for supporting quality. As such numerous object-oriented software development methods have been defined. Nevertheless, methods often provide a complexity by their own due to their large number of artifacts, method rules and their complicated processes. We think that automation of software development methods is a valuable support for the software engineer in coping with this complexity and for improving quality. This paper presents a summary and a discussion of the ideas that were raised during the workshop on automating object-oriented software development methods.

1 Introduction

Numerous object-oriented software development methods exist in the literature. Most popular methods have a general character, but some methods, like real-time system design, are targeted at specific application domains. Some methods are specifically defined for a given phase in the life cycle of software development, such as requirement analysis or domain analysis. It is generally accepted that these methods are useful for developing high-quality software.

Most methods include a number of different heuristic rules, which are needed to produce or refine different artifacts. Moreover, the rules are structured in different ways, leading to different software development processes. Although useful, applying methods is a complex issue, and does not necessarily lead to effective and efficient software development. Automated support for object-oriented methods will decrease this complexity, increase reusability, and provide better support for adaptability, customizability and continuous improvement. Unfortunately, apart from the many environments with diagram editors and visualization tools, existing object- oriented methods are basically

Á. Frohner (Ed.): ECOOP 2001 Workshops, LNCS 2323, pp. 41–56, 2002.

described in separate handbooks and manuals. Complete and integrated tools, which support the entire life cycle, are not yet present in practice.

This workshop aimed to identify the fundamental problems of automating methods and to explore the mechanisms for constructing case tools that provide full support for methods. The initial topics of interest were the following:

- Meta-models for software development methods
  - How to model software and management artifacts?
  - Which meta-models are needed?
  - Development process patterns.
- Active rule/process support for methods
  - How to formalize heuristic rules of methods?
  - How to integrate rules in case tools.
  - How to formalize process of methods.
- Method engineering
  - Tailoring and composing methods.
  - Refinement of methods to projects.
  - Inconsistencies in method integration.
- Case tools for method generation
  - Experiences with meta-case tools.
  - Design of meta-case tools.
- Automated support for quality reasoning
  - Tools for quality management
  - Automated support for alternatives selection.
- Existing case tools
  - Overview/comparison of existing tools with respect to method support
  - Extensions to existing case tools

In the following sections we will report on the ideas that were developed at this workshop. To understand the context we will first explain the basic elements of a method in Sect. 2 followed by the rationale for applying a method in Sect. 3. Section 4 will present the rationale for automating methods. In Sect. 5 we will provide the program of the workshop and present the categorization and discussion on the papers. Section 6 presents the discussions and the ideas that were developed during the workshop. We will conclude in Sect. 7.

2   What Is a Method?

In order to automate methods we need first to understand the basic elements of methods. Figure 1 represents a methodological framework for software development, which consists of four basic layers. The application layer represents the software product being developed using this methodological framework. The method layer includes process descriptions, notations, rules and hints to build the application with the existing computation models. The computation models represent the basic building blocks of the application and include the object-oriented features like objects, classes, messages and inheritance. The tools layer provides tools to support the horizontal layers, like dedicated compilers and CASE tools.

Using this methodological framework we can define a software development method in terms of the following aspects:

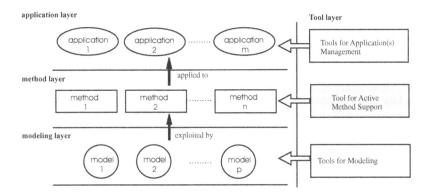

Fig. 1. Methodological framework for software development (adapted from [22])

Artifact Types

Artifact types are descriptive forms that the software engineer can utilize for producing artifacts. In this sense, artifact types reflect the properties of the artifacts in the system. For example, the Unified Process [14] provides artifact types for use cases, classes, associations, attributes, inheritance relations and state-charts. Artifact types are represented basically using textual or graphical representations. Artifact types include descriptions of the models in the modeling layer in Fig. 2. In addition to these, the method itself may define intermediate or subsidiary artifact types to produce the final software products. An intermediate artifact type in, for example, OMT [19] is the artifact type *Tentative Class*, which describes the entities that are potentially an artifact *Class*, but may which may later be eliminated or transformed to the artifact *Attribute*.

Method Rules

Method rules aim at identifying, eliminating and verifying the artifacts. Most methods define rules in an informal manner. Nevertheless, method rules can be expressed using conditional statements in the form IF <condition> THEN <consequent> [23]. The consequent part may typically be a selection, elimination or an update action. For example, the Unified Process advises the following rule to identify classes:

IF an entity in a use case model is relevant
THEN select it as a class

In general, most rules are *heuristic* rules [18]; they support the identification of the solution but there is actually no guarantee that the solution can be found by anybody at anytime by applying the corresponding heuristic rules. The heuristic rules are generally built up over a period of time, as experience is gained in using the method in a wider domain. The application of the heuristic rules depends on the interpretation of the engineer, which may differ because of the different backgrounds, and experiences of the engineers. Opposite to heuristic rules are algorithmic rules, which are derived from the concept of algorithm. An algorithm is a unique representation of operations, which will lead to clearly described result. An algorithmic rule is a rule, which can be transformed to an algorithm. Every rule that cannot be transformed to an algorithmic rule is a heuristic rule. Algorithmic rules work best in a predictable and limited environment and where there is full knowledge of all contingencies. Algorithmic rules fail however in unpredictable environments which contain uncertainty, change or competition. In general the gross of the rules in current software development methods are heuristic rules.

Software Process

Very often, the term *process* is used to indicate the overall elements that are included in a method, that is, the set of method rules, activities, and practices used to produce and maintain software products. Sometimes the term process is also used as a synonym for the term method. We make an explicit distinction between method and process. In the given methodological framework of Fig. 1 a process is part of a method. In this context, we adopt the definition of a process as a (partially) ordered set of actions for achieving a certain goal [10]. The actions of a process are typically the method rules for accessing the artifacts. Process actions can be causally ordered, which represents the time-dependent relations between the various process steps. We adopt the currently accepted term *workflow* to indicate such an ordering [14]. Workflows in software development are, for example, analysis, design, implementation and test. Formerly, this logical ordering of the process actions was also called *phase*. Currently, the term phase is more and more used to define time- related aspects such as milestones and iterations [14].

To support the understanding of software processes and improve the quality we may provide different models of processes [1]. Several process models have been proposed, including the traditional waterfall model and the spiral model, which have been often criticized because of the rigid order of the process steps. Recently, more advanced process models such as the Rational Unified Process [16] and the Unified Software Development Process [10] have been proposed.

Software development methods differ in the adopted artifact types, the corresponding method rules and the process that is enforced for applying the method rules. Consequently, automated support for methods can thus basically concern automating artifact management, automating method rules and/or automating the development process.

3   Rationale for Utilizing Methods

It is generally believed that the application of methods plays an important role in developing quality software products. The following are the fundamental technical reasons for this.

First, a method provides the designer a set of guidelines in producing the artifact and its verification against the requirements in the problem statement. This is particularly important for the inexperienced designer who needs assistance to capture the essential aspects of the design. From experimental studies it follows that experienced designers may often follow an opportunistic approach, but that is less effective for inexperienced designers who are not familiar with the problem domain [1][24]. A method directs the designer to produce the right artifact.

Second, since methods formalize certain procedures of design and externalize design thinking, they help to avoid the occurrence of overlooked issues in the design and tend to widen the search for appropriate solutions by encouraging and enabling the designer to think beyond the first solution that comes to mind.

Third, design methods help to provide logical consistency among the different processes and phases in design. This is particularly important for the design of large and complex systems, which is produced by a large team of designers. A design method provides a set of common standards, criteria and goals for the team members.

Fourth, design methods help to reduce possible errors in design and provide heuristic rules for evaluating design decisions.

Finally, mainly from the organizational point of view, a method helps to identify important progress milestones. This information is necessary to control and coordinate the different phases in design.

A method is mainly necessary for structuring the process in producing large scale and complex systems that involve high costs. Motivation for design methods can thus be summarized as directing the designer, widening possible number of design solutions, providing consistency among design processes, reducing errors in design and identifying important milestones.

4   Rationale for Automating Methods

Although methods may include the right process, artifact types and method rules, applying methods may not be trivial at all. Currently, software development is a human-intensive process in which methods are designed and applied by humans with their inherent limitations, who can cope with a limited degree of complexity. Software development is a problem-solving process in which the application of methods is a complex issue. The complexity is firstly caused by the complexity of the problems that need to be solved and secondly by the complexity of the methods themselves. Currently, a valuable and practical method usually includes over dozens of artifact types each corresponding with many method rules that are linked together in a complicated process, which is all together not easy to grasp for the individual mind. In addition these aspects may also not be explicitly described in the methods and likewise increase complexity. As such, applying the method may be cumbersome, which will directly impact the artifacts that are being produced.

Automating the software development methods can be considered as a viable solution to managing the complexity of the application of methods. Automating the methods will reduce the labor time and eliminate the source of errors in applying the method [7]. In addition, as a matter of fact, many activities in methods do not require specific and/or advanced skills and basically consists of routine work. It may then be worthwhile to automate all the activities so that the software engineer can focus on more conceptual issues. Naturally, there may also be activities that are hard to automate or even impossible for automation, e.g. forming concepts may be one candidate for this.

The software engineering community has an intrinsic tendency towards automating processes and providing tools to cope with the complexity. The so-called Computer Aided Software Engineering (CASE) tools basically aim at automating the various activities in the software development process. Automating methods essentially means that we need to build CASE tools for supporting the application of methods. This is shown in Fig. 2 through the gray rectangle in the tool layer.

Automation is inherent to software engineering since it basically automates the solutions for the real world problems. For this purpose, in the beginning of software engineering the major tool was the programming language itself. This was followed with compilers, editors, debuggers, and interpreters. Until the middle of 1980s tools were developed mainly for the lower level phases of the life cycle. With the exception of general purpose editing facilities almost no support was provided for the higher level phases. With the advent of interactive graphic tools automated support for graphical design notations appeared on the market in the late 1980s. A collection of related tools is usually called an *environment* [12]. Unfortunately complete and integrated tools that support the entire life cycle are not yet present in practice. This workshop aimed to identify the problems in these issues and try to come up with some reusable solutions.

5   Meta-modeling

Engineers build models to better understand the systems that are being developed [6]. In a similar way, to understand existing models we may provide models of these as well. This activity is called *meta-modeling*. Meta-models are thus abstractions of a set of existing models. They can be used to understand the relationships of the concepts in different modeling languages, for comparing and evaluating different models, for providing interoperability among different tools, or as conceptual schemas for modeling CASE tools and repositories.

To understand software development methods we may thus need to provide models of methods. An example of a model for software development methods is the model in Fig. 1. Method-modeling is typically an activity of method engineering, which is defined as an engineering discipline for designing, constructing and adapting methods, techniques and tools for the development of information systems [21].

To automate methods both method-engineering and meta-modeling can be applied. CASE tools can be developed for supporting a single method. However, since it is generally difficult to define an ideal method for all application domains and all processes, most CASE environments need to support several methods. To be able to support multiple methods, modern CASE environments basically adopt meta-models of these methods, which can be tailored by method designers. A typical example is the meta-model of the Unified Modeling Language (UML) [6]. The quality of meta- models basically depends on the scope of the models it can describe and its adaptability and extensibility with future requirements. Providing meta-models of existing models is not a trivial task, and method engineering knowledge may provide systematic activities to do this properly.

In the same way that meta-models describe models in a particular language, meta-meta-models express meta-models. To express these ideas the *four-level architecture* [5] has been accepted as an architectural framework for model, meta-models and meta-meta-models. This architecture is shown in Fig. 2. Hereby the rectangles represent the model layers, whereas the rounded rectangles represent the instantiations of these models.

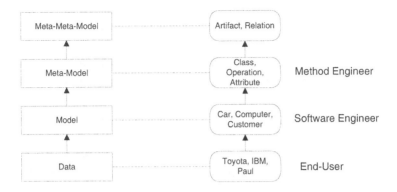

Fig. 2. The four level architecture for modeling

6 Workshop Program

The workshop topics were related to the background as presented in the previous section. We have received 14 papers from varying topics, that we classified into five groups. These papers were shortly presented during the morning. Based on the topics of the papers and the preferences of the participants we selected the discussion topics for the afternoon session. In the following we present the program together with a short summary and a discussion of each session. The sessions actually provide a refinement of the framework in Fig. 2.

6.1 Refining the Four-Level Architecture

9:00–9:20 Introduction, Bedir Tekinerdoğan

This presentation basically discussed the goals of the workshop and presented the basic elements of methods, the rationale for automating methods and a categorization of the submitted papers.

9:20–10:00 Group 1: Meta-modeling, Chair: Motoshi Saeki

- *Medical Reports through Meta-modeling Techniques: MetaGen in the medical domain*, N. Revault, B. Huet
- *Towards a Tool for Class Diagram Construction and Evolution*, M. Dao, M. Huchard, H. Leblanc, T. Libourel, C. Roume
- *Using UML Profiles: A Case Study*, L. Fuentes, A. Vallecillo
- *Abstraction Levels in Composition*, M. Glandrup

In Sect. 5 we have seen the importance of meta-modeling for designing methods. In this Meta-modeling session the first two papers concern the application of meta- models while the latter two discuss various aspects of meta-models. Fig. 3 summarizes the map of the discussions in the session, and in addition can be considered as a refinement to the four-layered architecture in Fig. 2.

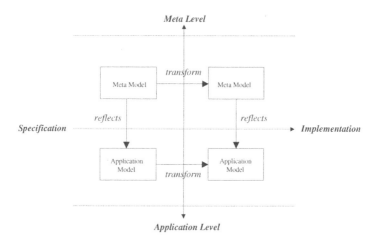

Fig. 3. Aspects of meta-models

The papers in this session consider two levels of reflection relations: meta-model and application model (meta-model layer and model layer in Fig. 2 respectively). The paper of Revault & Huet pointed out that at one level in the meta-modeling architecture different models exist that are transformed to other models at the same level. In addition, they make an explicit distinction between specification and implementation of the models. To develop application programs (semi-) automatically we need to model the transformation of meta-models from specification to implementation. Dao et. al. proposed automated CASE tool generation from a meta- model description so that the construction and the evolution of application models can be supported by manipulating and analyzing the meta-model. The other two papers presented by Glandrup, and Fuentes & Vallecillo, discussed several viewpoints of meta-models themselves. The former captured meta-models from a compositional view and set up five abstraction levels of meta-model composition; behavior, artifact, structure, expression power and expression language. The latter one discussed meta- models from UML profile view and proposed the concepts of basic model and composite one in UML profiles to define meta-models.

10:00–10:30 Group 2: Automatic Transformation of Models, Chair: Gerson Sunye

- *Automatic Code Generation Using an Aspect Oriented Framework*, O. Aldawoud, A. Bader, E. Tzilla
- *Automatic Transformation of Conceptual Models into Design Models*, J. Said, E. Steegmans

This session focuses more on the transformation of models within one level of the meta-modeling architecture of Fig. 2. Hereby, basically two topics were addressed: separation of concerns and traceability.

The first paper tries to formally separate the basic algorithm from special purpose concerns such as persistence, synchronization, real-time constraints, etc. This separation allows for the locality of different kinds of functionalities in the programs, making them easier to write, understand, and modify. Hereby, a method for using the separation of concerns at the design level is presented. Their work uses the different UML views to express different concerns. More precisely, they use statecharts to express the concurrency of a system and generate the specialization code for an application framework. Traceability is the degree to which a relationship can be established between two or more models during the development process. Said and Steegmans introduced a Java framework, which helps the development of transformational components, used to translate models from analysis to design. Since this framework can keep a trace of the transformed elements, it keeps traceability dependencies between software development activities.

10:30–11:00 Break

11:00–11:20 Group 3: Automatic Support for Patterns, Chair: Gerson Sunye

- *Meta-modeling Design Patterns: Application to Pattern Detection and Code Synthesis*, H. Albin-Amiot, Y. Gueheneuc
- *Object-Oriented Modeling of Software Patterns and Support Tool*, T. Kobayashi

Within one model one may identify patterns of models and patterns of transformations. This session focused on tool support for Design Patterns, which has been recently the subject of several research efforts. The goal of these tools is to help designers in several ways, using different approaches, such as code generation, validation and recognition. Automatic code generation focuses on automatically generating code from design patterns, which likewise releases designers from the implementation burden. Validation ensures that pattern constraints are respected, and since this may be easily overlooked automation may play an important supporting role. Finally, the recognition of pattern instances within source code avoid them to get lost after they have been implemented.

Independently of the approach it supports, a pattern tool must answer to at least two questions: (i) how (and what parts of) the definition of the pattern definition is represented and (ii) how a pattern instance is implemented/recognized. The tool presented by Albin-Amiot & Yann-Gal Gueheneuc uses a Java framework in order to represent the structure of a pattern in terms of Entities (essentially, classes and interfaces) and Elements (associations, methods and fields). In addition, some precise behavior (e.g. delegation) is represented by a Java class. Pattern methods are represented by a declarative description. Once a pattern is precisely represented in the framework, it is used to generate and recognize pattern instances. A similar tool was introduced by Takashi Kobayashi where design patterns are also represented by a Java framework. The representation of a pattern is used by a class-diagram editor, which allows instances of different patterns to be merged.

11:20–11:40 Group 4: Formal approaches/verification, Chair: Pim van den Broek

- *Prototype Execution of Independently Constructed Object-Oriented Analysis Model*, T. Aoki, T. Katayama
- *Regulating Software Development Process by Formal Contracts*, C. Pons, G. Baum

Generally, the transformation between the different models is required to be correct. This session focused on automating this verification and validation of the transformation of the models.

In the first paper, the authors propose a formal approach for object-oriented analysis modeling, consisting of formal analysis models, unification of these models, prototype execution of the resulting model, and a prototyping environment. It is shown how the analysis models are formalized, how they are unified into the unified model, and how prototyping execution of the unified model is performed. The purpose of the prototype execution is to ensure the validity of the constructed analysis model. To ensure that the constructed analysis model is correct, it should be verified, which is costly. Therefore the model is validated by prototype execution, and then verified. The prototype execution of the constructed analysis model is done with the functional programming language ML, whose higher order capabilities are useful for modeling application domains.

In the second paper, the authors propose to apply the notion of formal contract to the object-oriented software development process itself. This means that the software development process involves a number of agents (the development team and the software artifacts) carrying out actions with the goal of building a software system that meets the user requirements. Contracts can be used to reason about correctness of the development process and to compare the capabilities of various groupings of agents (coalitions) in order to accomplish a particular contract. The originality of process contracts resides in the fact that software developers are incorporated into the formalism as agents (or coalitions of agents) who make decisions and have responsibilities. Traditional correctness reasoning can be used to show that a coalition of agents achieves a particular goal. Single contracts are analyzed from the point of view of different coalitions with the weakest precondition formalism.

11:40–12:20 group 5: Process Support/Modeling, Chair: Bedir Tekinerdoğan

- *Empowering the Interdependence between the Software Architecture and Development Process*, C. Wege
- *Knowledge-Based Techniques to Support Reuse in Vertical Markets*, E. Paesschen
- *HyperCase- Case Tool Which Supports the Entire Life Cycle of OODPM*, O. Drori
- *Convergent Architecture Software Development Process*, G. Hillenbrand

This session focused on the concerns in process modeling and process support. In the first paper, Wege observes that the evolution of software artifacts may require the adaptation of the software development process. This may especially the case in the case of software architecture design, which has the largest impact on the overall software development process and which is generally followed by an analysis and design phase. Sometimes, like in Extreme Programming [3], even a constant architecture evolution may be required and it is important to interrelate the changes of the process to software architecture. Wege states that this interdependence between the software architecture and the development process should be made explicit and proposes to provide tool support for this.

Paesschen reflects on transformational and evolutionary dependencies of artifacts in the software development process, such as for example, the dependency between analysis and design. The interesting aspect here is, firstly that artifacts are structurally related, and secondly they may evolve independently. To provide the consistency it is required that the evolution of related artifacts are synchronized. In her paper she specifically focuses on the interdependence between domain models and framework code, and claims that currently the evolution link between the two is implicit but should be captured as knowledge to provide automated support for this. She suggests the development of an expert system that applies this knowledge to provide an explicit coupling between domain models and frameworks.

The last two papers in this session aim to provide tool support for the entire life cycle of the software development process. Drori basically points to the management and control of the various method elements in automating software development methods. He presents a tool called HyperCASE that assumes that the developer already uses a set of tools, and which are structured and managed.

Hillenbrand proposes to apply the so-called convergent architecture software development process that is based on convergent engineering, which aims a convergence between the business domain and the software domain. In the paper the process and the corresponding tool is shortly described.

12:20–12:30 Wrap-Up Morning Session

12:30–14:00 Lunch

6.2   Preparing Discussions

After the presentations in the morning and the lunch, the program for the afternoon was as follows:

14:00–14:30 Preparing Discussions, Motoshi Saeki
In this afternoon session we had planned to identify the important topics that the participants preferred to discuss and that could be considered as a refinement of the ideas that were presented or identified during the morning. Based on the morning presentations and interests of the participants, the following categories were selected as discussions topics:

1. Methodology, which would focus on methods and method engineering techniques.
2. Quality, whereby the quality concerns in applying methods were relevant.
3. Meta-models, which focused on defining meta-models for automating methods.

The basic goal for the discussions was a lively discussion and full information extraction. For this we proposed to utilize so-called index cards in which the following process would be followed: (1) Each member gets 5 index cards (2) On each index card every member writes a question that (s)he thinks is important (3) When everybody has finished writing the questions all the index cards are put on the table (4) Each time randomly an index card is picked up and the question is read by one person (5) The group discusses about the question and categorizes the question. After this, the next person gets the question, reads it and the group categorizes the question, until all index cards have been ordered and categorized. (6) The group tries to find answers for the questions in the different sub-categories, preferably by giving concrete examples.
The subsequent program was as follows:

14:30–15:30 Discussion

15:30–16:00 Break

16:00–17:00 Discussion

17:00–17:30 Presentations of the Conclusions of the Separate Groups

6.3 Discussion Results

Methodologies

Automating methods requires a thorough understanding of methods and as such this group focused on the important aspects of software development methods. The first observation is that different methods may be required for developing different applications and a considerable number of methods have been introduced for various purposes. The problem is that there is actually no universal method for each application and existing methods have been designed for as much as wide range of applications. Nevertheless, they may fail for individual applications. The best possible way is to develop or tailor a dedicated method for each problem domain, that is, engineer methods. This activity of *method engineering* is defined as an engineering discipline for designing, constructing and adapting methods, techniques and tools for the development of information systems [21].

Before we can apply method-engineering techniques and automate methods, it is first required to select the right method or method parts from the extensive set of methods. For this we need to do apply a systematic approach in which we can utilize techniques of domain analysis methods [2]. Domain analysis aims to select and define the domain of focus, and collect the relevant information to provide a domain model. A domain model provides an explicit representation of the common and variant properties of the systems in the domain. Domain analysis applied to software design methods means that we select and define the set of methods that we are interested in, and develop a *method domain model* that includes the commonality and the variabilities of the different methods in the selected domain.

Domain analysis on methods will lead to the observation that some methods are better able to be automated than others. To denote this difference we introduced the quality concept of *automatability*. We have defined automatability of methods as the degree on which methods can be automated. If we consider that every method consists basically of artifact types, method rules and a process as it is explained in Sect. 2, then the first reason for the lack of automatability may be due to the lack of sufficient number of artifact types, method rules and a process. However, this is not the only reason. While some methods are more rigid and seek for high predictability, other methods have by their nature a very flexible and agile process [9]. Flexible methods are less rigid in applying process actions and rely more on intuition of the persons who are involved in the corresponding process actions.

While flexible methods have a lower automatability degree this does not mean that automation is not possible at all. In this case, the kind of automation will only be different and basically focus on providing supporting tools for the human-centric processes. The bottom line however is that automation is useful for both rigid and flexible methods.

Rigid Method

High degree of
automatability

Flexible Methods

Low degree of
automatability

Fig. 4. Automatability of methods with respect to their rigidity

Quality Issues in Automating Methods

Like quality of the artifacts that are produced by software methods we can talk about qualities of methods. The previous section already described a quality factor of automatability. In this session, the group has basically focused on the traceability quality factor since this plays an essential role for supporting the automation process and the other quality factors. Traceability requires that the transformational links between the various artifacts must be made explicit and visible to understand their production and to provide automated support for this. The transformation of models exists on various abstraction levels of the four-level architecture in Fig. 2. In this session the group focused on transformation of artifacts within one layer, that is, the model layer of Fig. 2. As shown in Fig. 5 below, we can find two types of transformation relations among artifacts.

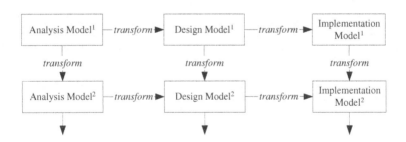

Fig. 5. Refinement of transformation of models

This figure can be seen as a further refinement of Fig. 3. The horizontal direction of the transformation in Fig. 5 is for making artifacts more concrete and its transformation goes along the progress of software development from an analysis model (requirements specification) to an implementation model (program), while the vertical direction holds the same abstraction level and indicates only the refinement of the same model.

In the horizontal transformation, it is important to preserve the quality from the *Analysis Model*[1] to the *Design Model*[1], and finally to the *Implementation Model*[1]. This preservation of quality can be supported by automating the preservation of transformation links, the storing of the various artifacts and the active rule support in producing and transforming artifacts.

The vertical transformation denotes model transformations of the same model. The reason for transformation may be due to introduction of evolutionary requirements or the need for a different representation of the same model. For example, in Fig. 5 *Analysis Model*[1] may be written in a natural language but transformed into *Analysis Model*[2] written in a formal language to reason and ensure the quality of the analysis model. Any inconsistencies in the original analysis model can then be easily detected and corrected. This may require bi-directional traceability of the artifacts. In the same sense, *Analysis Model*[2] may represent the analysis model with additional requirement. The updating of the artifacts may have direct impact on the subsequent models and require the retriggering of the transformation process. Automated support may be helpful to guide this process.

Meta-models

Like conventional modeling, meta-modeling by its own can be a means to formalize different aspects of the software development process in order to support its automation. Each meta-model has its own focus and scope and solves a particular problem. Meta-models can be utilized as conceptual schemas for repositories that hold knowledge on artifact production and manipulation. Meta-models may be defined for artifact types, like in the UML, but also for heuristic rule support or process support. Meta-modeling has basically focused on modeling artifact types, however, for an active support of software development methods it is required that also meta-models are generated for coping with heuristic rules and process support.

Meta-models may also be needed to couple different CASE tools and to provide interoperability. Since CASE tools may be based on different meta-models this results in the composability problem of meta-models. Current techniques for solving this issue is by providing Meta-CASE tools in which meta-models can be adjusted to the support the automation of different methods. Nevertheless, even then a change of the methods that are modeled might require the meta-models to change as well, and it may not be so easy to define an appropriate meta-model.

7 Conclusions

In this paper we have described the results of the workshop on automating methods. We have first presented the background on the notion of methods and identified that every method basically includes artifact types, rules and a process to produce artifacts. We have defined the rationale for applying methods and automating methods. It appears that automating methods requires knowledge on the software development methods, meta-modeling, method engineering techniques and knowledge on CASE tool development. We have explained the methodological framework for software development in Fig. 1 and showed our focus of interest on defining CASE tools for developing and managing methods. In Fig. 2 we have explained the four-level architecture of meta-modeling and refined this throughout the paper. Figure 3 has shown the various aspects of meta-models within one layer of the four-layered architecture. Hereby, software development is seen as a transformation of models, that might be themselves reflected on using meta-models to provide automated support. This observation highlighted several problems in automation of methods. Basically, we can define meta-models for artifact types, heuristic rules and the process.

We have introduced the quality factor of automatability, which refers to the possibility of automation for the corresponding methods. As a matter of fact some methods have a higher automatability degree than other methods. Nevertheless, automation might also be useful for flexible methods to support the human intensive but less conceptual activities.

Acknowledgements. It took us 302 e-mail communications to organize the workshop and finish this summary report. We would like to thank Hervé Albin-Amiot, Omar Aldawud, Christian Wege, and Toshiaki Aoki for their contribution to the discussion section in this report. The following persons attended the workshop:

1. Akşit, Mehmet, University of Twente.
2. Albin-Amiot, Hervé, Ecole des Mines de Nantes.
3. Aldawud, Omar, Lucent Technologies
4. Aoki,Toshiaki, JAIST
5. van den Broek, Pim, University of Twente
6. Dao,Michel, France Telecom R&D
7. Drori, Offer, Hebrew University of Jerusalem
8. Elrad, Tzilla , University of Chicago
9. Fuentes, Lidia, University of Malaga
10. Glandrup, Maurice, University of Twente
11. Hillenbrand, Gisela, Interactive Objects Software
12. Kobayashi, Takashi, Tokyo Institute of Technology
13. Libourel,Therese, LIRMM
14. Mughal, Khalid, University of Bergen
15. Van Paesschen, Ellen, Vrije Universiteit Brussel
16. Pons, Claudia, LIFIA
17. Revault, Nicolas, Univ. Cergy-Pontoise - LIP6
18. Roume, Cyril, LIRMM
19. Saeki, Motoshi, Tokyo Institute of Technology
20. Said,Jamal,K.U.LEUVEN
21. Sunye,Gerson,IRISA
22. Thierry, Eric, LIRMM
23. Tekinerdoğan, Bedir, University of Twente
24. Vallecillo, Antonio, University of Malaga
25. Wege, Chris, University of Tubingen
26. Yann-Gael Gueheneuc, Ecole des Mines de Nantes

The organizers would like to thank all the attendants for their participation to the workshop and the fruitful discussions that we had. Finally we would like to thank Manabu Ishida and Erik Ernst for their efforts in converting this document from MS-Word to Latex.

References

1. Adelson, B, & Soloway E.: The role of domain experience in software design. IEEE Trans. Software Engineering, SE-11(11), 1351-9, 1985.
2. Arrango, G.: Domain Analysis Methods, in: Software Engineering Reusability, R. Schafer, R. Prieto-Diaz, & M. Matsumoto (eds.), Ellis Horwood, 1994.
3. Beck, K.: Extreme Programming Explained, Addison-Wesley, 2000.
4. Berg, van den K.: Modeling Software Processes and Artifacts, In Bosch, J. and Mitchell, S. (Eds), ECOOP'97 Workshop Reader, LNCS 1357, Springer-Verlag, pp. 285-288, 1997.
5. Bezivin, J.: Who is afraid of ontologies, OOPSlA 1996 Workshop on Model Engineering, Methods, and Tool Integration with CDIF, 1998.
6. Booch, G., Rumbaugh, J., & Jacobson, I.: The Unified Modeling Language User Guide, Addison-Wesley, 1999.
7. Budgen, D.: Software Design, Addison-Wesley, 1994.
8. Chikofsky, E.J.; Computer-Aided Software Engineering (CASE). Washington, D.C. IEEE Computer Society, 1989.
9. Cockburn, A.: Agile Software Development, Addison-Wesley Longman, 2001.
10. Feiler, P.H., & Humphrey, W.S.: Software Process Development and Enactment: Concepts and Definitions, Software Engineering Institute, Carnegie Mellon University, Pittsburgh, PA, 1991.
11. Gane, C.: Computer-Aided Software Engineering: The Methodologies, the Products, and the Future, Englewood Cliffs, NJ: Prentice Hall, 1990.
12. Ghezzi, C., Jazayeri, M., & Mandrioli, D.: Fundamentals of Software Engineering. Prentice-Hall, 1991.
13. Humphrey, W.S.: Managing the Software Process, Addison-Wesley, 1989.
14. Jacobson, I., Booch, G., & Rumbaugh, J.: The Unified Software Development Process, Addison-Wesley, 1999.
15. Johnson, R., & Foote, B.: Designing Reusable Classes. Journal of Object-Oriented Programming. Vol. 1, No. 2, pp. 22-35, 1988.
16. Kruchten, P.: The Rational Unfied Process: An Introduction, Addison-Wesley, 2000.
17. Pressman, R.S.: Software Engineering: A Practitioner's Approach, Mc-Graw-Hill, 1994.
18. Riel, A: Object Oriented Design Heuristics, Addison-Wesley, 1996.
19. Rumbaugh, J., Blaha, M., Premerlani, W., Eddy, F., & Lorensen, W.: Object-Oriented Modeling and Design, Prentice-Hall, 1991.
20. Rumbaugh, J., Jacobson, I., & Booch, G.: The Unified Modeling Language Reference Manual, Addision-Wesley, 1998.
21. Saeki, M.: Method Engineering. in: P. Navrat and H. Ueno (Eds.), Knowledge-Based Software Engineering, IOS Press, 1998.
22. Tekinerdoğan, B. & Aksit, M.: Adaptability in object-oriented software development: Workshop report, in M. Muhlhauser (ed), Special issues in Object-Oriented Programming, Dpunkt, Heidelberg, 1998.
23. Tekinerdogan, B., & Aksit, M.: Providing automatic support for heuristic rules of methods. In: Demeyer, S., & Bosch, J. (eds.), Object-Oriented Technology, ECOOP '98 Workshop Reader, LNCS 1543, Springer-Verlag, pp. 496-499, 1999.
24. Visser, W., & Hoc, J.M.: Expert software design strategies. In: Psychology of Programming, Hoc, J.M., Green, T.R.G., Samuray, R., & Gilmore, D.J. (eds). Academic Press, 1990.

Adaptive Object-Models and Metamodeling Techniques

Nicolas Revault[1] and Joseph W. Yoder[2]

[1] University of Cergy-Pontoise (& Paris 6)
33 bd du Port 95011 Cergy-Pontoise Cedex, FRANCE
`Nicolas.Revault@lip6.fr`
[2] The Refactory, Inc.
209 W. Iowa Urbana, IL 61801, USA
`yoder@refactory.com`

Abstract. This article reports on the presentations and discussions of the workshop on "Adaptive Object-Models and Metamodeling Techniques", held in conjonction with Ecoop'01 in Budapest on June 2001. After overviewing the themes of the workshop, its organization is briefly presented. This is followed by a summary of the works presented and a section dedicated to develop the results of the workshop. The main conclusions are about comparing and locating one towards another three techniques of interest: – Reflection at the Language Level, – Adaptive Object-Models and – Meta-Tool Approaches to Meta-modeling. Moreover, a discussion on the needed levels of abstraction, and on their nature, is also developed in reference to the so-called "OMG four-layer architecture".

1 Overview

A system with an Adaptive Object-Model (AOM) has an explicit object model that it interprets at runtime. If you change the object model, the system changes its behavior. For example, a lot of workflow systems have an Adaptive Object-Model. Objects have states and respond to events by changing state. The Adaptive Object-Model defines the objects, their states, the events, and the conditions under which an object changes state.

There are various techniques that share common features with AOM's. Especially, those that capture business rules and build domain- or business-specific languages, namely – Grammar-Oriented Object Design (applied in the three major areas of configurable workflow, tier-to-tier mapping and object graph traversal) or – Meta-Tool Approaches[1], à la MetaEdit or à la MétaGen (applied in various fields of information system modeling: telecom, finance, medicine, etc.). There are other techniques which also describe ways to build systems that change behavior at runtime, namely – Reflection at the Language Level (mostly applied to programming language design). What is actually common to those various techniques is that they are leading to, or are driven by, meta-modeling principles and implementation using OO languages.

Adaptive Object-Models and other techniques such as Grammar-Oriented Object Design, Meta-Tool Approaches or Reflection at the Language Level, address at least one of the two following problems:

---

[1] sometimes also refered to as "Meta-CASE Tool Approaches".

Á. Frohner (Ed.): ECOOP 2001 Workshops, LNCS 2323, pp. 57–71, 2002.
© Springer-Verlag Berlin Heidelberg 2002

- Capturing (business) rules for user modeling and/or building (Domain/ Business) Specific Languages;
- Building systems that need to change requirements and reflect those requirements as quickly as possible, i.e. runtime or dynamic adaptability.

The workshop focused on identifying, cataloging and comparing these techniques one towards another. We looked at establishing some conclusions on the conditions of use of these techniques, on where they meet or overlap, and hopefully on some cross-fertilization ideas of benefit for each technique. What is generally common to these techniques is that they actually implement or use meta-modeling principles through OO languages capabilities.

Workshop position papers were presented that addressed one or more of the following:

- Examples of the different techniques;
- Concrete development reports with lessons learned;
- How can these techniques support one another;
- Prerequisites or needs for each technique;
- Pros and Cons of the different techniques;
- Comparison of the different techniques showing similarities and differences.

This paper is actually highlighting the submitted papers along with the result of our findings that address the above mentioned points.

2 Workshop Organization

The workshop was first organized around the history of the workshop, the building of a common vocabulary and context for the workshop, along with the objectives of the workshop. We then looked at some details for two of the subfields of interest, followed by presentations from works in the subfields from submitted papers[2]. We then broke into some groups for discussions and synthesized our results to be presented at the end of this paper.

2.1 History of the Workshop

From 1998 to 2000, AOM's have been discussed in various workshops [24,23,22,25]. Metadata and Adaptive Object-Model workshops at the University of Illinois in 1998 and at OOPSLA '98 and '99 were devoted to "pattern mining" some of these ideas. The workshop at ECOOP '00 was oriented toward a broader analysis of the possible uses of the Adaptive Object-Model technology, based on the examination of a range of examples. The discussions their led to establish some "dimensions of abstraction in Adaptive Object-Models, Reflection and OMG's meta-modeling architecture". Further along after these discussions, we came out with a wider idea of comparison of the techniques of interest: meta-modeling appearing to be the core feature of each technique, it has naturally been tackled as the next stepping problem.

---

[2] Available position papers from workshop participants [9,12,13,21] can be found at http://www.adaptiveobjectmodel.com/ECOOP2001.

2.2 Context for the Workshop

In order to fix a common vocabulary and settle the basis of the work for the workshop day, we recalled – 1. what we mean while using the "meta" prefix and what main idea is behind it for us, and – 2. the various techniques that deal with meta-modeling, defined in the workshop as the "subfields of interest". We also recalled the common problems we think these techniques intend to all address.

The main idea we have in mind while using the "meta" prefix is related to class-based object-oriented programming languages (OOPL). In these, we are used to differentiate between the "instance level" and the "class level". Briefly, the instance level is the one of runtime, where objects virtually exist in the computer memory, as instances of their class. The class level is the one of programming time, where classes are defined as "shapes" or "molds" for their future instances with references to other classes and actually planning (programming) the way objects will be created and will evolve at runtime. The operational link thus defined between instances and their class, is the one we call the "meta" link. This particularly makes sense when considering classes themselves as objects, instances of other classes (usual in some OOPL, e.g. Smalltalk): classes of the objects being classes are always called metaclasses.

The techniques dealing with meta-modeling we are interested in (as "subfields of interest") are those presented in the overview. Namely, Reflection at the Language Level, Grammar-Oriented Object Design, Adaptive Object-Models and Meta-Tool Approaches (à la MetaEdit or à la MétaGen), each one applied in some privileged areas. The main problems these techniques address are – Capturing (business) rules for user modeling and/or building (Domain/Business) Specific Languages and – Building systems that need to change requirements and reflect those requirements as quickly as possible, i.e. runtime or dynamic adaptability.

2.3 More on the Objectives of the Workshop

In addition to the general objectives presented in the overview section (identifying, cataloging and comparing techniques), some more specific objectives were given as part of the introduction to the workshop. These were mainly related to AOM's along with Meta-Tool Approaches.

A first idea was on the way of "going bottom up from" AOM's, in the sense that they allow to define operational domain (or business) specific languages. One of the specific objectives here is to make clear, and hopefully systematic, the way(s) this kind of languages can be supported by tools.

Another idea was on the way of "going top down from" Meta-Tool Approaches. Indeed, these generally offer meta-modeling and generating environments, in the sense that they allow to build operational user-customized model editors. One objective on that subject is to explicit the way(s) to get the operationality for models: how code generators can be systematically specified and what are the most suitable forms for them?

In addition, another objective concerning interaction between the two sets of techniques was declared: "how to interact somewhere in the middle ?". Issues such as how the techniques might support one another while setting differences and overlapping (if any) were actually asked.

Finally, setting the potential answer as another objective, we wondered on how to integrate and locate the other techniques of interest, which have either some similar goals or some similar means.

3 Summary of Contributions

The workshop brought together researchers and practitioners from a variety of areas in order to explore the themes that underlie the various techniques of interest.

A good sign that a technical area is ripening is that a number of people independently discover or explore it. This would seem to be the case with AOM's and meta-modeling. In the main, participants focused on comparisons between the Adaptive Object-Model's approach and those of Reflection and meta-modeling through Meta-Tools. It emerged that indeed all three approaches share the same levels of abstraction.

The following is a more detailed view of the main experiences/positions that were presented for participation at the workshop.

3.1 Reflection at the Language Level

Reflection is one of the main techniques used to develop adaptable systems and, currently, different kinds of reflective systems exist[3]. Compile-time reflection systems provide the ability to customize their language but they are not adaptable at runtime. On the other hand, runtime reflection systems define meta-object protocols to customize the system semantics at runtime. However, these meta-object protocols restrict the way a system may be adapted before its execution, and they do not permit the customization of its language.

The system presented by Ortin et al. [12] implements a non-restrictive reflection mechanism over a virtual machine, in which every feature may be adapted at runtime. No meta-object protocol is used and, therefore, it is not needed to specify previously what may be reflected. With this reflective system, the programming language may be also customized at runtime.

3.2 Adaptive Object-Model Architecture

Today, users themselves often seek to dynamically change their business rules without the writing of new code[4]. Customers require that systems are built that can adapt more easily to changing business needs, that can meet their unique requirements, and can scale to large and small installations.

On the other hand, the same technique is adequate for the slightly different purpose of producing a whole line of software products: of course, a line of products may be obtained by variously instantiating a unique abstract model, but also by adapting a given initial system to various requirements that appear simultaneously instead of evolving in time. Moreover, the diversification of a successful product may also be seen as a form of reengineering.

---

[3] This work was presented by F. Ortin, on the basis of his workshop submission [12]

[4] This work was presented by J. Yoder, on the basis of his workshop submission [21]

Black-box frameworks provided early solutions for the design of flexible implementation of business rules [17]. Recent research in the different types of architectures to meet such requirements from an object-oriented perspective has been catalogued as Adaptive Object-Models [2,3,1,7,23]. An Adaptive Object-Model is where the object representation of the domain under study has itself an explicit object model (however partial) that is interpreted at runtime. Such an object model can be changed with immediate (but controlled) effect on the system interpreting and running it. Note that Adaptive Object-Models usually requires a thorough analysis of the domain at hand, which may very well include a black-box framework as an initial stage.

Objects have states and respond to events by changing state. The Adaptive Object-Model defines the object model, i.e. the objects, their states, the events, and the conditions under which an object changes state, in a way that allows for dynamic modification. If you change the object model, the system changes its behavior. For example, such a feature makes it easy to integrate a workflow mechanism, which proves useful in many systems [10,19].

Adaptive Object-Models successfully confront the need for change by casting information like business rules as data rather than code. In this way, it is subject to change at runtime. Using objects to model such data and coupling an interpretation mechanism to that structure, we obtain a domain-specific language, which allows users themselves to change the system following the evolution of their business.

Metadata[5] is then often used in adaptive object-models to describe the object model itself. When runtime descriptions of these objects are available, users can directly manipulate these objects. Since the system can interpret the metadata to build and manipulate these runtime descriptions, it is easy to add new objects to the adaptive object-model, and make them immediately available to users. This approach has been validated by several successful industrial projects (see submissions to [24] and [25] along with [19, 14]).

Adaptive Object-Model architectures are usually made up of several patterns: *TypeObject* [7] is used to separate an Entity from an EntityType, Entities have Attributes, which are implemented with the *Property* pattern [3], and the *TypeObject* pattern is used a second time to separate Attributes from AttributeTypes. As is common in Entity-Relationship modeling, an Adaptive Object-Model usually separates attributes from relationships.

The *Strategy* pattern [4] is often used to define the behavior of an EntityType. These strategies can evolve to a more powerful rule-based language that gets interpreted at runtime for representing changing behavior. Finally, there needs to be support for reading and interpreting the data representing the business rules that are stored in the database

---

[5] MetaData can be described by saying that if something is going to vary in a predictable way, store the description of the variation in a database so that it is easy to change. In other words, if something is going to change a lot, make it easy to change. The problem is that it can be hard to figure out what changes, and even if you know what changes then it can be hard to figure out how to describe the change in your database. Code is powerful, and it can be hard to make your data as powerful as your code without making it as complicated as your code. But when you are able to figure out how to do it right, metadata can be incredibly powerful, and can decrease your maintenance burden by an order of magnitude, or two. [R. Johnson]

and there is usually an interface for non-programmers to define the new types of objects, attributes and behaviors needed for the specified domain.

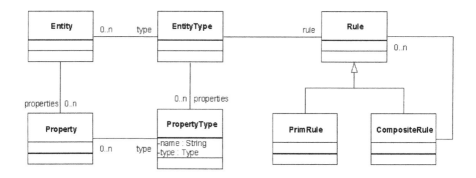

Fig. 1. Type square

Figure 1 is a UML diagram of applying the *TypeObject* pattern twice with the *Property* pattern and then adding *Strategies/RuleObjects* for representing the behavior. We call this resulting architecture the *TypeSquare* pattern and it is often seen in adaptable systems with knowledge levels as described in this paper.

Metadata for describing the business rules and objects model is interpreted in two places. The first is where the objects are constructed otherwise known as instantiating the object-model. The second is during the runtime interpretation of the business rules.

The information for describing the types of entities, properties, relationships, and behaviors are stored in a database for runtime manipulation, thus allowing for the business model to be updated and immediately reflected in applications interpreting the data.

Regardless of how the data is stored, it is necessary for the data to be interpreted to build up the adaptive object-model that represents the real business model. If an object-oriented database is used, the types of objects and relationships can be built up by simply instantiating the *TypeObjects*, *Properties*, and *RuleObjects*. Otherwise, the metadata is read from the database for building these objects, which are built using the *Interpreter* and *Builder* pattern.

The second place where the *Interpreter* pattern is applied is for the actual behaviors associated with the business entities described in the system. Eventually after new types of objects are created with their respective attributes, some meaningful operations will be applied to these objects. If these are simple *Strategies*, some metadata might describe the method that needs to be invoked along with the appropriate *Strategy*. These *Strategies* can be plugged into the appropriate object during the instantiation of the types.

As more powerful business rules are needed, *Strategies* can evolve to become more complex such that they are built up and interpreted at runtime. These can be either primitive rules or the combination of business rules through application of the *Composite* pattern. If the business rules are workflow in nature, you can use the Micro-Workflow architecture as described by Manolescu [10]. Micro-Workflow describes classes that represent workflow structure as a combination of rules such as repetition, conditional, sequential, forking, and primitive rules. These rules can be built up at runtime to represent a particular workflow process.

Adaptive Object-Models are usually built from applying one or more of the above patterns in conjunction with other design patterns such as *Composite, Interpreter*, and *Builder* [4]. *Composite* is used for either building dynamic tree structure types or rules. For example, if your entities need to be composed in a dynamic tree like structure, the *Composite* pattern is applied. *Builders* and *Interpreters* are commonly used for building the structures from the meta-model or interpreting the results.

But, these are just patterns; they are not a framework for building Adaptive Object-Models. Every Adaptive Object-Model is similar to a framework of a sort but there is currently no generic framework for building them. A generic framework for building the *TypeObjects, Properties*, and their respective relationships could probably be built, but these are fairly easy to define and the hard work is generally associated with rules described by the business language. This is something that is usually very domain-specific and varies quite a bit.

3.3   Meta-modeling through Meta-tool Approaches

For about the last 10 years, meta-modeling environments have been developed, sometimes originally for specific application areas (see e.g. [6,18,16,5,9])[6]. These environments generally share two main features: – they allow explicit meta-modeling, where meta-models and models are fully reified at instance level, and – they allow to derive (full or partial) application code from the models being specified in their editors.

In order to illustrate this kind of specification tools, a particular tool has been presented at the workshop: the MétaGen system [16]. This meta-tool has for specificity to address the problem of code generation by model transformation, this process being itself expressed in the form of a (first-order logic) rule-based system. And like other meta-tools, it allows model edition and modeling language (meta-model) prototyping, by supporting dynamically model/meta-model articulation.

For being concrete, a simple but illustrative example has been used to show the various components of the tool. The example is about a reduced dataflow modeling language, where simple *operators* (standard arithmetic ones) might be used in connection through *flows* to *constants* or *variables*, for building models of equations. Two models expressed in the language were given as examples of equations: one with just a simple operation and two variables as input and one as output ($a * b = c$, Fig. 2), the second with several operations, for representing the way an amount of installments can be computed from an initial capital, a rate and a number of installments (not shown here). Both of the models for the corresponding equations were in turn automatically operationalized as a Smalltalk application, with the necessary GUI built for giving arbitrary values to the relative input variables.

Each of the dataflow models has been used for explaining how the transformation process operates for finally generating the application code. Actually, the initial model is used as input of a first step in the transformation: it is transformed into another model,

---

[6] This work was presented by N. Revault, as an introduction to that subfield of interest

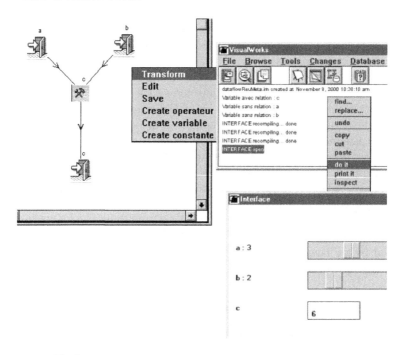

Fig. 2. Example of a model operationalization, input and output

representing the same "core" equation, but with some more information, added in order to express the way to edit the equation elements, e.g. standard sliders for input variables, or simple text fields for output variables. The new model is expressed in another modeling language, "Appli", used for specifying the application more in details. It is actually an intermediate that is in turn used as input of the second step in the generation: it is straight fully interpreted for generating the Smalltalk code for implementing the equation and allowing to edit its parameters.[7]

On the practical aspect, the transformation operates on objects reifying the models. These objects are instances of classes that are called "model classes". The model classes are in fact the implementation of a meta-model for the modeling language in use, the dataflow language or Appli in our example. The meta-models are themselves reified as objects in the environment (Fig. 3). They are specified as instances of constructs of the meta-modeling language of the tool: Pir3 in MétaGen, which roughly allows to define classes and set associations between them [15].

What is particular to the MétaGen tool is that the transformation process is preferably expressed with first-order logic (forward-chaining) rules. The rules are expressed on the basis of the meta-models' elements: in our example, one of the rules states for instance that a variable of a dataflow model without any input flow relation is to be treated such that the intermediate model must include a slider connected to it, and

---

[7] Note that there might be several possible interpretations here, e.g. for generating code towards another support language: it was shown for Java for instance.

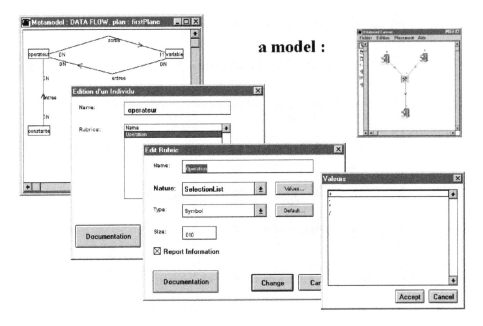

Fig. 3. Example of meta-model specification

thus that such a GUI component must be used for graphically representing it in the final application... Of course, it is the execution of the various rules that operates the automatic model transformation.

Finally, in order to illustrate adaptable model edition and actually dynamic modeling language prototyping, an evolution of the representation for variable intervals was presented: min, max and step values, initially treated within a single blank-separated string, were restructured as a record or "struct" data type. Naturally, it would be necessary to update the transformation rules for taking that evolution in account in order to make the generation process consistent.

As a summary, Fig. 4 shows a schema for the whole implementation of the example. It is actually an archetypal schema for a lot of the projects developed with the MétaGen tool.

3.4 Composable Meta-modeling Environment

Domain-Specific Design Environments (DSDE) capture specifications and automatically generate or configure the target applications in particular engineering fields[8]. Well known examples include Matlab/Simulink for signal processing and LabView for instrumentation, among others. The success of DSDEs in a wide variety of applications in diverse fields is well documented. Unfortunately, the development of a typical DSDE is very expensive. To solve this problem, Ledeczi et al. advocate the idea of a Configurable Domain-Specific Development Environment (CDSDE) that is configurable to a wide

---

[8] This work was presented by A. Ledeczi, on the basis of his workshop submission [9]

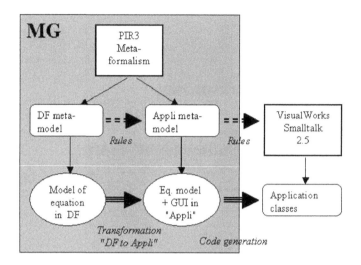

Fig. 4. Schema of the dataflow example implementation in MétaGen (MG)

range of domains. The Generic Modeling Environment (GME 2000) is a configurable toolkit for creating domain-specific design environments. The configuration is accomplished through metamodels specifying the modeling paradigm (modeling language) of the application domain. GME 2000 follows the standard four-layer metamodeling architecture applied in the specification of CDIF and UML. It is thus representing another particular Meta-Tool Approach.

The metamodeling language in GME 2000 is based on the UML class diagram notation including OCL constraints. Just as the reusability of domain models from application to application is essential, the reusability of metamodels from domain to domain is also important. Ideally, a library of metamodels of important sub-domains should be made available to the metamodeler, who can extend and compose them together to specify domain languages. These sub-domains might include different variations of signal-flow, finite state machines, data type specifications, fault propagation graphs, petri-nets, etc. The extension and composition mechanisms must not modify the original metamodels, just as subclasses do not modify base classes in OO programming. Then changes in the metamodel libraries, reflecting a better understanding of the given domain, for example, can propagate automatically to the metamodels that utilize them. Furthermore, by precisely specifying the extension and composition rules, models specified in the original domain language can be automatically translated to comply with the new, extended and composed, modeling language.

To support metamodel composition, some new UML operators are necessary. The equivalence operator is used to represent the union of two UML class objects. The two classes cease to be separate entities, but form a single class instead. Thus, the union includes all attributes, compositions and associations of each individual class. Equivalence can be thought of as defining the "join points" or "composition points" of two or more source metamodels.

New operators were also introduced to provide finer control over inheritance. When the new class needs to be able to play the role of the base class, but its internals need not be inherited, interface inheritance is used. In this case, all associations and those compositions where the base class plays the role of the contained object are inherited. On the other hand, when only the internals of a class are needed by a subclass, implementation inheritance is used. In this case, all the attributes and those compositions where the base class plays the role of the container are inherited. Notice that the union of these two new inheritance operators is the "regular" UML inheritance.

It is important to observe that the use the equivalence and new inheritance operators are just a notational convenience, and in no way change the underlying semantics of UML. In fact, every diagram using the new operators has an equivalent "pure" UML representation, and as such, each composed metamodel could be represented without the new operators. However, such metamodels would either need to modify the original metamodels or require the manual repetition of information in them due to the lack of fine control over inheritance. These metamodels would also be significantly more cluttered, making the diagrams more difficult to read and understand.

4   Workshop Results

Following the workshop, we came to several conclusions on various themes. Hereafter, we present the main ones:

- on comparing techniques of Reflection at the Language Level and AOM techniques, the former being seen as a more transversal case of the latter (or the later as a more application specific case);
- on paralleling the relationship between AOM's definition/utilization and meta-model/model of Meta-Tool Approaches to the relationship between interpreted and compiled expressions in programming languages; and finally
- on discussing about abstraction levels, in reference to the standard OMG 4-layers architecture.

Considering the ins and outs of activities using Reflection at the Language Level (RaLL) on the one hand (e.g. [12] and also its references), and those of AOM based developments on the other hand (see references of [21]), some commonalities appear between the two sets of works. In particular, in both kinds of works a main concern is put on the property of (dynamic) adaptability, where a developed system is supposed to automatically adjust (at runtime) to new specifications of its users. Moreover, for achieving the above property, both sets of works lead to define and develop some kind of an interpreter for runtime adaptation: the one specified by a Meta-Object Protocol (MOP) in the first case [8], and a more application specific one in the second case (e.g. for the developed health system for the Illinois Department of Public Health [20]).

For these reasons, and because of the differences we explain just below, we might see RaLL techniques as some more general or transversal cases of AOM techniques, or *a contrario*, AOM techniques as more specific cases of RaLL techniques.

The main differences between the techniques are concerning their scope wideness, their application domains, and also their applicability. Indeed, RaLL techniques are definitely more powerful in scope that AOM techniques, in the sense they are mainly developed for general programming languages design, whereas AOM's are more restricted for them being developed for particular application domains. Another difference is about complexity and applicability: RaLL techniques are actually complex and not easy to manage and apply in business oriented developments, precisely for their wideness of scope, whereas AOM's, as offset by their restriction to particular application domains, reduce complexity and increase applicability in business.

For observing both the techniques for AOM based developments and for projects where Meta-Tool Approaches have been used, we came also to parallel their relationship to that which exists between interpreted expressions in programming languages and compiled expressions.

Indeed, both techniques essentially share a common objective: defining a business-specific language for "operational business modeling" (see details for each technique in the relative sections of this document). On the other hand, the means used by each technique for that purpose are quite different: – in the case of AOM's, the language is in some sense "pulled up" from the implementation of an interpreter and in that way driven by the (operational) semantics; – in the case of Meta-Tool Approaches, the language is specified by a meta-model and in the some sense "pushed down" from it whereas its semantics is fixed by a third-party artifact, a model transformer and/or code generator, which can be viewed as an actual model compiler.

Finally, we can find the same kind of differences between AOM's (a) and Meta-Tool Approaches (b) than between interpreted expressions (a') and compiled expressions (b') in programming languages:

- the specifications (models or expressions) and their usage are more interactive in case of (a) and (a'), whereas there is a more static usage in case of (b) and (b');
- some direct executions might be obtained for (a) and (a') whereas they are delayed by definition for (b) and (b').

Of course, this parallel is to be treated with caution because of the scale of specification which is much larger in the case of the techniques we are interested in - (a) and (b) - than in the case of (a') and (b'), and also because of their modeling orientation and business concern.

As we also had some points on the various levels of abstraction needed for each technique, here is a summary of what appeared to some of us. First, we made the assessment that on a -precise- operational point of view (while using class-instance based OOPL), there are only two levels of abstractions: roughly, the two levels cover the class level and the instance level, as introduced in the context section of this document (while talking about the "meta" prefix). Programming is what occurs at the first level, which is the definition level, where classes are specified, and runtime is about the second level, the execution level, where instances are actually "activated" (at least as the current context for execution). Then, especially while dealing with meta-programming or meta-modeling, we need to settle a conceptual framework where more levels are available in order to isolate things well.

That's is why the OMG's 4-layers architecture is certainly justified and why we might like to conform to it [11]. However, we must keep in mind that when implementing such a conceptual framework or part of it, the various conceptual levels of abstractions are finally all projected onto the two operational levels of classes and instances.

Finally, we think it might also be useful to have in mind that on top of the standard 4-layer architecture, whatever its implementation is, each layer is actually aggregating a dual representation: indeed, on the one hand a model (or expression) at one level is being composed of instances of the classes of the level above, and on the other hand, it is also defining classes for the level below. For example, a meta-model (resp. a model) is built of instances of a meta-modeling language (resp. a modeling language), whereas it describes itself classes of a modeling language (resp. an object model or class diagram).

There are an infinite number of modeling languages. A metamodeling language is just another modeling language. A metamodel specifies one specific modeling language. If that specific modeling language is the metamodeling language, then its metamodel is called the meta-metamodel. In that sense, it is often the case that the fourth layer is not needed; the third layer (the metamodeling layer) is the top layer and it can describe itself.

5   Conclusions

A dominant theme was that the need to confront change is forcing system architects to find ways to allow their systems and users to more effectively keep pace with these changes. A way to do this is to cast information like business rules as data rather than code, so that it is subject to change at runtime. When such data are reflected as objects, these objects can, in time, come to constitute a domain-specific language, which allows users themselves to change the system as business needs dictate.

A major accomplishment of this workshop was to finally get this disparate group together, and to establish this dialog. However, we've only begun the task of fleshing out these architectural issues, uncovering the patterns, and of better defining our vocabulary. It was noted that principles of Reflection and Meta-Modeling could be used to better support the goals of AOM's and vice-versa. We are looking forward to reconvening the members of this community to continue this work. The focus of the next meeting will be around on seeing where these communities meet and how they can support one another for achieving the goal of building dynamically adaptable systems.

References

1. Francis Anderson. A Collection of History Patterns. In *Collected papers from the PLoP '98 and EuroPLoP '98 Conference, Technical Report #wucs-98-25*. Dept. of Computer Science, Washington University, 1998.
2. Brian Foote and Joseph Yoder. Architecture, Evolution, and Metamorphosis. In J. M. Vlissides, J. O. Coplien, and N. L. Kerth, editors, *Pattern Languages of Program Design 2*. Addison-Wesley, Reading, MA., 1996.
3. Brian Foote and Joseph Yoder. Metadata and Active Object-Models. In *Collected papers from the PLoP '98 and EuroPLoP '98 Conference, Technical Report #wucs-98-25*. Dept. of Computer Science, Washington University, 1998.
4. E. Gamma, R. Helm, R. Johnson, and J. Vlissides. *Design Patterns: Elements of Reusable Object-Oriented Software*. Addison-Wesley, Reading, MA, 1995.

5. W.E. Grosso, H. Eriksson, R.W. Fergerson, J.H. Gennari, S.W. Tu, and M.A. Musen. Knowledge Modeling at the Millennium (The Design and Evolution of Protege-2000). Internal report SMI-1999-0801, Stanford Medical Informatics, 1999.

6. P. Jeulin, M. Khlat, and L. Wilhem. GRAPHTALK, GQL et GKNOWLEDGE: Des techniques d'Intelligence Artificielle au service d'un environnement de Génie Logiciel. Technical report, Rank Rerox France, 1989.

7. R.E. Johnson and B. Woolf. Type Object. In R. Martin, D. Riehle, and F. Buschmann, editors, *Pattern Languages of Program Design 3*. Addison-Wesley, Reading, MA., 1998.

8. Kiczales, Riviers, and Bborow. *The art of the MOP*. MIT Press, Cambridge, MA, 1991.

9. Akos Ledeczi, Peter Volgyesi, and Gabor Karsai. Metamodel Composition in the Generic Modeling Environment. Comm. at workshop on Adaptive Object-Models and Metamodeling Techniques, Ecoop'01, Budapest, Hungary, 2001.

10. D. Manolescu. *Micro-Workflow: A Workflow Architecture Supporting Compositional Object-Oriented Software Development*. PhD thesis, Computer Science Technical Report UIUCDCS-R-2000-2186, University of Illinois at Urbana-Champaign, Urbana, IL, October 2000.

11. OMG. Meta-Object Facility (MOF) Specification v.1.3. TC Document ad/99-09-05, OMG, 1999.

12. Francisco Ortín-Soler and Juan Manuel Cueva-Lovelle. Building a Completely Adaptable Reflective System. Comm. at workshop on Adaptive Object-Models and Metamodeling Techniques, Ecoop'01, Budapest, Hungary, June (18) 2001.

13. John D. Poole. Model-Driven Architecture: Vision, Standards And Emerging Technologies. Comm. at workshop on Adaptive Object-Models and Metamodeling Techniques, Ecoop'01, Budapest, Hungary, 2001.

14. Reza Razavi. Active Object-Models et Lignes de Produits. In *OCM'2000*, Nantes, France, May 2000. http://www-poleia.lip6.fr/$\sim$razavi.

15. N. Revault, X. Blanc, and J.-F. Perrot. On Meta-Modeling Formalisms and Rule-Based Model Transforms. Comm. at workshop Iwme'00, Ecoop'00, Sophia Antipolis & Cannes, France, 2000.

16. N. Revault, H.A. Sahraoui, G. Blain, and J.-F. Perrot. A Metamodeling technique: The Méta-Gen system. In *Tools 16: Tools Europe'95*, pages 127–139, Versailles, France, 1995. Prentice Hall. Also RR LAFORIA95/01.

17. D. Roberts and R. Johnson. Evolving Frameworks: A Pattern Language for Developing Object-Oriented Frameworks. In R. Martin, D. Riehle, and F. Buschmann, editors, *Pattern Languages of Program Design 3*. Addison-Wesley, Reading, MA., 1997.

18. K. Smolander, P. Marttiin, K. Lyytinen, and V. Tahvanainen. MetaEdit - a flexible graphical environment for methodology modelling. In *Caise'91*, pages 168–193, Trondheim, Norway, 1991. Springer Verlag, Berlin.

19. M. Tilman and M. Devos. A Reflective and Repository Based Framework. In *Implementing Application Frameworks*, pages 29–64. Wiley, 1999.

20. J.W. Yoder, F. Balaguer, and R.E. Johnson. Architecture and Design of Adaptive Object-Models. In *Proceedings of the 2001 Conference on Object-Oriented Programming Systems, Languages, and Applications (OOPSLA '01)*. ACM Press, 2001.

21. J.W. Yoder, F. Balaguer, and R.E. Johnson. The Architectural Style of Adaptive Object-Models. Comm. at workshop on Adaptive Object-Models and Metamodeling Techniques, Ecoop'01, Budapest, Hungary, June (18) 2001.

22. J.W. Yoder, B. Foote, D. Riehle, M. Fowler, and M. Tilman. Metadata and Active Object-Models. Workshop report, http://www.adaptiveobjectmodel.com/OOPSLA99, OOPSLA'99, 1999.

23. J.W. Yoder, B. Foote, D. Riehle, and M. Tilman. Metadata and Active Object-Models Workshop. In *OOPSLA '98 Addendum*. ACM Press, 1998.

24. J.W. Yoder and R.E. Johnson. MetaData Pattern Mining. Workshop report, `http://www.joeyoder.com/Research/metadata/` `UoI98MetadataWkshop.html`, University of Illinois at Urbana-Champaign, Urbana, IL, May 1998.
25. J.W. Yoder and R. Razavi. Metadata and Active Object-Model pattern mining. In *Ecoop'00 Workshop Reader*. Springer-Verlag, 2000.

Workshop Participants

Our workshop gathered researchers from Adaptive Object-Modeling with others from Meta-Tool Approaches and Reflection. Table 1 below shows the list of all participants to our workshop:

Table 1. Workshop participants

surname	first	company	email
Alvarez	Dario	University of Oviedo	darioa@pinon.ccu.uniovi.es
Gabor	Andras	University of Debrecen	gabora@dragon.klte.hu
Gerhardt	Frank		fg@acm.org
Jonas	Richard	University of Debrecen	jonasr@math.klte.hu
Kollar	Layar	University of Debrecen	kollarl@math.klte.hu
Ledeczi	Akos	Vanderbilt University	akos@isis.vanderbilt.edu
Madacas	Bodnar	IQSoft	bodnari@iqsoft.hu
Oliver	Ian	Nokia Research Center	ian.oliver@nokia.com
Ortín	Francisco	University of Oviedo	ortin@pinon.ccu.uniovi.es
Revault	Nicolas	Univ. Cergy-Pontoise - LIP6	Nicolas.Revault@lip6.fr
Vereb	Kriantian	University of Debrecen	sparrow@math.klte.hu
Yoder	Joseph	The Refactory	yoder@refactory.com

Specification, Implementation, and Validation of Object-Oriented Embedded Systems

Sébastien Gerard[1], Alexandre David[2], and François Terrier[1]

[1] CEA-LIST/DTSI/SLA/L-LSP, CEA/Saclay, F-91191 Gif sur Yvette Cedex, France
Sebastien.Gerard@cea.fr, Francois.Terrier@cea.fr
[2] Department of Computer Systems, Uppsala University, Box 325, 751 05 Uppsala, Sweden
adavid@docs.uu.se

Abstract. This workshop is the third one of a series of workshops which objective is to identify the main lacks of UML for developing real-time embedded systems and the main prospective directions for research to these difficulties. For that, it aims to gather academics and industrial people to discuss on industrial needs, on formalisms prospects and on advanced solutions. It tries to tackle the three main part of a development cycle: specification/analysis, design/implementation and validation.

Two main common issues have emerged from the workshop submissions The first one developed in the morning of the workshop was focused on real-time features specification of real-time embedded systems. The afternoon of the workshop was then dedicated to component modeling issues when targeting real-time embedded system.

Workshop Organizers

Dr. Sébastien GERARD, CEA-LIST Saclay
Laboratoire " Logiciels pour la Sûreté des Procédés "
DRT-LIST/DTSI/SLA/L-LSP - CEA/Saclay, F-91191 Gif sur Yvette Cedex, France
E-mail: Sebastien.Gerard@cea.fr

Pr. Dr. François TERRIER, CEA-LIST Saclay
Laboratoire " Logiciels pour la Sûreté des Procédés "
DRT-LIST/DTSI/SLA/L-LSP - CEA/Saclay, F-91191 Gif sur Yvette Cedex, France
E-mail: Sebastien.Gerard@cea.fr

Bran SELIC, Rational Software
340 March Road Kanata, Ontario
K2K 2E4, Canada
E-mail: bran@objectime.com

Pr. Dr. Werner DAMM, OFFIS e.V.
Escherweg 2, D-26121 Oldenburg , Germany
E-mail: Wermer.Damm@OFFIS.de

Dr. Udo BROCKMEYER, OFFIS e.V.
Escherweg 2 D-26121 Oldenburg, Germany
E-mail: Udo.Brockmeyer@OFFIS.de

Á. Frohner (Ed.): ECOOP 2001 Workshops, LNCS 2323, pp. 72–85, 2002.
ⓒ Springer-Verlag Berlin Heidelberg 2002

Pr. Dr. Wan YI, Department of Computer Systems
Uppsala University, Box 325, 751 05 Uppsala, Sweden
Email: yi@docs.uu.se, URL: www.docs.uu.se/~yi
Dr. Paul PETTERSSON, Department of Computer Systems
Uppsala University
Box 325, 751 05 Uppsala, Sweden
Email: paupet@docs.uu.se, URL: www.docs.uu.se/~paupet

Workshop Participants

- Omar ALDAWOUD, Lucent Technologies, oaldawud@lucent.com
- Ahmad ALKHODRE, L3I / INSA-Lyon, France,
  ahmad.alkhodre@if.insa-lyon.fr
- Jean-Philippe BABAU, L3I / INSA-Lyon, France,
  jbbabau@if.insa-lyon.fr
- Yvan BARBAIX, Dept. of Comput. Science, K.U.Leuven, Belgium,
  yvan.barbaix@cs.kuleuven.ac.be
- Alexandre DAVID, Dept. of Computer Systems / Uppsala Uni., Sweden,
  adavid@DoCS.UU.SE
- Vieri DEL BIANCO, Politecnico di Milano, Italy,
  delbianc@cefriel.it
- Sébastien GERARD, CEA-LIST Saclay, France,
  Sebastien.Gerard@cea.fr
- Rédha HAMOUCHE, LaMI / Uni. Evry Val d'Essonne, France,
  hamouche@lami.univ-evry.fr
- Bernhard JOSKO, OFFIS, Germany,
  Bernhard.Josko@OFFIS.Uni-Oldenburg.DE
- Janis OSIS, Riga Technical University, Meža iela 1/3, Riga Latvija, LV-1048,
  osis@egle.cs.rtu.lv
- Ian OLIVER, Nokia Research Center It amerenkatu 11-13 Helsinki, Finland,
  Ian.Oliver@nokia.com
- Jean-Paul RIGAULT, I3S / Uni. of Nice Sophia Antipolis and CNRS UMR 6070,
  France, jpr@essi.fr
- François TERRIER, CEA-LIST Saclay, France,
  Francois.Terrier@cea.fr
- David URTING, Dept. Of Comput. Science, K.U. Leuven, Belgium,
  david.urting@cs.kuleuven.ac.be
- Stefan VAN BAELEN, Department Of Computer Science, Katholieke Univ.
  Leuven, Belgium Stefan.VanBaelen@cs.kuleuven.ac.be
- Guy VIDAL-NAQUET, Uni. of Paris V, France,
  vidalnaq@supelec.fr

1   Summary of the CFP

Among the organizers of the workshop were people participating in the AIT-WOODDES project (http://wooddes.intranet.gr). AIT-WOODDES project focuses on the high level specification of embedded real-time systems allowing evolving design of product applications so as to quickly and easily adapt the product to the market evolution and to master increasing complexity of such products. The project will deliver an environment for the design of embedded systems using, where possible, existing standards, techniques and products. This environment will offer system description and development tools providing a homogeneous and continuous support for the development process of embedded systems. The project is tackling this problem by using the UML (Unified Modeling Language) notations, to completely describe embedded and real time characteristics of such systems and also to benefit from the advantages of a component based approach. The results of the project are expected to have major impacts on:

- development time and cost
- quality of delivered products
- continuity of the development process

To be competitive, companies need to decrease time to market. To achieve this, the project proposes to optimize the use of different actors' know-how in design and development techniques:

- to investigate and adapt the UML notations towards a development process for embedded systems with real-time constraints
- to implement homogeneous modeling tools for data exchange between people from different areas using different data administration systems
- to extend validation tools to be used early in the process (during the prototyping phase) and to cover both component validation and integration

The case study we propose is system aiming to regulate the car speed to a preselected setpoint value reflecting the normal velocity at which the driver wishes to travel. The complete specification of this case study may be found on the web site of AIT-WOODDES project:
`http://wooddes.intranet.gr/conferences.htm`

2   About Contributions

The papers that retained for the workshop were focused mainly on two aspects of real-time systems development. Either they were proposals describing a given approach to model real-time systems , or their focused on the validation issues of such systems.

2.1   Modeling Method for Real-Time Systems Development

J.-P. BABAU and A. ALKHODRE have submitted a paper relating a method called PROSEUS. This method addresses engineers needing to build prototypes of embedded systems. The method, combining UML and SDL formalisms, defines the different stages of the development process it advocates and the order in which to chain them up. At each stage, the method gives the formalism to use and how to use it: UML is used to model the system and SDL to implement UML diagrams. In fact, SDL is seen here as an intermediate language between UML and the final generated target code. The SDL model may also be used for simulation, verification and code generation depending on the tool used.

R. HAMOUCHE (with B. MIRAMOND, B. DJAFRI from LaMI / Univ Evry Val d'Essonne – France) presents a proposal for heterogeneous system design called ModelJ describing a component-based approach combined with aspect oriented concepts. The component approach addresses the system complexity and improves reusability whereas aspect concepts deal with the heterogeneity of application domains. By separating system features (function, communication, timing and computation properties), systems can be refined in separate manners. This work is in keeping with a global methodology that can have UML diagrams as input. After a short description of ModelJ, the example of an automotive case study is presented.

D. URTING (with S. VAN BAELEN and Y. BERBERS from Dept. Of Computer Science, K.U. Leuven, Belgium) describes in his position paper a component oriented approach for the modeling of the *regulator* case. The modeling method is one of the results of the SEESCOA project, sponsored by the Flemish IWT and 6 industrial partners. In this project we investigate the development of embedded software using high-level software concepts.

The SEESCOA method is in part based on a combination of Component Based Development and Contract Based Development. The approach in this paper does not show a new method for modeling the *functional* part of an application since it is based on UML for Real-Time. However, UML for Real-Time does not have explicit constructs for annotating *non-functional* requirements (like timing and memory). In this approach this is enable by using a contract based method: timing requirements are put into contracts. These contracts have a specification meaning but also a runtime meaning (they are used to monitor timings in an application at runtime).

G. VIDAL-NAQUET (with H.G. MENDELBAUM from Jerusalem College of Technology (Israel) & IUT Versailles / Univ Paris V – France) has introduced a methodology to design, build, validate and run embedded systems through 'temporal-components' which may contain physical and software parts. The embedded systems are designed in terms of hierarchical temporal-components, which are described as synchronous subsystems validated through the use of temporal logic. The concept of temporal-component is an extension of the concept of UML active-objects, it is made of four parts : (i) a declarative part giving the local variables and the links with other components, (ii) a set of local operations (hard/soft), (iii) a requirements part named 'Goals' and (iv) a working specification part named 'Behavior' or 'Controller', these two last parts are written using TCOM an "engineering dialect" of the temporal logic. The validation process consists in proving that the behavior specification of the whole embedded system satisfies its main goal using all the subcomponents' Goals (for this, one can use an automatic prover such as the Stanford's STeP prover). The temporal-components (parts i, ii, iv) can be translated in UML active-objects for running. A Speed-Controller case study example is presented.

J.-P. RIGAULT (with M.-A. PERALDI-FRATI and C. ANDRE from I3S Uni. of Nice Sophia Antipolis, and CNRS UMR 6070 – France) has proposed a methodology mixing solutions coming from the UML, ROOM, and synchronous modeling. They adopt the *Use Case diagrams* of UML for expressing the functionality of the system and *textual scenarios* as instances of use cases. From ROOM, they have adopted *capsules*, *ports* and *protocols* and the ROOM-like *structure diagrams* are used for expressing connections between instances of capsules. For expressing the relations between capsules, they have chosen to keep the class diagram of UML. For expressing the *dynamic behavior* of objects the synchronous model *SyncCharts* is used instead of Statecharts and *Sequence Diagrams* are extended with synchronously sound constructs akin to Message Sequence Charts. *SIB* (*Synchronous Interface Behavior*) is the name of this new model. They had also modeled the speed regulating system in order to demonstrate the usability of their approach.

O. ALDAWOUD (with A. BADER from Lucent Technologies and E. TZILA from IIT Concurrent Systems Group) has presented a formal method for specifying and validating of concurrent software systems based on Aspect Oriented (AO) modeling via automatic code generation, where the design and the generated code confirms to the requirements of these systems. The formal methodology described supports also aspectual behavioral modeling for concurrent software systems.

Their approach allows explicit representation of aspects within the system model, each aspect in the system will have to be represented and designed separately from its functional components. Statecharts are used to describe the behavior of both aspects and functional components. Using Statecharts is essential to the approach, since they are used to describe the objects/aspects behavior and are part of the system model thus can be used to automatically generate code using any CASE tool that supports statecharts.

V. DEL BIANCO (with L. LAVAZZA and M. MAURI from CEFRIEL and Politecnico di Milano (DESS - ITEA project) – Italy) are currently involved in the ITEA DESS project (Software Development Process for Real-Time Embedded Software Systems), whose goal is to develop a methodology for developing real-time software systems. In the DESS project they are mainly involved in defining methods for the representation of requirements of real-time software, and in the definition of methods for analysing real-time specifications. The DESS environment allows analysts to model real-time systems using an extension of UML, which can support the translation of models into formal notations. In this way they retain the expressiveness and ease of use of UML, while gaining the power to use formal methods, which can be employed for verifying properties of specifications, for deriving test cases, etc.

First, they have proposed a classification of real-time systems complexity. For that purpose they have analysed three different case studies: the speed regulator proposed as support of the workshop, the usual Generalized Railroad Crossing (GRC) case study, and one sample extracted from the DESS project constituted of two "activities" that work concurrently on a mono-processor architecture: a Filter and a Corrector.

And second, they have reported an experience aiming at modelling the speed regulator system with the methodology they are contributing to in the context of the DESS project.

Y. BARBAIX (with S. VAN BAELEN and K. DE VLAMINCK From Dept. of Computer Science, K.U. Leuven, Belgium) propose the position that the simple mechanism of virtual timers is powerful enough to annotate, analyze and verify (at run-time) the majority of the timing constraints. Their approach is based on the notion of *virtual Timer.* They justify their position by the fact that thinking about timing constraints in a fine grained way, timing always requires two points of an execution trace; a start and end points. So a simple timing constraint may though as a constraint on some stop-watch that is started at some point and is halted at a second point.

As a majority of the timing constraints are not restricted to deadline specification, they propose also a mapping from the timing constraints to the semantics of virtual timers.

2.2 Validation of Real-Time Systems

I. OLIVER focused his position paper on the need for embedded systems builders to be sure their system will run the first time. For that purpose, Nokia has investigated the possibility to apply existing real-time analysis techniques such like RMA (Rate-Monotonic Analysis) to object-oriented models and even UML models. In order to perform this work, since the OMG work targeting to define a RT-UML profile was not yet available, they have also decided to define their own real-time UML profile. They have also specified a set of tagged values a modeler could use to annotate a UML model in order to validate it. The second point they had to solve in order to apply RMA on UML models was to define a transformation strategy between the user UML model and a task model that can be analyzed with RMA.

They have applied their technology on the speed regulating system proving their proposal may be useful to validate a real-time systems modeled with UML.

A. DAVID (with T. AMNELL, E. FERSMAN, P. PETTERSSON and W. YI from Dpt of Information Technology from Uppsala Univ. and O. MÖLLER from Dpt of Computer Science - Aarhus Univ.) described a real-time extension of UML statecharts to enable modeling and verification of real-time constraints. For clarity, they consider a reasonable subset of the rich UML statechart model and extend it with real-time constructs: clocks, timed guards, invariants and real-time tasks. In addition, they have developed a rule-based formal semantics for the obtained formalism, called hierarchical timed automata (HTA). To use the existing tool UPPAAL they have developed, HTA are also transformed to enriched timed automata model. For that purpose, they have used an XML based implementation of the translation from HTA to a network of timed automata. By the way, they also present a prototype implementation of the code synthesis for the legOS platform.

B. JOSKO (with U. BROCKMEYER from OSC, I. SCHINZ from OFFIS and J. KLSE and B. WESTPHAL from Uni. Oldenburg.) described a work aiming to do verification by model checking on UML models. For that purpose, they wanted to reuse a tool they had already developed and which targeted verification on STATEMATE specification. But a UML model contains more information than a STATEMATE one. Indeed, in addition of a behavioral specification, a UML model may also contain structural, interaction, deployment, ... models. Moreover, they have used a specific formalism in order to enable the user to express timing properties to check. Specification can also be given as temporal logic e.g. under the form of Live Sequence Charts.

3   Organization of the Workshop

Twelve position papers have been selected for the workshop. They express the opinion of the authors on the different topics relevant for the workshop. The day was divided into two sessions and two participants were also chosen, one for each session, in order to present their position paper as an introduction of an open discussion where each participants was invited to express their position or/and questions on the both issues addressed by the workshop.

The morning has been dedicated to discussion on real-time features and properties of embedded systems. Vieri Del Bianco from Politecnico di Milano has given a short presentation of 30-40 minutes on this subject in order to introduce the discussion. After that, an open discussion started.

The format of the afternoon has be similar but it was then focused on the second identified theme i.e. component issues in real-time embedded systems. For that discussion, G.Vidal-Naquet from Paris V University has given a presentation about 30-40 minutes also in order to introduce the discussions.

4   Summary of the Debates

4.1   Morning Session: Real-Time Aspects (directed by Sébastien Gérard)

The first paper presented was "A Classification of Real-Time Specifications Complexity" by Vieri Del Bianco, Luigi Lavazza, and Marco Mauri. The talk was focused on the ITEA DESS project (Software Development Process for Real-time Embedded Software Systems) whose purpose is to define methods for the representation of requirements of real-time software and for analyzing real-time specifications. Real-time systems are modeled using an extension of UML that is translated into formal models. The main tasks involved are modeling using UML, specifying properties, and verifying the properties. The modeling and verification stages do not have any major obstacle. The main difficulty of the method is to derive satisfactory specifications, in particular those involving the behavior in time. The question is then to choose the appropriate approach.

The issues addressed were the type of constraints and the independence of components. In particular, correlation constraints are long and complex to express for a translation to Kronos, even if the translation UML to timed automata is easily understandable. Testing these constraints does not seem to be satisfactory and people want an analysis of them. A solution is to identify a set of constraints meeting people usual needs. Concerning the component issue, one should add the constraints and the components together and construct the model with sets of components.

After this introduction, an open discussion directed by Sébastien Gérard was begun. The discussion was then focused on the interesting time constraints that one would want. For people such as Alcatel, interested in reliability, quality of service, and maintainability, the prior constraint is the *order of events* that they specify with MSCs. The question is then how to *choose an appropriate formalism*. The use of temporal logic formalism suits this purpose however in a way where small formulae are used to prove partial results further reused to prove other properties. The point is to keep the formulae rather short and understandable while obtaining scalable proofs. The problem is the power of expression of such a formalism. There are basically two ways to reach this: choose a simple formalism and push the limits of its expressiveness, or choose a rich formalism and push the limits of what is provable. The *synchronous approach* is preferred since it makes things simpler. One can fit constraints into synchronous charts, extend scenarios, and generate observers. The synchrony hypothesis should be checked however. The advantage is to be able to code everything functional, including properties. Though it is possible to represent asynchronous events in the synchronous paradigm, the synchronization mechanism that have to be coded in this case are complex.

In the continuation of the difficulty to specify, it is difficult as well to write down the formulae themselves, i.e. writing them correctly in a given formalism. It is a non-trivial exercise to translate a complex English temporal specification, still understandable, into LTL without making mistakes. The issue addressed is the *difficulty of the formalism*. Several attempts have been done to use graphical composers of temporal logic but they proved to be of little help. Another problem is to be able to express a property *precisely* since when one writes a property, one often does not say everything. The time automata formalism is of high complexity and life sequence charts were proposed as an alternative. They allow to distinguish between events that may happen or not. They are not easy to use but still very expressive.

From the experience on case studies on embedded systems, the arrival time of events are proven to be useful but also *the separation time between two events*. Unfortunately it is hard to use formalisms to express this though they are common, e.g. input/output constraints. This is related to components that are considered as black boxes with their own threads. We need for them to link inputs to outputs and the simple behavioral description is not enough. Timing specifications are needed as well.

The question of *applicability of formal techniques*, and in particular with timed system, was raised. The timed constraints in UML context are most useful to answer the question: is the system schedulable or not? However the only tool available for the target is a C compiler that does not necessarily give guarantees with respect to the model. There is a gap between what we get from validation and verification techniques and the poor tools used for the target platforms. It appears that it is better to think what class of engineers needs techniques, and at which level.

To improve the analysis of timed systems, the use of *virtual timers* was discussed. The point is to know at which point the verification holds, but not at an event point. Requirements have to be annotated to keep track of the results. Virtual timers are not part of the system but are use to measure time only. A timer is considered as a virtual object.

On the modeling aspect, *extensions of MSCs* with timing information were discussed, such as annotations for processing time, or sending time for messages. A number of verifications from this extension are then possible, e.g. transformation to state machines, or runtime verification of timing constraints based on the ROOM modeling. In this latter case MSCs are annotated with *timing contracts* that are hooks, e.g. send, receive, or end of processing. These contracts are expressed as formulae translated to code for the runtime verification. When modeling with scenarios, contracts are attached to components. When checking these scenarios at runtime, only one scenario at a time is treated due to the overhead. Other approaches are underway to integrate deadlines in the code generation process.

An attempt to classify time constraints was made:
General constraints in real-time/distributed systems: events have to occur after/before other ones. Specify which other events, in the sense which occurrences more precisely. Two events occur at the same time: what is simultaneity? Two events in a sequence with the same time stamp? The notion of observability has to be defined.

Constraints on data: data is available within a given time interval, freshness of data. This is useful in the case of outputs produced from inputs within a certain given time to be considered valid. This can be called end-to-end deadline. Moreover it is problematic to express the notion of freshness of data even in natural language. Correlation constraints between events should be taken into account: outputs have to be produced by inputs that have been generated within a given time interval. On the input side, one has to consider that all input samples should be taken within a certain time interval to be able to guarantee an upper bound between the occurrence of a real event and the instant this event is recognized by the software, i.e. system event. More generally, one wants to define time intervals between a set of inputs/outputs as {inputs, inputs} or {inputs, outputs} or {outputs, outputs}.

Event constraints: model that nothing happens within an amount of time. This is the absence of event case. It is useful in the case when an event does not occur within a given time to take action and raise an exception for example. Constraints on execution time can be classified here due to periods, interleaving of events, repetition of events, and constraints on periods.

An open question remains, namely the mapping with object models. This concerns mainly the basic concepts for the execution model formalism. One has to define the mapping with the end users' notion used at specification stages and one has to distinguish between various levels such as logical versus physical.

4.2   Afternoon Session: Components for Embedded Systems (directed by François Terrier)

The second presentation was based on the paper "Validation of Temporal-Component Based Embedded Systems" by G. Vidal-Naquet and H.G. Mendelbaum. The content of the paper was not presented in detail but rather issues related to temporal components were raised. The paper describes the TCOM methodology to design, build, validate and run embedded systems through "temporal-components" that may contain physical and software parts. The embedded systems are designed in terms of hierarchical temporal-components, which are described as synchronous subsystems validated trough the use of temporal logic. The concept of temporal-component is an extension of the concept of UML active-objects and is made of four parts: (1) a declarative part giving the local variables and the links with other components, (2) a set of local operations (hard/soft), (3) a requirements part named "Behavior" or "Controller". The two last parts are written using TCOM, an "engineering dialect" of the temporal logic. The validation process consists in proving that the behavior specification of the whole embedded system satisfies its main goal using all the sub-components' goals. The temporal components can be translated in UML active objects for running. The TCOM notation is intended to be clear and natural for real-time engineers, close enough to classical notations to be used relatively easily by temporal provers, and integrated in UML. Finally their main idea relative to component development is: "Complex embedded systems can be built gradually using a composition of validated components. To obtain this, in a realistic way, we propose in the TCOM methodology a "simple, clear and natural notation" that is close enough to the way of expression of the industrial engineer (for requirements and specifications). So that, these properties of the system and of the components can be easily translated into formulas of temporal logic which can be accepted by a prover".

This presentation was also to introduce an open discussion directed François Terrier and focused on the issues of using component-based development approaches to build embedded systems.

The live cycle of components in the context of embedded systems was tackled. From an existentialist point of view, the question "what do objects do?" arises. What is the relationship between objects and components? Generally we associate one object per component, but not necessarily. As embedded systems are basically reactive, it desirable to define relationships on incoming and outgoing data flows. How is the component updated in the processing? Furthermore, to describe object the use of UML and object related concepts seem appropriate to get a smoother development process. Concerning the validation, the notion of component should help the validation process. The underlying model is vital and validation tools are based on statecharts. This poses the big problem of compositionality of proofs.

The scope of the discussion should be focused: the communication, interaction and structure of the system are specific issues to distributed systems and should not be addressed here. We should address the specific issues of temporal components and not components in general. Unfortunately, this path was difficult to follow.

The four following items summarize the main ideas that was raised and discussed during this afternoon:

Use of Components. Components are used for abstraction approaches and are able to cope with heterogeneity of systems. Autonomy of components is required and they are to be connected with each other, though not only by method calls. Components should be self-contained without references to objects outside. Big specified components are appreciated to use. However, to be usable, a component should carry an appropriate description, which can be obtained by different levels of descriptions, one of them being MSCs. In the definition of usable components, one should consider *replaceable and reusable* units, preferably large units. So in this view a component is different from one object, it rather contains a number of them. Sophisticated interfaces are required because they are used like objects, i.e. one may want to use components several times, with different states, several instances, and still be able to replace them by others.

Embedded Systems. They have constraints due to their embedded and reactive nature. The question is what kind of new constraints are added with components, in particular their interaction with each other. Which kind of requirements do we need for these components? Quality of service can be one way to specify such requirements to guarantee a certain quality when connecting several components on an embedded system. Absence of deadlocks is a desired property. Another point is the question: do components provide something useful for real-time systems, is it worth the trouble? Yes it is, for critical components. Notice that first, real-time systems have already an inherent complexity due to their reactive nature and keeping this though different heterogeneous components is challenging (think of Ariane launcher), second, real critical systems are implemented in hardware, not software and they are hardwired mechanically. The advantage of components lies here in its replacement capabilities where it is hopefully easier to track down problems (think of Ariane launcher again).

Description of Properties. We need to describe the behavioral properties of real-time components, how? Logical properties are easier to check than real-time ones. One can check that components are properly plugged, with proper protocols, but the question is what more needs to be done with real-time constraints. Today it is unknown how to compose components and the critical path is often considered. Too much information is needed too often to carry out a precise analysis. We cannot do anything sophisticated, at least because of the cache usage of processors.

Design Issue. Components should be used in a top-down design. A number of questions arise then: how to connect them, what is the size of a typical component? Concerning the size a major condition must be met: the cost to learn how to use a component must be less than the cost to write what is needed from scratch. Components should obviously be organized in a hierarchical way. The question concerns the hierarchy in the sense of the composition: structural view of compositional hierarchy?

Conclusion. The following points were considered important:
  Components versus objects: component can represent associations of objects.
  Use of components: components must have interfaces in the form of input/output, in particular output interfaces do not yet exist. These include possible protocols of use and behavioral properties (contracts) expected from the environment. Components must be linked to the context of use and must have limited dependencies with the rest of the system, which means high cohesion inside the component and loose coupling with other components. They should be usable alone or with other components they contain, or, if they are defined in one other component with components defined at the same level.
  What is particular to real-time components that distinguish them from "ordinary" components? It is a basic question not so easy to answer: real time properties, but which ones? Real-time in components is present in the interface and services that have real-time constraints. Quality of service takes into account timing constraints. In the definition of autonomous entities, the notion of concurrency is addressed.
  The interest is to have ultimately certified, trusted components, though what makes a real-time certification on components is another question.

The choice of the modeling language and formalism seems to be UML. We have though a problem in the validation process due to the lack of practical tools and techniques.

Workshop Conclusions. Even, if all the participants agree on the fact that UML will become the de facto standard for modeling applications and that its potential advantages for building component based development techniques for real time systems, it is also clear for all the participants that a lot of work remains to done in order to reach the objectives of both automating, optimizing application implementation and of reducing cots and time developments.

In particular, new UML profiles must be proposed to support higher level modeling of application, integration of advanced validation techniques and integration of particular needs such as connection with data flow based modeling or definition of probabilistic timing features.

Presentations performed during the workshop have shown that both the research community and the industry or tool vendors are very active on these subjects. Incoming conferences and workshop (such as SIVOOES'2000 held at ECOOP2000 or FDTRT associated to the UML'2000 conference) will probably provide more and more precise responses. This provides a very favorable context to obtain during the next years efficient and industrial solution for this particularly important application domain that takes a more and more important place in the market of the computer based systems

5   References and Pointers on Related Works

5.1   Web Sites

Description of the web site	Web site address
Dedicated to AIT-WODDES an IST Program project (IST-1999-10069) of the 5th PCRD	http://wooddes.intranet.gr/conferences. htm
ACOTRIS - French project (RNTL)	http://www.acotric.c-s.fr
CIUML'2001 (workshop associated with the UML'2001 conference)	http://wooddes.intranet.gr/uml2001/ Home.htm
RT-TOOLS'2001 (workshop assocated with the UML'2001 conference)	http://www.docs.uu.se/ paupet/rttools-2001/
UML'2001	http://www.cs.toronto.edu/uml2001/
CONCUR'2001	http://concur01.cs.auc.dk
CiaoLab	http://www.ciaolab.com

5.2   Contribution Papers

All the following papers are available on the web site of the workshop
(http://wooddes.intranet.gr/ecoop2001/sivoes2001.htm):

1. J.-P. Babau, A. Alkhodre, A development method for PROtotyping embedded SystEms by using UML and SDL (PROSEUS) - L3I, INSA Lyon - FRANCE
   SubmittedPapers/A development method for PROtotyping embedded SystEms by using UML and SDL.doc

2. R. Hamouche, B. Miramond, B. Djafri , ModelJ: Component-Based Modeling for Embedded Systems - LaMI / Univ Evry Val d'Essonne - FRANCE
   SubmittedPapers/ModelJ-Component-based Modeling for Embedded Systems.doc
3. V. del Bianco, L. Lavazza, M. Mauri, A classification of real-time specifications complexity - CEFRIEL and Politecnico di Milano (DESS - ITEA project) - ITALY
   SubmittedPapers/A Classification of RT specification complexity.pdf
4. V. del Bianco, L. Lavazza, M. Mauri , An application of the DESS modeling approach: The Car Speed Regulator - CEFRIEL and Politecnico di Milano (DESS - ITEA project) - ITALY
   SubmittedPapers/AnApplicationOfDESS.pdf
5. G.Vidal-Naquet and H.G.Mendelbaum, Validation of Temporal-Component Based Embedded Systems - SupElec ; Jerusalem College of Technology (Israel) & IUT Versailles / Univ Paris V - FRANCE
   SubmittedPapers/Validation of Temporal-Component based Embedded Systems.doc
6. M.-A. PERALDI-FRATI, C. ANDRE, J.-P. RIGAULT, Modeling a Speed Regulator System with "Synchronous" UML: A case Study - Laboratoire d'Informatique, Signaux et Systèmes (I3S) University of Nice Sophia Antipolis, and CNRS UMR 6070, France
   SubmittedPapers/Modeling a Speed Regulator System with Synchronous UML.doc
7. O. Aldawoud, A. Bader, Aspect-Oriented Modeling to Automate the Implementation and Validation of Concurrent Software Systems - Lucent Technologies and Dr. Elrad Tzila - IIT Concurrent Systems Group
   SubmittedPapers/AOMtoAutomateImplementationAndValidationOfCOnurrent SoftwareSystems.doc
8. Y. Barbaix, S. Van Baelen and K. De Vlaminck, Handling Time Constraints with Virtual Timers - Dept. of Computer Science, K.U.Leuven, Belgium
   SubmittedPapers/Handling TimingConstraints With Virtual Timers.pdf
9. D. Urting, S. Van Baelen and Y. Berbers, Embedded Software using Components and Contracts - Dept. Of Computer Science, K.U. Leuven, Belgium
   SubmittedPapers/Embedded Software using Components and Contracts.doc
10. I. Oliver, An Example of Validation of Embedded System Models Described in UML using Rate Monotonic Analysis - Nokia Research Center Itämerenkatu 11-13 Helsinki, Finland
    SubmittedPapers/AnExampleOfValidationOfEmbeddedSystemModelsDescribedIn UMLLusingRMA.ps
11. T. Amnell, A. David, E. Fersman, P. Pettersson, W. Yi and M. O. Möller, Tools for Real-Time UML: Formal Verification and Code Synthesis - Dpt of Information Technology from Uppsala Univ. and Dpt of Computer Science - Aarhus Univ.
    ../ReceiptPaper/ToolsForRTUML-FormalVerification AndCodeSynthesis.pdf
12. U. Brockmeyer, B. Josko, I. Schinz, J. Klse and B. Westphal, Towards Formal Verification Of Rhapsody UML Designs – OSC, OFFIS, Uni. Oldenburg.
    SubmittedPapers/TowardsFormalVerification OfRhaspodyUML_Design.pdf

5.3 Papers about Real-Time Specification

1. A. Alhodre, J-P Babau, J. Schwarz, "Modeling of real-time embedded systems by using SDL" internal search rapport, L3i laboratory, INSA Lyon, April 2001.
2. R. Alur and T.A. Henzinger. "Logics and models of real time: a survey", J.W. de Bakker, K. Huizing, W.-P. de Roever, and G. Rozenberg, editors, Real Time: Theory in Practice, LNCS vol. 600, pages 74–106. Springer-Verlag, 1992
3. C. André. "Representation and Analysis of Reactive Behaviors: A Synchronous Approach" *IEEE-SMC Computational Engineering in Systems Applications (CESA),* Lille (F), July 1996, pp 19–29.

4. C. André, M.A. Peraldi-Frati, J.P. Rigault *"Scenario and properties checking of real-time systems using synchronous approach"* IEEE International Symposium on Object-Oriented Real-Time Distributed Computing, ISORC 2001, Magdeburg, Germany, May, 2–4, 2001, pp 438–444.

5. J.-P. Babau, J. L. Sourrouille "Expressing Real-time Constraints in a Reflective Object Model" Control Engineering Practice Vol 6, pp 421-430.

6. B.P. Douglass. Doing Hard Time: Developing Real-Time Systems with UML, Objects, Frameworks and Patterns. Addison Wesley, 1999.

7. S. Gérard, "Modélisation UML exécutable pour les systèmes de l'automobile", PhD. Report, University of Evry-Val-d'Essonne, October 2000.

8. G. Kiczales, J. Lamping, A. Mendhekar, C. Maeda, C. Lopes, J.-M. Loingtier, and J. Irwin, Aspect-Oriented Programming. In Proceedings of ECOOP '97. LNCS 1241. Springer-Verlag, pp. 220-242.

9. A. Lanusse, S. Gérard, and F. Terrier, "Real-Time Modeling with UML : The ACCORD Approach", UML'98, Mulhouse, France.

10. P. Lanchès et al.: Client/Server Architecture - Managing New Technologies for Automotive Embedded Systems - A Joint Project of Daimler-Benz & IBM; In Proc. of the 1998 International Congress on Transportation Electronics, No 98C015, pp. 111-120, Warrendale, USA. Society of Automotive Engineers, 1998.

11. L. Lavazza, "An introduction to the DESS approach to the specification of real-time software", CEFRIEL report, April 2001.

12. H.G. Mendelbaum, Introduction to a CAD object-oriented method for the development of real-time embedded system. 1st Israeli-IEEE conf. On software engineering , Herzlya (1986)

13. B. Selic et al., "Real-time Object-Oriented Modeling", John Wiley & Sons, Inc., ISBN: 0471599174, Feb. 1994.

14. B. Selic, J. Rumbaugh "Using UML for Modeling Complex Real-Time Systems", Mars 1998 http://www.objectime.com/otl/technical/umlrt.html

15. F. Terrier and al., "A Real-Time Object Model", TOOLS EUROPE '96, , Paris, France, pp.127-141, 1996.

16. OMG UML v.1.3 specification, available as http://www.omg.org/cgi-bin/doc?ad/99-06-08.pdf

17. UML^TM Profile for Action Semantics for the UML", Object Management Group document ad/98-11-01. See answers at: http://www.kc.com/as_site/

18. UML^TM Profile for Scheduling, Performance, and Time - ad/2001-06-14.

19. J. Rumbaugh and B. Selic, "Using UML for Modeling Complex Real-Time Systems", "White paper" available at http://www.objectime.com/otl/technical/umlrt.pdf

5.4 Papers about Components Issues

1. B. Djafri, R. Hamouche, J. Benzakki: "Object Oriented Modeling for System Design", Proc. of Information Systems Analysis and Synthesis (ISAS'99), pp. 307-313, Orlando, Fl, July 1999.

2. R. Hamouche, B. Miramond, B. Djafri, J. Benzakki, "ModelJ: An Embedded Design Methodology ", Research Report RR 60-2001, University of Evry, March 2001.

3. C. Szyperski. "Component Software: Beyond Object-Oriented Programming", Addison-Wesley, 1999.

4. SEESCOA, "Working Definition of Components", Deliverable D 1.4, March 2000

Feature Interaction in Composed Systems

Elke Pulvermueller[1], Andreas Speck[2], James O. Coplien[3], Maja D'Hondt[4], and
Wolfgang De Meuter[4]

[1] Universitaet Karlsruhe, Postfach 6980 Karlsruhe, Germany
`pulvermueller@acm.org`
[2] Intershop, Intershop Tower Jena, Germany
`A.Speck@intershop.de`
[3] Bell Laboratories, Naperville IL, USA
`cope@research.bell-labs.com`
[4] Vrije Universiteit Brussel, Pleinlaan 2 Brussel, Belgium
`mjdhondt@vub.ac.be, wdmeuter@vub.ac.be`

Abstract. The history of computer science has shown that decomposing software applications helps managing their complexity and facilitates reuse, but also bears challenging problems still unsolved, such as the assembly of the decomposed features when non-trivial feature interactions are involved. Examples of features include concerns or aspects, black box or white box components, and functional and non-functional requirements. Approaches such as object-oriented and component-based software development, as well as relatively new directions such as aspect-oriented programming, multi-dimensional separation of concerns and generative programming, all provide technical support for the definition and syntactical assembly of features, but fall short on the semantic level, for example in spotting meaningless or even faulty combinations. At previous ECOOPs, OOPSLAs and GCSEs dedicated events have been organised around the aforementioned technologies, where we experienced a growing awareness of this feature interaction problem. However, feature interaction is often merely dismissed as a secondary problem, percolating as an afterthought while other issues are being addressed. The intention of this workshop was to be the first co-ordinated effort to address the general problem of feature interaction in composed systems separately from other issues.

1 Introduction

In the domain of telecommunications the problem of interfering features was first explicitly explored in the beginning 1990s. In a series of workshops (the first was held in 1992) the difficulty to manage implicit and unforeseen interactions between newly inserted features and the base system have been examined [3,9,1,5]. However, the problem is not limited to the telecommunications domain only, but occurs when decomposing software applications in general.

The history of computer science has shown that decomposing software helps managing their complexity and facilitates reuse, but also bears challenging problems still unsolved, such as the assembly of the decomposed features when non-trivial feature interactions are involved. Examples of features include concerns or aspects, black-box

Á. Frohner (Ed.): ECOOP 2001 Workshops, LNCS 2323, pp. 86–97, 2002.

or white-box components, and functional and non-functional requirements. Approaches such as object-oriented and component-based software development [15], as well as relatively new directions such as aspect-oriented programming [8], multi-dimensional separation of concerns [16] and generative programming [2], all provide technical support for the definition and syntactical assembly of features, but fall short on the semantic level, for example in spotting meaningless or even faulty combinations. At previous ECOOPs, OOPSLAs and GCSEs dedicated events have been organised around the aforementioned technologies, where we experienced a growing awareness of this feature interaction problem. However, feature interaction is often merely dismissed as a secondary problem, percolating as an afterthought while other issues are being addressed. This workshop is the first co-ordinated effort to address the general problem of feature interaction in composed systems separately from other issues.

Examples of currently known feature interaction problems include the combination of features in feature-oriented programming [11], the combination of aspects, the combinations of subjects, black-box composition of components, combining mixins, or more generally the combination of class hierarchies and the combination of several meta programs.

This document reports on the first workshop on feature interaction in composed systems. In the next section (Sect. 2) we describe the setup of the workshop, i.e. the goals of the workshop, the topics of interest, the workshop structure, and its relation to other workshops that were organised at ECOOP 2001. The following two sections (Sect. 3 and Sect. 4) list the members of the programme commitee concerned with reviewing the position papers and the workshop participants, respectively. Section 5 contains a classification of the submitted materials, where each position paper and presentation hereof is summarised. Section 6 summarises the discussions that were held by two groups in the second half of the workshop. In Sect. 7 we attempt to discuss the most important issues that were raised and some preliminary conclusions that were reached, the most important ones being terminology and definitions (7.1), and examples (7.2). We conclude in Sect. 8. Finally this document lists some important links and all the position papers that were submitted.

2 Setup of the Workshop

Goals of the Workshop.

- Bring together the researchers in the different domains facing this problem.
- Select, collect and classify the different problems in the area of feature composition in research and practice.
- Provide a platform to exchange the problems and experiences in this field.
- Select and communicate the different approaches to ensure valid component compositions.
- Promote and encourage the ongoing collaborations to deal with this multifarious and cross-cutting problem.
- Discuss further open issues.

Topics of Interest.

- Composition and interaction problems in research and industry.
- Artificial intelligence supporting the developer in this problem.
- Theoretical foundation of composition and interaction verification.
- The role of interfaces in the interaction validation domain.
- Methods to assure certain qualities of service after composition.
- Measurement and categorisation of feature interaction problems.
- The usage of pre- and post-conditions in identifying and tackling feature interactions.

Programme. Since it is the first workshop on feature interaction in composed systems, we decided to let all the participants introduce themselves and present the work they submitted. This was followed by group discussions, based on subjects that came up during the presentations or were offered by the participants explicitly. The discussions were followed by presentations of the group results.

Since feature interaction also occurs in the domain of advanced separation of concerns, where these features are of the more cross-cutting and systemic kind (such as aspects), we expected some overlap with the workshop on Advanced Separation of Concerns. Organisers of both workshops acknowledged this overlap and agreed to a organise joint session at the end of both workshops.

There is also an overlap with the workshop on Component-Oriented Programming, were the issue of feature interaction is considered as a topic of interest in the context of component-oriented programming.

3 Programme Committee

The submissions, listed at the end of this report, were reviewed by an international committee of experts in the field of feature interaction or related fields.

- Don Batory, University of Texas at Austin (USA)
  Email: `dsb@cs.utexas.edu`
  WWW: `http://www.cs.utexas.edu/users/dsb/`

- Johan Brichau, Vrije Universiteit Brussel (Belgium)
  Email: `Johan.Brichau@vub.ac.be`
  WWW: `http://prog.vub.ac.be/`

- Lee Carver, IBM T. J. Watson Research Center (USA)
  Email: `leeca@pnambic.com`
  WWW: `http://www.pnambic.com/leeca/`

- Krzysztof Czarnecki, DaimlerChrysler AG (Germany)
  Email: `czarnecki@acm.org`
  WWW: `http://www.generative-programming.org`
  or: `http://www.prakinf.tu-ilmenau.de/~czarn/`

- Erik Ernst, University of Aalborg (Denmark)
  Email: eernst@cs.auc.dk
  WWW: http://www.cs.auc.dk/~eernst/

- Patrick Steyaert, MediaGeniX (Belgium)
  Email: patrick.steyaert@vub.ac.be
  WWW: http://www.mediagenix.com

- Shmuel Tyszberowicz, Tel-Aviv University (Israel)
  Email: tyshbe@post.tau.ac.il
  WWW: http://www.math.tau.ac.il/~tyshbe/

4 Participants

The workshop counted 22 participants, whose names, affiliations and e-mail addresses are listed below:

- Danilo Beuche, Universitaet Magdeburg (Germany)
- Marie Beureton-Aimar, Université de Bordeaux (France)
- Lynne Blair, University of Tromso (Norway) and Lancaster University (UK)
- Johan Brichau, Vrije Universiteit Brussel (Belgium)
- Matthias Clauss, Intershop Research (Germany)
- Wolfgang De Meuter, Vrije Universiteit Brussel (Belgium)
- Maja D'Hondt, Vrije Universiteit Brussel (Belgium)
- Erik Ernst, University of Aalborg (Denmark)
- José Luiz Fiadeiro, ATX Software and University of Lisbon (Portugal)
- Andreas Hein, Robert Bosch GmbH (Germany)
- Tom Mahien, Katholieke Universiteit Leuven (Belgium)
- Amparo Navasa Martinez, University of Extremadura (Spain)
- Miguel Angel Perez Toledano, University of Extremadura (Spain)
- Elke Pulvermueller, Universitaet Karlsruhe (Germany)
- Ralf Reussner, Universitaet Karlsruhe (Germany)
- Silva Robak, Technical University of Zielone Gora (Poland)
- Andreas Speck, Intershop Research (Germany)
- Judy Stafford, Carnegie Mellon University (USA)
- Clemens Szyperski, Intershop Research (Germany)
- Antti-Pekka Tuovinen, Nokia Research Center (Finland)
- Ragnhild Van Der Straeten, Vrije Universiteit Brussel (Belgium)
- Julien Vayssiere, INRIA and Sophia Antipolis (France)

5 Classification of the Submitted Materials

5.1 Features and Feature Interaction

L. Lorentsen, A. Tuovinen, J. Xu:
Modelling Feature Interactions in Mobile Phones

This position paper is about feature interaction in the user interface of mobile phones. The authors identify a feature as a functionality of such a phone, that can be activated through keystrokes on a simple keypad. Feature interaction occurs easily because several functionalities of the phone can be intertwined (e.g. using the calendar while performing calls) or logically depend on each other. This makes the design and development of user interfaces a non-trivial concurrent activity. Features are identified with displays, softkeys, note, etc. Feature interactions include disabling of certain features, disabling certain keys, and so on.

The authors present a classification of feature interactions and a graphical tool to simulate features and their interactions interactively. The tool is based on coloured Petri nets. The tool is succesfully used to detect interaction patterns in UIs of phones.

L. Blair, G. Blair, J. Pang, C. Efstratiou:
Feature Interactions Outside a Telecom Domain

This position paper reminds us that the original notion of feature interaction originates from the domain of telecommunications, and that the knowledge and techniques developed in this community can potentially be generalised to other areas of computer science. The authors identify mobile systems, multimedia systems, component based middleware and reflective middleware as initital candidates of such areas. The techniques developed in the telecom world include off-line (or design time) techniques, on-line (or run-time) techniques, and hybrid techniques. With off-line techniques, the properties the system should exhibit are specified in a modelling language. When these properties are less well known in advance, an on-line technique is probably more adequate because in this case, adaptive (dynamic) strategies can be used. These strategies are typically supported by a knowledge base. Hybrid techniques try to combine the advantages of both.

M. Clauss:
A Proposal for Uniform Abstract Modeling of Feature Interaction in UML

This position paper proposes an extension of the UML (based on the standardised extension mechanisms) for feature modelling and for modelling variability in software products.

E. Ernst
What's in a Name

This paper argues that many feature interaction problems can be reduced to name collision problems. When two features are combined that both contain an entity under the same name, then the question arises how exactly the features can be combined in the presence of this name collision and how exactly the binding for the name will look like in the combined feature. The position paper surveys the treatment of such problems in several programming languages. The author defends the position that such problems should be detected statically because problems due to name collisions give rise to errors that are extremely difficult to trace at run time.

5.2   Feature Composition

J. Stafford, K. Wallnau
Predictable Assembly from Certifiable Components

This paper considers the qualitative problems arising from wiring together different binary component implementations. The so-called quality attributes of a software system are argued to be determined by the properties of the underlying component interactions. The paper proposes that some form of compositional reasoning (i.e. reasoning about a composition based on the properties of constituents) should lead to a better prediction and ensurance of the quality attributes of interactions in composed systems. It proposes PACC (*Predictable Assembly from Certifiable Components*) as an abstract reference model to achieve this. Furthermore, two concrete approaches to instantiate the PACC model have been explored and reported upon.

M. Perez, A. Navasa, J. Murillo
An Architectural Style to Integrate Components and Aspects

This paper argues that both component-based development (CBD) and aspect-oriented programming (AOP) are good tools to make complex systems more comprehensible and composable, but that little work has been done to integrate them. The paper proposes a way to integrate AOP en CBD by introducing the concept of an *aspect component*. The paper presents an architectural style to support both functional and aspect components and presents a way to document and search aspect components in a repository.

L. Andrade, J. Fiadeiro
Feature Modelling and Composition with Coordination Contracts

The authors argue that feature interaction is inherent to compositional technologies because it is exactly the interaction of the constituting components that we are after when composing a system. Hence, feature interaction is not a problem to be solved, but a phenomenon to be controlled. Some feature interactions are wanted whilst others are not.

The paper presents *coordination contracts* to control feature interaction. Such a contract is superposed "on top of" a suite of features. Depending on actions undertaken by these features (messages sent, variables read/written,...), the contract can lead to a triggering of actions to be undertaken by the contract.

D. Beuche
Feature Based Composition of an Embedded Operating System Family

In this work, the authors describe their experiences of using a feature model for a family of operating systems for embedded systems. In the position paper they recognise the usefulness of feature modelling, but see many remaining problems especially when it comes to selecting the right components with respect to system efficiency, an extremely important property of embedded systems.

5.3   Product Lines

S. Robak, B. Franczyk
Feature Interaction and Composition Problems in Software Product Lines

The paper explains how features can be organised in different kinds of feature diagrams containing trees of features which are mandatory or optional to a resulting system. Implementing a member of a software family largely consists of selecting the optional features. Of course, only a subset of the possible set of combinations of optional features will lead to complete and correct configurations. The authors argue that "reducing the n:m-relation between feature and variation point would help organising scalable and traceable software models according to the principles of separation of concerns with less intertwined feature trees". They further argue that techniques like aspect-oriented programming, subject-oriented programming and frame engineering may play an important role here.

A. Hein, J. MacGregor, S. Thiel
Configuring Software Product Line Features

The authors start by differentiating between development *for* reuse and development *with* reuse. They state that the former has been the topic of research for quite a while, but that the latter is relatively new. They continue by supporting the view that encoding domain knowledge and the integration of solutions from artificial intelligence in the product line can help in partially automating the derivation of new products in the development with reuse process. Their goal is to adapt feature models with AI techniques to enable product derivation from product line assets.

5.4   Logic Models

Y. Jia, Y. Gu
Representing and Reasoning on Feature Architecture: A Description Logic Approach

The paper denounces the lack of formalisms to support feature-oriented software development. It then proposes descriptive logics to formalise feature relationship types. These have sound and complete inference systems. The paper also presents a descriptive logic based reasoning procedure for the feature interaction problem. Feature interaction is defined as one feature influencing another.

R. Van Der Straeten, J. Brichau
Features and Features Interactions in Software Engineering Using Logic

This paper reports on two experiments using logic to formalise features models. The first approach proposes description logic as a formalisation of feature models in the problem domain, so that reasoning about features becomes possible. The second approach uses a Prolog variant to represent feature code (solution domain) and uses the Prolog engine to reason about that code in order to detect feature interactions.

6   Summary of the Discussions

6.1   Models for Features and Feature Interaction

Subject. This subject involves the notations and techniques that exist for modelling features and more importantly, feature interactions. Since unwanted feature interactions need to be detected, these models should support feature interference detection.

Participants. Danilo Beuche, Matthias Clauss, Wolfgang De Meuter, Andreas Hein, Amparo Navasa Martinez, Andreas Speck, Ragnhild Van Der Straeten.

Summary of Discussion. A large part of the discussion was spent on the definition of a feature. Because this is a recurring issue in the workshop, we elaborate on this explicitly in Sect. 7.1.

Modeling features boils down to two major points: first the modelling medium, and second how to model existing features of a system, in other words reverse engineering of features that are already implemented.

Features can be modelled using for example the *feature diagrams* of Feature-Oriented Domain Analysis [7]. A major part of this kind of diagram are constraints, such as *require*, *mutex*, and so on, which have to be described in a formal way, for example by using logic or temporal logic.

Reverse engineering of implemented features could be achieved by a number of techniques. One could annotate existing features in the code. The drawback of this approach is that it requires a certain discipline from the developer to document the code that is rarely found. Another, more sophisticated approach, is *logic meta programming* [4], a technology that consists of a base language in which the application is implemented and a logic meta language that is able to reason about the base code, more specifically it is able to query the base code. With a library of well-designed queries, this approach should be able to detect features and feature interference in an application.

6.2   Comparison of Different Approaches in Feature Interaction

Subject. This subject concentrates on the different approaches that can be taken for detecting and solving feature interference.

Participants. Marie Beureton-Aimar, Lynne Blair, Johan Brichau, Maja D'Hondt, Erik Ernst, José Fiadeiro, Tom Mahien, Miguel Angel Perez Toledano, Elke Pulvermueller, Ralf Reussner, Silva Robak, Judy Stafford, Clemens Szyperski, Antti-Pekka Tuovinen, Julien Vayssiere.

Summary of Discussion. During this group session there was also some time spent on discussing the definition and nature of a feature. Again this is further investigated in 7.1. This group also touched the subject of reverse engineering of implemented features, as did the other group, and identified feature mining, identification, and decomposition as important issues.

Typically, there are three approaches for building systems with respect to feature interaction: the first is to worry about feature interference at run-time, trying to detect unwanted side-effects and trying to solve them then, and the second approach is to do so before run-time. Basically, it boils down to trying to find the balance between proving the system is correct and testing the correctness of a system by simulation, or in other words verification versus validation. The former approach requires a complete semantic model of the software application, whereas the latter is more informal. When constructing a formal model of a software application, an important issue is establishing the boundaries of the model. Moreover knowledge about the features and to a certain degree about their environment has to be described. When sufficient information about features is at hand, the first approach is more suitable.

7 Workshop Results

7.1 Terminology and Definitions

The workshop statement of one of the earlier feature interaction workshops in the telecommunications domain reads: *"feature interaction occurs when one telecommunication feature modifies or subverts the operation of another one"*. Another definition found in the telecommunications community is the following: *"The feature interaction problem can be simply defined as the unwanted interference between features running together in a software system."* A simple example given in [14] is a mailing list echoing all emails to all subscribers. If one of the subscribers has enabled the vacation program (without first suspending messages from the mailing list) an infinite cycle of mail messages between the mailing list and the vacation program will occur. In [17] a feature is defined as *"an extension to the basic functionality provided by a service"* while a service is explained as *"a core set of functionality, such as the ability to establish a connection between two parties"*.

In the context of composed systems in general, we distinguish between a *feature*, a *component*, a *service*, and an *aspect*. In [10] the following definition of a feature is given: *"A feature is something especially noticeable: a prominent part or detail (a characteristic). A feature is a main or outstanding attraction, e.g. a special column or section in a newspaper or magazine"*. Its origin is from the Latin word *factura* which means the "act of making" or from *facere* which means "to make, do". Based on this definition we use the term feature in a broader sense than just as an extension to some basic functionality: It is *"an observable and relatively closed behaviour or characteristic of a (software) part"*. In software, it is not just an arbitrary section in the code except this code section *"makes something of outstanding attraction"*. A component can implement several features, but it should implement at least one. A component implements functionality and has non-functional properties (e.g. real-time properties, platform-dependence). Consequently, a feature may be functional or have a non-functional nature. A feature is a service if it is localised in one component and if it realises some functionality. However, a feature may be implemented in several components, in which case it *cross-cuts* the component structure and we can refer to it as an aspect.

There is a difference between problem domain features and features on the implementation level. Several implementation features may realise the higher-level problem domain features. A problem domain feature may be implemented by one or more implementation features.

We have to distinguish between intended feature interactions which contribute in a positive way to the resulting application, and unintended *feature interferences* leading to faulty applications. Several approaches might prove suitable in detecting feature interferences.

7.2   Examples of Feature Interference

In the following some examples of undesirable or unforeseen feature interactions are listed. These examples are taken from different application domains, giving an impression of the range of the feature interaction problem.

Modularised Corba Functionality. This example is discussed in [12]. In order to keep an application independent from the communication technique the communication code may be separated in aspects applying aspect-oriented programming. When a client wants to access a service exposed by a specific server the client has to obtain an initial reference to the server. This can be done either via a name server or via a file-based solution (the reference is stored as a string in a file which is accessible for clients and server). Aspects realising one of these two alternatives are exclusive. This is already known at design and implementation time. Let us assume that this knowledge was not captured at design time. As a consequence it might happen that the developer configures the system during the deployment phase with both mutual exclusive features. It might happen that even the compilation or weaving doesn't report this as an error. However, the running system behaves in an unforeseen way.

Telecommunication. Feature interaction is a typical problem in the telecommunications domain. Due to high competition and market demand telecommunication companies are urged to realise a rapid development and deployment of features. A list of features in the telecommunication domain may be found in [6]. Examples of features are forwarding calls, placing callers on hold, or blocking calls. It's obvious that some of the features lead to effects which are unforeseen if combined.

Configuration. In [13] a system called *VT* is described which configures elevator systems at the Westinghouse Elevator Company. An elevator has cables which have some weight. This weight influences the traction ratio needed to move the car. The traction ratio influences the cable equipment (also the cable weight). Therefore, we have a circular feature dependency. In case we would like to improve the security standards and therefore increase the cable quality (which results in a higher cable weight) we have an interaction with the traction ratio which might be unforeseen if this dependency is not specified and documented. VT uses artificial intelligence (propose-and-refine approach) to deal with this problem. Individual design parameters and their inferences are represented as nodes in a network.

8   Conclusions

Athough this was the first workshop on Feature Interaction in Composed Systems, the interest of the software engineering and object-oriented programming communities was significant, as is shown by the number of submissions and participants. The main objectives of this workshop, to serve as a platform where people with an interest in this topic can meet and exchange ideas, and to raise feature interaction to a first-class problem, have been achieved. Moreover, initial discussions were held on terminology and definitions, examples of feature interaction, and approaches to detect feature interference. Nevertheless, a lot of work needs to be done in this area, enough to make further workshops useful.

Links

- The Feature Interaction in Composed Systems Workshop Web Site:
  http://i44w3.info.uni-karlsruhe.de/~pulvermu/workshops/ecoop2001/cfp.html
- The Feature Interaction WIKI:
  http://www.easycomp.org/cgi-bin/FeatureInteraction

List of Position Papers

1. Luís Filipe Andrade(1) and José Luiz Fiadeiro(1,2) ((1)ATX Software, Linda-a-Velta, Portugal (2)University of Lisbon, Portugal),
   Feature Modelling and Composition with Coordination Contracts
2. Danilo Beuche (University of Magdeburg, Germany), *Feature Based Composition of an Embedded Operating System Family*
3. Lynne Blair(1), Gordon Blair(1), Jianxiong Pang(2), and Christos Efstratiou(2) ((1)University of Troms, Norway (2)Lancaster University, UK), *'Feature' Interactions Outside a Telecom Domain*
4. Matthias Clauss (Intershop Research, Jena, Germany), *A proposal for uniform abstract modelling of feature interactions in UML*
5. Erik Ernst (Aalborg University, Denmark), *What's in a Name?*
6. Andreas Hein, John MacGregor, and Steffen Thiel (Robert Bosch GmbH, Frankfurt am Main, Germany), *Configuring Software Product Line Features*
7. Yu Jia and Yuqing Gu (Chinese Academy of Science, Beijing, China), *Representing and Reasoning on Feature Architecture: A Description Logic Approach*
8. Louise Lorentsen(1), Antti-Pekka Tuovinen(2), and Jianli Xu(2) ((1)University of Aarhus, Denmark (2)Nokia Research Center, Finland), *Modelling Feature Interactions in Mobile Phones*
9. Miguel A. Perez, Amparo Navasa, and Juan M. Murillo (Extremadura Universidad, Spain), *An Architectural Style to Integrate Components and Aspects*
10. Silva Robak(1) and Bogdan Franczyk(2) ((1)Technical University Zielona Góra, Poland (2)Intershop Research, Jena, Germany),
    Feature Interaction and Composition Problems in Software Product Lines

11. Judith Stafford and Kurt Wallnau (Carnegie Mellon University, Pittsburg, USA), *Predictable Assembly from Certifiable Components*
12. Ragnhild Van Der Straeten and Johan Brichau (Vrije Universtiteit Brussel, Belgium), *Features and Feature Interactions in Software Engineering using Logic*

References

1. Calder M., Magill E. (editors), Feature Interactions in Telecommunications and Software Systems VI, IOS Press, 2000.
2. K. Czarnecki and U.W. Eisenecker, Generative Programming, Springer, 2000.
3. Dini P., Boutaba R., Logrippo L. (editors), Feature Interactions in Telecommunications Networks, IOS Press, 1997.
4. Theo D'Hondt, Kris De Volder, Kim Mens, Roel Wuyts, Co-Evolution of Object-Oriented Software Design and Implementation, Proceedings of TACT Symposium, Kluwer Academic Publishers, 2000.
5. University of Glasgow, Feature Interaction Workshop, http://www.cs.stir.ac.uk/mko/fiw00, 2000.
6. University of Glasgow, The Feature List, http://www.dcs.gla.ac.uk/research/hfig/, 2001.
7. K. Kang, S. Cohen, J. Hess, W. Nowak, and S. Peterson, Feature-Oriented Domain Analysis (FODA) Feasibility Study, Technical Report, CMU/SEI-90-TR-21, Software Engineering Institute, Carnegie Mellon University, Pittsburgh, Pennsylvania, November 1990.
8. Kiczales G., Lamping J., Mendhekar A., Maeda C., Lopes C., Loingtier J., Irwin J., Aspect-oriented programming, In Proceedings of ECOOP,1997.
9. Kimbler K., Bouma L. G. (editors), Feature Interactions in Telecommunications and Software Systems V, IOS Press, 1998.
10. Merriam-Webster OnLine, Merriam Webster's Collegiate Dictionary, http://www.m-w.com/, 2001.
11. Christian Prehofer, Feature-Oriented Programming: A Fresh Look at Objects, In Proceedings of ECOOP, 1997.
12. E. Pulvermueller, H. Klaeren, and A. Speck, Aspects in Distributed Environments, In K. Czarnecki and U.W. Eisenecker (editors), Proceedings of the GCSE'99, First International Symposium on Generative and Component-Based Software Engineering, LNCS 1799, Erfurt, Germany, September 2000. Springer.
13. M. Stefik, Introduction to Knowledge Systems, Morgan Kaufmann Publishers Inc., 1995.
14. University of Strathclyde, Feature Interaction Group, http://www.comms.eee.strath.ac.uk/~fi/, 2000.
15. Clemens Szyperski, Component Software: Beyond Object-Oriented Programming, Addison-Wesley, 1998.
16. P. Tarr, H. Ossher, W. Harrison and S.M. Sutton, N Degrees of Separation: Multi-Dimensional Separation of Concerns, Proceedings of the International Conference on Software Engineering (ICSE'99), May, 1999.
17. University of Waterloo, Feature Interaction Problem, http://se.uwaterloo.ca/~s4siddiq/fi/, 2001.

6th Workshop on Component-Oriented Programming

Jan Bosch[1], Clemens Szyperski[2], and Wolfgang Weck[3]

[1] University of Groningen, Netherlands
Jan.Bosch@cs.rug.nl
[2] Microsoft Research, USA
cszypers@microsoft.com
[3] Oberon microsystems, Zurich, Switzerland
weck@oberon.ch

WCOP 2001, held in conjunction with ECOOP 2001 in Budapest, Hungary, was the sixth workshop in the successful series of workshops on component-oriented programming. The previous workshops were held in conjunction with the respective ECOOP conferences in Linz, Austria; Jyväskylä, Finland; Brussels, Belgium; Lisbon, Portugal; and Sophia Antipolis, France. WCOP'96 had focussed on the principal idea of software components and worked towards definitions of terms. In particular, a high-level definition of what a software component is was formulated. WCOP'97 concentrated on compositional aspects, architecture and gluing, substitutability, interface evolution, and non-functional requirements. WCOP'98 had a closer look at issues arising in industrial practice and developed a major focus on the issues of adaptation. WCOP'99 moved on to address issues of component frameworks, structured architecture, and some bigger systems built using components frameworks. WCOP 2000 focussed on component composition, validation and refinement and the use of component technology in the software industry. This latest instance, WCOP 2001, continued the move from the basics to the hard problems that arise when applying component technology, including problem sets that overlap with other view points, such as aspectual separation of concerns.

WCOP 2001 had been announced as follows:

> WCOP 2001 seeks position papers on the important field of component-oriented programming (COP). WCOP 2001 is the sixth event in a series of highly successful workshops, which took place in conjunction with every ECOOP since 1996.
>
> COP has been described as the natural extension of object-oriented programming to the realm of independently extensible systems. Several important approaches have emerged over the recent years, including component technology standards, such as CORBA/CCM, COM/COM+, JavaBeans/EJB, and most recently .NET, but also the increasing appreciation of software architecture for component-based systems, and the consequent effects on organizational processes and structures as well as software development business as a whole. After WCOP'96 focused on the fundamental terminology of COP, the subsequent workshops expanded into the many related facets of component software.

Á. Frohner (Ed.): ECOOP 2001 Workshops, LNCS 2323, pp. 98–106, 2002.
© Springer-Verlag Berlin Heidelberg 2002

WCOP 2001 has an explicit focus on the connection between software architecture and component software: are these the flip sides of the same coin? Two exemplary problem areas are the use of components versus generators to address architectural variability and the distinction between components and connectors.

To enable lively and productive discussions, attendance will be limited to 25 participants. To participate in the workshop, acceptance of a submitted position statement is required and at most two authors per accepted submission can participate.

All submissions will be formally reviewed. High-quality position statements will be considered for publication in conjunction with transcripts of workshop results.

A continuing observation made in the past two WCOP reports is the increasing shift in focus away from the characteristics of components as such and towards the means to control composition such that desirable or required properties are achieved and undesirable properties are avoided.

17 papers from 9 countries of overall high quality were submitted to the workshop and formally reviewed. Fifteen papers were accepted for presentation at the workshop and publication in the workshop proceedings. About 35 participants from around the world participated in the workshop.

The workshop was organized into four morning sessions with presentations, one afternoon breakout session with five focus groups, and one final afternoon session gathering reports form the breakout session and discussing future direction.

1 Presentations

This section summarizes briefly the contributions of the fifteen presenters, as grouped into four sessions, i.e. Containers, Dynamic Reconfiguration, Conformance, and Qualities.

1.1 Containers

The first session consisted of three papers. The first paper, by Ralf Reussner, introduced the notion of parameterized contracts that link the provided to the required interfaces of a components. The claim is made that if parametric dependencies can be expressed, then finer-grained components become feasible.

The second paper of Denis Conan (presenter), Erik Putrycz, Nicolas Farcet, and Miguel DeMiguel covered the integration of non-functional properties in containers: by handling such properties in containers rather than business components, the authors claim, the mismatch between technology and business lifecycle requirements can be resolved.

Finally, in the third paper Ran Rinat and Scott Smith (presenter) discuss aspects of their Cell project. In particular, cells are components that have distinct late-link-time interfaces that establish what can and cannot be done between two cells at run-time. Late linking supports the notion of component instances (cells) being discoverd and connected on demand. Most importantly, no cells will engage in any run-time (post-link) activities, unless *both* accepted the respective other cell at late link time.

1.2 Dynamic Reconfiguration

The second session consisted of four papers, covering various facets of dynamic reconfiguration. The first paper by Pascal Costanza focused on the dynamic replacement of objects while retaining references. Two ideas form the key: separating identity (the target of references) from objects and a notion of implementation-only classes. The latter are classes that do not introduce a type and therefore can only be used in constructor calls but not to type any variables. Such classes prevent dependencies that wouldn't survive object replacement.

In the second paper, Chris Salzmann considered architectural abstractions that are suitable for wide-area component systems. Starting from the observation that systems based on the emerging standards for web services are substantially different from traditional distributed systems, the author observes that there is actually little architectural foundation for the proper engineering of web-service-based systems. In particular, the notions of discovery and binding introduce a high level of dynamicity that enables the on-the-fly exchange of system components without disrupting service provisioning. The author then proceeds to identify sandboxes, channels, binding & hosting, and environments as key architectural abstractions for this new area. Followed by thoughts on deployment the paper concludes with a first look at a development environment that aims to support these concepts and abstractions.

Looking at hot swapping for JavaBeans the third paper by L. Tan, Babak Esfandiari (presenter), and B. Pagurek introduced SwapBox, a test container and framework for hot-swappable JavaBeans. Since JavaBeans are connected by means of event adapters, the SwapBox has to disconnect and reconnect such adapters when disconnecting an old bean instance and then connecting a new one. A second concern is the need to transfer state from the old to the new instance. Both, changing connections and transferring state, need to be performed in a way that allows for some differences between the old and new instance's component.

Concluding the session, the fourth paper by Noel De Palma (presenter), P. Laumay, and L. Bellissard considered how to ensure consistency when supporting dynamic reconfiguration. The primary approach proposed is to ensure application consistency by establishing an extended transactional model that strongly isolates the effects of reconfigurations. For applications that don't require full ACID transactions, they propose to create custom transaction models that may ensure no more than strong isolation.

1.3 Conformance

The third session consisted of four papers, covering aspects of conformance and classification. The first paper by Vicente de Lucena introduces a new scheme for component classification that is based on facet and targets components for the industrial automation domain.

The second paper by Antonio Albarrán, Francisco Durán (presenter), and Antonio Vallecillo focuses on a process for implementing systems that allows the progressive replacement of components that are simulated based on their specification by actual implementations of such components. The basis for their approach is Maude, their executable specification language based on rewriting logic language that, they claim, is particularly well suited for the specification of object-oriented open and distributed systems. Their implementation simulates components specified in Maude in a CORBA environment, enabling progressive implementation of CORBA components, while always retaining a running system.

Přrmysl Brada, in the third paper, discusses the issues of automatically assessing the compatibility of components. The focus is on forward/backward compatibility between a given component and a suggested replacement; either a different version or a different component entirely. Rather than aiming at making generic claims, the approach takes assembly-specific context into account. Differences that are irrelevant in a particular assembly, but that would suggest incompatibility in general can thus be masked appropriately. The author introduces a method for determining compatibility that uses an analysis of differences in specifications that have been structured into traits of related declarations.

In the fourth and last paper of the session, Roel Wuyts (presenter), Stéphane Ducasse, and Gabriela Arévalo report on their experience when using declarative definitions of component-oriented software architecture. The authors experimented in the context of embedded devices. They briefly describe COMES, their model and how it uses logic rules to describe architecture.

1.4 Qualities

The fourth session consisted of four papers, exploring aspects of system qualities. The fourth paper could be seen as standing on its own, focussing on the emerging model of web services.

In the first paper, Torben Weis proposes a model to support vendor-side tayloring of components as requested by clients. Based on a description of the possible configurations of a component and the selected configuration, a custom-taylored component is generated without having to make the basis for such generation available to clients. The descriptions are UML based and a tool supports the validation of configurations, ensuring that all dependencies are addressed. The proposed generator is aspect oriented.

Stephan Herrmann, Mira Mezini, and Klaus Ostermann (presenter) address issues of modularity in the second paper. They observe an increasing divergence of industrial component technologies that focus on server-side, container-based component frameworks and academic approaches based on advanced forms of software decomposition. They aim to provide first steps toward a common reference framework that would integrate these two separately emerging approaches.

In the third paper, Kurt Wallnau, Judith Stafford (presenter), Scott Hissam, and Mark Klein analyze the relationships between software architecture and component technology. In particular they note that component technology focuses largely on enabling the wiring process when assembling systems from components, but does little to predict the properties of the assembled system. Software architecture focuses on just that: the prediction of system properties resulting from particular assemblies. The link between the two–requiring implementations to *conform* to architecture–is weak; there is little that relates concrete implementation components to abstract architecture components.

In the last paper of both this session and the workshop, Francisco Curbera (presenter), Nirmal Mukhi, and Sanjiva Weerawarana discuss several of the aspects of the emerging Web services component model and present a brief overview of the Web services platform. They then examine the suitability of components and component-oriented architecture to underpin Web service implementations.

2   Breakout Session

The following five breakout groups were formed (with the number of group members as indicated – that is, 30 attendees participated in this session):

1. Components and WAN/Internet/Web (6)
2. Components and Architecture / Qualities (5)
3. Components and ASOC/AOP + frameworks (8)
4. Dynamic reconfiguration (6)
5. Variability / customization (5)

All groups had a designated scribe and a designated moderator. The following subsections summarize each groups findings. The material is intentionally presented in bullet form to remind the reader that this is not the result of planned writing, but the summary of a workshop breakout session. (It is also evident that the groups had scribes of varying output efficiency.)

2.1   Components and WAN/Internet/Web

The first group discussed[1] the possible implications of wide-area systems on components, component composition, and software architecture. The discussion continued from the statements of several of the position papers–in particular, Curbera/Mukhi/Weerawarana, Rinat/Smith, and Salzmann.

2.2   Components and Architecture/Qualities

The second breakout group addressed the key question as to how to conclude from local component properties to global properties of the architecture.

1. Bottom-up and top-down approaches should be combined.
2. Properties depend on one or more of the following: style, components, and interactions.
3. There are different ways of implementing global properties, in terms of component, style, and interaction properties (n:m mappings are possible).
4. Traceability is important.
5. A desirable way of thinking about extra-functional properties is by using the ISO 9126 definitions.

---

[1] The full notes from this breakout group weren't available at the time of report writing–see the list of accepted papers for where to find these and other additional information on the Web.

2.3   Components and ASOC/AOP + Frameworks

Faced with an increasing overlap of top-level claims between component and aspect separation approaches, this breakout group aimed to clarify things from the component viewpoint. The group organized its discussion into four areas, itemized below.

1. Aspects need to be seen in scope. Different scopes correspond to different granularity and need to be handled differently:
   (i) Per component: weaving.
   (ii) Across components: Factor into separate specialized components; service/ property of container/framework; or distribute aspect by weaving.
2. Orthogonality of Aspects?
   (i) Not realistic to assume in general case. Thus, cannot handle automatically.
   (ii) Might find a linguistic approach to ease aspect composition. (Such as monad transformers in functional languages.)
3. Who is in Charge?
   (i) Aspect Declaration, Join-Point Declaration, Component Declaration. (How much needs to be exposed to enable such factoring?)
   (ii) Need to be able to assign the blame. (What is the proof obligation?)
   (iii) What can be done by means of automatic checking? (For example, aspect type systems.)
4. Aspects: What do they do for us? – Aspects and AOP do *not* provide a solution to problems around components and composition (of components), but they *do* provide a clean way to think about these.

2.4   Dynamic Reconfiguration

1. USA & USSR working group–USA: Unanticipated Software Adaptation; USSR: Unanticipated Software System Reconfiguration.
2. Basic patterns:
   (i) Object reuse: sharing via forwarding. (Client references redirected to new object, which forwards to old object to access old object's state.)
   (ii) Object replacement: state swapping. (Client references redirected to new object; state transferred from old to new object.)
3. Basic technology issues:
   (i) Reference transparency;
   (ii) Interface mismatch;
   (iii) State capture, busy state.
4. Identity control:
   (i) Benefits of reference tables;
   (ii) Need for comparands;
   (iii) Importance of unique OID.
5. Transparent Forwarding: Self reference of reused object. (Should refer to the wrapper; automatically!)
6. State capture, busy state:
   (i) Mapping rules;
   (ii) Need to reach an idle state;

    (iii) Need to modify the VM;

    (iv) Need to know it advance (hooks).

    (v) Is it really important? Is it always possible? (Needed: theory for a swap critical section.)

7. Atomicity:

    (i) When you need to swap one or more component;

    (ii) Need for a transaction/commit concept;

    (iii) No distinction between object and component then?

8. Interface mismatch:

    (i) Problem when the interface is fixed;

    (ii) Rewiring possible when higher level reconfiguration;

    (iii) Downgrading problem;

    (iv) Flexibility vs. type-safety.

9. Applications–Yes, why bother?

    (i) Washington's Old Axe aphorism;

    (ii) Highly available systems (telecom, avionics);

    (iii) At least good to know if impossible!

    (iv) Can avoid replacing a whole sytem (e.g. PBX);

    (v) Once it is there, it will be used;

    (vi) Pervasive computing.

2.5 Variability/Customization

The group identified three top-level issues: the needs to analyze and design variability, as well as the required variability mechanisms. Based on a closer investigation of these three areas, a discussion of the use of generator approaches followed.

1. Analysis of variation–need to distinguish problem domain from solution domain:

    (i) Interactions are almost infinite–need to work out positive and negative implications, interaction chains.

    (ii) Bounding/scoping problem–infinite flexibility versus bounding. (Trade-offs?)

    (iii) At least two ways of dealing with variation. (Feature-based versus use-case.)

2. Design of variation–important parts of variation relate to the open and closed principle:

    (i) One way to deal with this is to capture variation (in the problem domain) and decide where to deal with it (in the solution domain–e.g., architectural design, detailed design, implementation etc.) (Difficulty here is the n-to-n relationship between variation analysis and variation implementation.)

    (ii) Another way is to spend time in the problem domain and automate the production (disposable software)

    (iii) Cost of variation is important–ultimately a business decision.

3. Variability mechanisms–in practice the mechanisms for implementing variability tend to be limited to one (not always without good reasons–complexity management for example). Many mechanisms exist (the PhD taxonomy). Therefore there is a need to understand:

    (i) Variation types (e.g., architectural, component etc.)–at what level does the variation occur?

   (ii) Variation patterns (mechanisms applicable in particular contexts)–when to use a particular mechanism?
   (iii) Where and when to bind the variation?
 4. Generator discussion–several levels of generation exist:
   (i) Plug-in that comes with a generator to generate a variant plug-in;
   (ii) Component generator;
   (iii) System generator.

The group concluded that the variability space, if left uncontrolled, is quickly outgrowing any reasonable capability. It is therefore important to understand the larger business case/goals, analyze and design appropriately, and in awareness of what available mechanisms can and cannot do. Generators are a particularly interesting approach to handle variability at various stages from ahead-of-time to just-in-time generation of specialized code.

3   Concluding Remarks

This sixth workshop on component-oriented programming was a successful event. Some of the breakout groups retained their mission beyond the workshop day and are still collaborating. Despite its sixth iteration, the workshop hadn't lost its teeth: the solid attendance and high level of interest, motivation, and aggregate competence of the participants combined to make this event enjoyable and productive for all.

At least two larger challenges remain ahead: predictable system properties from properties of assembled components and partial reorientation of technologies along the lines of Web services.

Accepted Papers

The full papers and additional information and material can be found on the workshop's Web site:
http://www.research.microsoft.com/users/cszypers/events/WCOP2001/.
   This site also has the details for the Microsoft Research technical report that gathers the papers and this report.

1. Antonio Albarrán *Junta de Andalucía, Spain*, Francisco Durán, and Antonio Vallecillo *Universidad de Málaga, Spain*. "On the Smooth Implementation of Component-Based System Specifications."
2. Přemysl Brada *University of West Bohemia, Pilsen, Czech Republic*. "Towards Automated Component Compatibility Assessment."
3. Denis Conan, Erik Putrycz *Institut National des Télécommunications, Évry, France*, Nicolas Farcet, and Miguel DeMiguel *THALES Corporate Research Labs, Orsay, France*. "Integration of Non-Functional Properties in Containers."
4. Pascal Costanza *University of Bonn, Germany*. "Dynamic Object Replacement and Implementation-Only Classes."
5. Francisco Curbera, Nirmal Mukhi, and Sanjiva Weerawarana *IBM T.J. Watson Research Center, Hawthorne, NY*. "On the Emergence of a Web Services Component Model."

6. N. De Palma, P. Laumay, and L. Bellissard *INRIA Rhône-Alpes*. "Ensuring Dynamic Reconfiguration Consistency."
7. L. Tan, B. Esfandiari, and B. Pagurek *Carleton University, Ottawa, Canada*. "The SwapBox: A Test Container and a Framework for Hot-swappable JavaBeans."
8. Stephan Herrmann *Technical University of Berlin, Germany*, Mira Mezini *Technical University of Darmstadt, Germany*, and Klaus Ostermann *Siemens, Germany*. "Joint efforts to dispel an approaching modularity crisis. Divide et impera, quo vadis?"
9. Vicente Ferreira de Lucena Jr. *University of Stuttgart, Germany*.
   "Facet-Based Classification Scheme for Industrial Automation Software Components."
10. Ralf H. Reussner *Karlsruhe University of Technology, Germany*.
    "The Use of Parameterised Contracts for Architecting Systems with Software Components."
11. Ran Rinat and Scott F. Smith *John Hopkins University, U.S.A.*. "The Cell Project: Component Technology for the Internet."
12. Chris Salzmann *Munich University of Technology, Germany*. "Towards an Architectural Abstraction for Wide Area Component Systems."
13. Kurt Wallnau, Judith Stafford, Scott Hissam, and Mark Klein *Software Engineering Institute, Carnegie Mellon University, Pittsburgh, U.S.A.* "On the Relationship of Software Architecture to Software Component Technology."
14. Torben Weis *University of Frankfurt, Germany*. "Component Customization."
15. Roel Wuyts, Stéphane Ducasse, and Gabriela Arévalo *Universität Bern, Switzerland*. "Applying Experiences with Declarative Codifications of Software Architectures on COD."

Advanced Separation of Concerns

Johan Brichau[1], Maurice Glandrup[2], Siobhan Clarke[3], and Lodewijk Bergmans[4]

[1] Vrije Universiteit Brussel, Pleinlaan 2, B-1050 Brussel, Belgium
johan.brichau@vub.ac.be
[2] University of Twente, Dept. of Computer Science/Software Engineering, PO Box 217, 7500
AE Enschede, Netherlands
glandrup@cs.utwente.nl
[3] Department of Computer Science, Trinity College, Dublin 2, Ireland
Siobhan.Clarke@cs.tcd.ie
[4] University of Twente, Dept. of Computer Science/Software Engineering, PO Box 217, 7500
AE Enschede, Netherlands
bergmans@cs.utwente.nl

Abstract. This document describes the results of the two-day workshop on Advanced Separation of Concerns at ECOOP 2001. The workshop combined presentations with tigthly focused work in small groups on these predefined topics: requirements and challenges for ASoC technologies, conventional solutions for ASoC problems, feature interaction, design support for ASoC and design decisions for ASoC models.

1 Introduction

Recent approaches such as adaptive programming, aspect-oriented programming, composition filters, hyperspaces, role-modelling, subject-oriented programming and many others, have enhanced object-oriented programming by providing separation of concerns along additional dimensions, beyond "objects". A series of related workshops on "Composability in OO", "Aspect-Oriented Programming" and "Aspects & Dimensions of Concerns" that have been held at ECOOP, as well as related workshops at ICSE and OOPSLA, indicate a fast growing interest in this area. This year another workshop on this topic was organised, entitled "Advanced Separation of Concerns" (ASoC).

During ECOOP 2000 a predecessor of this workshop was held. In that workshop, two days were spent mostly on group work, delivering concrete joint results [30]. This year we decided to continue this successful set-up: the workshop combined tightly focused work in small groups with regular short plenary sessions. The following agenda shows how group work and presentations were interwoven, with plenary discussions at the end of each day:

Day 1
Introduction, division in groups, other organisational stuff
Invited talk: *Harold Ossher*
Group work
Invited talk: *Awais Rashid*
Group work

Á. Frohner (Ed.): ECOOP 2001 Workshops, LNCS 2323, pp. 107–130, 2002.
© Springer-Verlag Berlin Heidelberg 2002

Invited talk: *Olivier Motelet*
Group discussion: "Strategic Issues for the ASoC Community"
(*Gregor Kiczales*)

Day 2
Invited talk: *Kris De Volder*
Group work
Invited talk: *Klaus Osterman*
Group work
Invited talk: *Bart De Win*
Wrap up: all groups present their findings
Panel discussion "What have we learned, where should we go?"
(chair: *Mira Mezini*)
Collaboration with the Workshop on Feature Interaction

The group work took place in 6 different focus groups, with 5 to 6 people each. The topics for the focus groups had been determined before the workshop. The following list summarises all focus groups:

1. Challenge problems for ASoC models
2. Requirements for ASoC models
3. Conventional solutions and counter examples
4. Characteristics and design decisions of ASoC models
5. Design support for applying ASoC
6. Feature Interaction for ASoC models

At the end of the first day, there was a session, led by Gregor Kiczales, on strategic issues for the ASoC community. Most of the session was dedicated to his reflection upon the current and future position of the ASoC community: he noted that the ideas are spreading with tremendous speed, and many people from both research and practice are interested in, experimenting with and/or working on ASoC technology. Examples of the growing interest are articles on ASoC (AOP) that appear in a broad range of publications, and the first conference on Aspect-Oriented Software Development, to be held at the University of Twente, The Netherlands, on 23rd to 26th of April, 2001. However, he warned that this success could backfire, because the research community has almost no time to develop and test the ideas and techniques rigorously. In particular, there are essentially no real industrial applications of ASoC techniques that can proof the applicability in practice.

The second day was concluded be a number of plenary sessions: first a wrap-up where all the focus groups presented their findings. The reports of the focus groups can be found in Sect. 3 of this paper. This was followed by a brief panel discussion, intended to raise controversial issues in AOSD. The panellists were representatives of each of the focus groups.

The panel mainly discussed the following two subjects:

– Are overlapping concerns equal to crosscutting concerns? (or: what is the definition of 'crosscutting'): An example was given where two concerns, implemented using

ASoC techniques, only needed to be composed together to form the system. Hence, they were not really crosscutting, they simply overlapped. Now, is an overlapping concern really crosscutting or not? The main response was that a crosscutting concern should at least 'partially overlap' with 'possibly many' other concerns. Hence, overlapping concerns would be a specific case of crosscutting concerns where they only crosscut one single other concern.

– Explicit hooks (calls) versus implicit places (obliviousness): Can you achieve separation of concerns without 'obliviousness'? The main response here was that ASoC techniques require 'oblivousness' because otherwise full separation between the concerns cannot be achieved.

The final agenda item was a joint session with the Feature Interaction workshop. This session was inspired by the fact that the problem of feature interaction is particularly relevant to the ASoC community. This is mainly because new forms of composition introduce new composability problems, and particularly because there is a strong relation between crosscutting aspects and features. For the contents of this session we refer to the report of the focus group on "Feature Interaction for ASoC Models" in Sect. 3.2 and the workshop report of the feature interaction workshop (elsewhere in this volume).

This workshop report consists of summaries of the presentations in Sect. 2, and reports for each of the focus groups in Sect. 3. An overview of the position papers and their authors is shown at the end of this report. The position papers are available at the workshop website:
(http://trese.cs.utwente.nl/Workshops/ecoop01asoc/).

2 Presentations

This section contains summaries of each of the invited presentations at the workshop. For further details we refer to the position papers that were submitted by the presenters.

2.1 Some Micro-Reuse Challenges

Presenter: Harold Ossher

One of the advantages of advanced separation of concerns approaches is that the modules they provide are often better units of reuse than traditional modules. This is because what one often wants to reuse is a *collaboration*, which involves multiple classes or objects, but only fragments of each. Such collaborations can be encapsulated by modules in ASoC technologies, suggesting that their reuse will be eased. However, to realise reuse, it is necessary to be able to compose these modules in multiple different ways in different contexts, often multiple times within the same program. This presents some new challenges to the composition-mechanisms of such technologies.

Consider the implementation of a 'Link' feature, which implements the ability to chain objects together using links stored within the objects. Secondly, it also counts the number of times its next() method is called.

```
public class Link {
    private Link _link;
    private int _count=0;
    public link next() {count++; return _link;}
    public void setNext(Link l) { _link = l;}
}
```

Clearly, Link is a highly reusable abstraction. Composing it with another class adds a link capability to that class (e.g. using Hyper/J). But within a single system, one might want to add links to many different classes or even to the same class (e.g. if a class should be doubly linked). In many cases, different problems arise:

1. What if Link is composed with a class D that already has a _link instance variable? Do we want them to be shared or should they be different? In most cases this will be the latter, but we could think of situations were the opposite is wanted. In such a case, an even more difficult issue arises: The class D may well contain accesses to its _link variable. But the Link class' access counter _count depends on the protocol that all access to the _link variable occur through the next() method. Thus, accesses in class D to _link will not be counted.
2. If Link is composed twice or more with the same class, do we want them to share their _link and _count instance variables or not? Clearly, in case of a doubly linked chain of objects, we do not want _link to be shared, but we might want to share _count.

It becomes even more difficult if _count is static (one _count per class):

```
private static _count=0;
```

1. If Link is composed with a class and a subclass of this class, do we want separate _count variables for the class and the subclass or should _count be shared by the class and its subclass?
2. Or should _count be unique for the entire system? This amounts to interpreting the "static" relative to the Link class, rather than the classes with which it is composed.

Many subtle and important issues arise when one is trying to use composition or weaving to achieve reuse. As soon as the same fragment is composed in different ways into different contexts, issues arise how to specify exactly the desired semantics, especially of sharing. Many possible alternatives exist and we should allow any of them to be expressed.

2.2 Sophisticated Crosscuts for E-Commerce

Presenter: Olivier Motelet

Expressing crosscutting modularity of a certain concern involves the definition of where (or when) a certain action should be performed. ASoC technologies should support sufficient expressive power to separate this definition of the crosscut from the action definitions. Inadequate expressive power for crosscut definitions will most often lead to action definitions containing part of the crosscut definition. This is illustrated in the context of a simple example:

Consider an e-commerce application running a shop's website where clients can buy products online using a web browser. A concrete usage scenario can be as follows: The client searches for a specific product and orders it, then performs another search that he cancels and finally he purchases the result of a third search. This scenario can be expressed using the following sequence of events:

```
search; buy; search; back; search; buy
```

The given scenario illustrates the base functionality of the application. Additional behaviour, like a discount and security policy, are crosscutting the base functionality and are most preferably handled using ASoC technologies. In the example, the ASoC technology that is used to implement them is event-monitor based. This means that the base program generates events during its execution (such as those shown in the example above). A crosscut is defined as a pattern of events and hence, and aspect is defined as follows:

```
aspect = when aPatternOfEvents perform action
```

The event-monitor traces the events and executes the `action` when `aPatternOfEvents` occurred. First, we present the implementation (in a Java-like syntax) of the discount policy using a simple crosscut mechanism:

```
aspect Discount {
        boolean firstbuy = true;
        float discountRate = 1.0;

        when buy perform {
          if (firstbuy)
            firstbuy = false;
          else
            discountRate -= 0.01;
            price *= discountRate; }
        }
}
```

This aspect is executed each time a user buys a product. It applies a discountRate to the price of the product after the second purchase of the user. However, the action-code (after the perform keyword) of this aspect still contains book-keeping code to check if this buy-event is not the first buy-event. In other words, the action code still contains code to define a sophisticated crosscut "all buys, except the first". A more sophisticated crosscut definition mechanism should separate the definition of the crosscut and the action. This is illustrated using the same Discount aspect example:

```
aspect Discount {
        float discountRate = 1.0;
```

```
when enableDiscount() perform {
  discountRate -= 0.01;
  price *= discountRate; }

Crosscut enableDiscount() {
  Event e = nextEvent(buy);
  return enableDiscount2(); }

Crosscut enableDiscount2() {
  Event e = nextEvent(buy);
  {return new Crosscut(e);
   |||
   return enableDiscount2()}
}
```

Here, the action code is no longer tangled with book-keeping code. The pattern of events is implemented by the function enableDiscount(). This function skips the first occurrence of the buy-event and calls the enableDiscount2() function. The latter returns a crosscut when a buy-event occurs and does a recursive call in parallel. This ensures that the action is executed and that future buy-events are also captured.

This separation makes the aspects easier to understand: the programmer can read crosscuts and actions separately. The aspect specifications are also more reusable since actions and crosscuts can be modified separately.

Position Statement: ASoC tools should provide a sufficiently expressive crosscut mechanism that supports the definition of sophisticated crosscuts, allowing a clear separation between the crosscut-code and the action-code of an aspect.

2.3 Code Reuse, an Essential Concern in the Design of Aspect Languages?

Presenter: Kris De Volder

Code-scattering, that results from cross-cutting concerns, includes *code replication* and *code tangling*. Code replication means that the same code is repeated in different locations, while code tangling means that code for different concerns is located in the same location. To implement crosscutting concerns in a satisfactory way, an ASoC technique needs to address both these issues. Code-tangling can be addressed by crosscutting modularization mechanisms, whereas code-replication can be addressed by mechanisms of genericity that make a piece of code reusable in different contexts.

Consider the implementation of a method that searches for an element in an enumerable data structure:

```
public boolean search(Object e) {
    boolean found = false;
    Enumeration elems = this.elements();
    while (!found && (elems.hasMoreElements()))
        found = e.equals(elems.nextElement());
    return found; }
```

This method should be located in many different classes (e.g. all classes that understand the *elements()* message). Since these classes are not located in the same class-hierarchy, it clearly is a crosscutting concern and it should be modularised using a crosscutting modularisation technique. This simple example illustrates both the issues of separation (the code is scattered across different classes) and replication (the scattered code is similar or, in this case, even identical).

A Logic Meta-Programming (LMP) approach can support both separation and replication in a natural way:

Separation: The representation of a base program as a set of logic facts allows for naturally crosscutting modularity structure because the facts can be grouped into logic modules without being constrained by the modularity structure of the program they describe. In the example this means that we will have a logic module consisting of the following facts:

```
method(Stack,boolean,search,[Object],[e],
      { boolean found=false ... return found }).
method(Array,boolean,search,[Object],[e],
      { boolean found=false ... return found }).
method(WidgetList,boolean,search,[Object],[e],
      { boolean found=false ... return found }).
...
```

Replication: Even if we can group facts together in logic modules, we will frequently end up with recurring patterns of code (as shown in the example). The generative power of logic rules and logic variables enables an expressive mechanism to deal with replication. Applying this to the example, we end up with the following rule:

```
method(?Class,boolean,search,[Object],[e],
      { boolean found=false ... return found; }) :-
   class(?Class),
     hasMethodSignature(?Class,Enumeration,elements,[]).
```

In this example, scattered code is identical in all classes. But it is significantly harder if the scattered code variates from location to location. An example of this is the accept-method in a Visitor design pattern:

```
method(?Visited,void,accept,[?AbstractVisitor],[v],
      { v.visit<?Visited>(this) }) :-

   abstractVisitor(?AbstractVisitor),
   visitorVisits(?AbstractVisitor,?Visited),
   concrete(?Visited).
```

There are three variation-points in the above example: the name of the receiver class (?Visited), the type of the visitor being accepted (?AbstractVisitor) and the name of the visit-method (visit<?Visited>) which depends on the receiver class.

Position Statement: The issue of replication in aspect languages is as fundamental as the issue of separation. Besides a crosscutting modularization technique, a good aspect language should offer a mechanism of genericity and parameterisation.

2.4   Risk Management in Component-Based Development

Presenter: Awais Rashid

There have been many promises associated with component-based development, for example, instant productivity gains; accelerated time to market; lower development costs; simple and rapid mechanism for increasing the functionality and capability of a system; and low risk development strategy. This presentation addressed the claim of a low risk development strategy in particular. The reality of component-based development is that there are significant risks to organisations that are particularly threatening to small organisations. These risks stem from four main factors: the black-box nature of COTS software; the quality of COTS software; the lack of component interoperability standards; and the disparity of customer-vendor evolution cycles. By considering these risks as crosscutting concerns across the whole development cycle, it can be demonstrated that crosscutting concerns do not only occur within artefacts at each development stage. Higher-level, more abstract, crosscutting concerns can also be identified and managed using ASoC principles.

The risks relating to CBD can be organised in six main categories: evaluation (E), integration (I), context (C), quality (Q), evolution (Evol) and process (P) risks. Evaluation risks are associated with problems of evaluating off-the-shelf software for use in system development. Integration risks relate to the problems of composing systems from COTS software. Context risks relate to the problems of using similar components in different application contexts. Process risks are associated with the problems of using inappropriate development process. Quality risks stem from the perceived reliability of COTS components and the ease with which their capabilities can be verified. Evolution risks are related to the extended development and management of component-based applications.

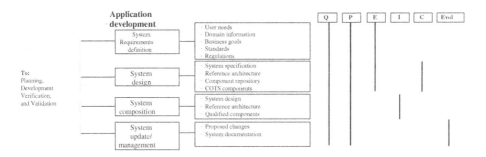

Fig. 1. Crosscutting and overlapping nature of risks in CBD

Figure 1 maps the different categories of CBD risks to development stages in a generic CBD cycle. The risks are shown to the right of the diagram. Black vertical lines indicate the development stage affected by the risk category. It should be noted that the various types of risks overlap as they affect the same development stages at times.

Separation of concerns is an approach to manage these risks. Categorising the various CBD risks into individual categories makes it possible to identify risk management mechanisms for each individual risk category (details of risk management mechanisms are in position paper 18. The individual risk management strategies may then be integrated into a single global strategy by factoring out the common mechanisms underlying the various individual strategies. Some of the core principles of advanced separation of concerns (i.e. separating crosscutting concerns in order to reason about them in isolation, with subsequent composition of the results) were demonstrated, therefore, as being useful for more than just development artefacts. The higher-level, more abstract, concern of risk management in component-based development also benefits from the approach.

2.5 Object-Oriented Composition is Tangled

Presenter: Klaus Ostermann

This presentation examined standard object-oriented composition mechanisms, such as inheritance, object composition, and delegation, and assessed difficulties associated with them within the context of advanced separation of concerns. One significant difficulty relates to the construction of mechanisms for untangling code (the standard goal for ASoC mechanisms) that are built on top of composition mechanisms that are themselves inherently tangled. A fixed set of five composition properties of standard composition mechanisms was discussed, followed by examples illustrating tangled composition scenarios in these approaches. These composition properties describe the relation that holds between two modules M and B (classes and/or objects) to be composed, where B denotes the base module, M denotes the modification module, and M(B) denotes the composition. The composition properties are:

Overriding: The ability of the modification to override methods defined in the base. In M(B), M's definitions hide B's definitions with the same name. Self invocations within B ignore redefinitions in M.

Transparent Redirection: The ability to transparently redirect B's this to denote M(B) within the composition.

Acquisition: The ability to use definitions in B as if these were local methods in M(B) (transparent forwarding of services from M to B).

Subtyping: The promise that M(B) fulfils the contract specified by B, or that M(B) can be used everywhere B is expected.

Polymorphism: The ability to (dynamically or statically) apply M to any subtype of B.

What is frequently needed is a set of composition properties which is not provided by any of the predefined mechanisms. The presentation discussed the need to clean up the primary composition mechanisms before introducing additional ASoC composition mechanisms. This requirement was underpinned through the illustration of a number of examples. It *is* possible to solve all the different composition requirements for each of the different scenarios using standard composition mechanisms such as inheritance, delegation, etc.

However, the result is deemed unsatisfactory for a number of reasons. First, depending on the desired mixture of composition properties, different architectures were used. Indeed, even where the same mixture of composition properties was required, it is possible for different designers to come up with different architectures. This problem is further compounded when a later change to the required composition features may necessitate switching to another architecture. This may require far reaching changes in the code. Even without considering the architectural issues, the design gets complex as soon as a non-standard composition is required. Together, all these problems affect the understandability, and hence the maintainability of object-oriented programs.

The basic idea that was introduced to counteract these difficulties is based upon the separation of composition properties at *language* level. With explicit linguistic means to render individual composition properties, they may be independently applicable in any architecture. This approach removes the tangling properties associated with composition mechanisms, which will therefore provide a better basis on which additional ASoC composition mechanisms may be built.

2.6   Building Frameworks in AspectJ

Presenter: Bart De Win

This presentation demonstrated the benefits that can be obtained when combining the capabilities of AspectJ with the notion of frameworks. Software reuse is an important goal in software engineering, and it was illustrated how frameworks provide mechanisms to enhance the reusability of aspects. AspectJ has mechanisms to support the coding of reusable crosscutting code with abstract aspects. Where crosscutting code requires co-operation from an application in order to work, some code is also required that is specific to a particular application (e.g., the specification of concrete pointcuts, etc.). In order to improve the reusability of aspects, a common approach is to extract the generic part of an aspect from the application specific part. One approach to deploying the reusable parts of an aspect might be to present them as a library of functions and classes. However, framework technology can improve this approach. The main advantage of frameworks over libraries is that the former can encode and enforce (to some degree) how the code should be used.

The challenge for aspect programmers within this model is therefore to design a solution in such a way that it is possible to combine a general specification with a specialised specification. First, the generic core structure should be designed using aspects. Specific concern implementations should also be provided. Then, at deployment time, any additional mechanisms may be implemented if necessary, as pointcuts specify which mechanisms to use and where. A security example, with crosscutting behaviour of access control and confidentiality, was presented to illustrate the approach. The AspectJ constructs supporting abstract pointcuts, together with aspect inheritance were shown to support the specification of reusable frameworks.

However, some difficulties of using AspectJ as a reusable framework were discussed as well. For example, when the pointcut definition is part of the framework, it is often difficult to foresee what type of parameters will be required (see Fig. 2). It is recommended that a more open mechanism than parameter passing should be considered.

Another problem that has been encountered is related to the use of pointcut definitions. Pointcut definitions are static, and may therefore only be referenced and extended in a static way (see Fig. 3).

pointcut checkAccessCut(int i): executions (* Resource1.foo(i)) ;
pointcut checkAccessCut(String s): executions (* Resource2.bar(s)) ;

abstract pointcut checkAccessCut(?) ;

Fig. 2. Abstract generalizations that are hard to predict.

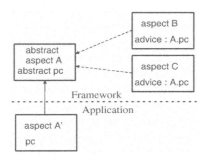

Fig. 3. Pointcut definitions are static

This makes it impossible to isolate an abstract pointcut definition into a separate construct, and rely on delegation to select one of many concrete versions, depending on where the original pointcut is used. A more open weaving process was suggested, such that pointcut definitions can be the result of a function evaluation over a representation of the application structure.

3   Focus Groups

3.1   Challenge Problems for ASoC Models

Group Members: Johan Fabry, John Zinky, Soren Top, Lahire Philippe, Marie Beurton-Aimar
Issues: Type of challenge problems, characteristics of these problems, categorise these challenge problems

The challenge problems focus group started with enumerating the issues considered important by the attendants. They are listed below:

– A first major issue was the apparent simplicity of current ASOC tools, and the clear need to go towards more advanced solutions. This would need to include support for composition of different, possibly overlapping, aspects and make it possible for the developer to get 'the big picture' of how the different aspects interact.
– A second issue is the use of existing techniques: we consider AOP, for example, to be very good at what it does: putting pieces of code in 'strange places'. However, we can not ignore the benefits of OOP, for example. The code which is weaved in should ideally contain only out-calls to code written in a 'classical' way.

– The third and final issue is the current lack of support for runtime aspects. We consider that the moment at which code gets weaved to be orthogonal to the idea of ASoC. ASoC should not be restricted only to compile-time weaving, but should also include weaving at runtime.

We envision future ASoC solutions to be more domain-driven: aspect programmes contain higher level information, domain knowledge is contained in the aspect definition, and the weaver would reason about the high-level information according to the aspect definition. Aspect definitions are now parameterise-able at a higher level: the parameters are values that are relevant for that domain. A domain expert would define a given domain as an aspect by first finding the right sets of parameters for that domain, second determine some kind of mapping from sets or ranges of parameters to an algorithm, and third define the join points. Note that this allows for a repository of algorithms that can be reused, even across different domains. The domain expert would also be responsible for determining how different aspects are composed. He can define a number of composition parameters, which allow for composition control by the programmer, where necessary. We realise that this proposed system differs strongly from current ASoC solutions. However, a first step towards our proposal would be the inclusion of libraries of aspects, which extend the current ASoC solutions.

3.2 Feature Interaction

Group Members: Johan Brichau, Guenter Kniesel, Olivier Motelet, Eddy Truyen, Mehmet Aksit
Issues: Measurement and categorisation feature interaction problems, methods to assure quality

Research in feature interaction deals with the unanticipated addition of features to a system. A feature in this context is a characteristic of the system. The focus of this research-domain is the automatic detection of conflicts between different features when a new feature is added to the system. Although feature modelling originated in the telephony domain, it is now also commonly used in software product-lines where a software product is tailored to the needs of the user who selects the desired features from a predefined set.

In the context of ASoC software development, ideally, every feature of the software system should map to one concern. Hence, in an ideal ASoC environment, the addition of a new feature to a software product means the introduction of one concern. Because ASoC technologies are improving the modularization of all concerns, the problems with feature interactions are becoming more important in ASoC research. A better separation of concerns obviously introduces more abstraction units in the implementation of a software product. Since composition always introduces interactions, the number of interactions is likely to be much higher when using ASoC compared to using more traditional techniques. What is even more important is that each feature is explicitly handled in an isolated concern and that the composition may raise issues that cannot be easily determined when the features are considered in isolation.

In order to allow detection of conflicts between features in a software product, each feature should be annotated with semantic information that defines what the feature is about. The main problem is the definition of some canonical model to specify the annotations. The problem here is two-fold:

– What should the annotations specify to allow detection of conflicts? i.e. what are the annotations about?
– What medium is most appropriate to annotate the different concerns to allow reasoning for feature interaction? i.e.: what is the language to use?

What Should Features Annotate? Features could conflict on many different levels, i.e. the conflict can be implementation-specific as well as domain-specific Therefore features should be specified at different levels of observation which can be coarse-grained or fine-grained. In the most fine-grained level we can specify every detail of the implementation (maybe even the program source code itself). More coarse-grained levels can omit the details and focus on higher level descriptions of the features (such as collaborations, architectures, use cases, domain models, etc. . .). This is illustrated in Fig. 4.

Abstract models (e.g architecture, domain models)

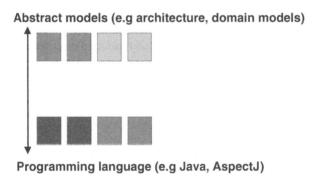

Programming language (e.g Java, AspectJ)

Fig. 4. Features can be defined – and conflict – at multiple levels

Consider a simple example, in which a certain class C implements a container that we extend with a 'linking' feature that implements the operations to form linked-list of containers. We also extend the same container with a 'back-linking' feature that allows backward linking in the list of containers. Obviously, operations on the list (e.g. delete, insert, . . .) that are implemented by both features will interfere. E.g., the insert operation of the linking feature only manipulates the forward-links of the list, which results in inconsistent backward-links.

A checker should detect such a 'feature interaction' problem, but the implementation itself is not sufficient. A high-level domain description is necessary, which in this case could be in a graph-language.

What Language to Use? Adding a new feature to a system means transforming a system. Features could then be described in terms of transformers. While it is generally impossible to prove that a system will work correctly after applying the transformations, we should limit the reasoning to the changes made by the transformations and check if they do not conflict in transformation. The transformations should specify their output as well as what triggers them. A possible strategy would be to say that they do not conflict if for each possible order of the application of the transformations, the end result is semantically the same.

Conclusion and Final Notes. Features of a software system will always interact and interfere due to issues that could not be observed when the features were considered in isolation. These issues can be implementation-specific as well as domain-specific. Therefore, features should annotate their impact on different levels of detail to allow conflict-detection.

Given this reasoning framework, there are still a lot of open research questions:

- Which category of features may interfere?
- What are the desired specification levels?
- How do we define an interference specification language in a particular (generic) domain?
- How to ensure conformance and traceability of refinement among the levels?
- How do we implement the checker algorithm in a practical way?
- How to implement the 'Feature interaction resolution' as a separate concern, once a certain conflict has been detected?

3.3   Design Support for Applying ASoC

Group Members: Maurice Glandrup, Siobhán Clarke, Constantinos Constantinides, Awais Rashid, Amparo Navasa Martinez
Issues: Type of requirements for ASoC models; examples of requirements for ASoC models; technologies to support ASoC requirements

The design support for applying ASoC focussed on the following type of questions:

- How should the different kinds of concerns be modelled at different stages of the software life cycle and in particular at 'design time'.
- Identify ASoC issues in the specification, analysis and design phases of the software development process.

The aim was to get a set of scenarios that highlight requirements on ASoC support across the life cycle; a set of issues and trade-offs to be addressed in providing such support; requirements on solutions. The heart of the problem in providing design support for ASoC can be summarised as follows:

Aspect (or concern)-orientation can be seen as a new direction in software development that requires its own process, modelling techniques and tooling environment. This is, in a way, similar to object-orientation that also went through this process to set-up an environment to develop quality software. Recognising aspect/concerns in problems and modelling the solution with help of the recognised concerns, is largely an unknown area. There are very little design heuristics to develop applications in a concern-oriented manner. This also accounts for process and modelling techniques.

To illustrate one view on the problems, we use an example: One of the issues to consider in aspect-oriented modelling and designing are the concerns that different stakeholders involved in the development of the software have, and how these concerns crosscut. For example, suppose in an imaginary project the following stakeholders with their concerns (in the remainder of the example we focus on the Cost concern):

Stakeholder	Viewpoint (concerns of stakeholder ordered by importance)			
Marketer	Cost	Functionality	Evolution	
Customer	Functionality	Technology	Cost	Cost
Architect/ designer	Evolution	Technology	Functionality	Cost
Programmer/ developer	Performance	Technology		

The domain knowledge of every stakeholder gives the stakeholder a certain viewpoint on a concern. For instance, the marketer wants low cost for a certain functionality to make a good profit, whereas the customer wants functionality he can use that is realised in a non-proprietary technology with low cost. Architects and programmers do not have cost as their primary concern, however, they realise that cost drives their development.

Certain design decisions are guided through cost. For example, design decisions that make the design more flexible, take often more time to develop than straight forward design constructs that are less flexible. What design decision to take depends on, for instance, the cost concern. Cost does influence design decisions, but it is hard to make cost explicit in the design of software. When giving design support for applying ASoC it is important to know how cost is "valued" in the project.

Analysing the above, we can say that different stakeholders recognise the same or similar concerns, but because of their domain knowledge and their viewpoint, concerns are valued differently. Concerns can crosscut stakeholder viewpoints; not in terms of meaning, but in terms of value in the project. The value of a concern expresses its dominance for a stakeholder.

Concerns should be modelled using the most suitable technique. However, translating the value of a concern in such a way that it is comparable with other concerns is a problem. In our example, the architect values the evolution concern very high, while cost is a lesser concern, the marketer will do vice versa. Modelling evolution is fundamentally different from modelling cost. Because of this difference, comparing and valuing evolution and cost is difficult. A number of issues must be considered during comparison and valuing, one of them is the value of a stakeholder to determine its decision influence for a certain concern.

To conclude the work of the discussion group, we define some research areas with possible research directions for design support for applying ASoC:

– When giving design support for applying ASoC, we need to make the concerns of the stakeholders explicit. This also accounts for the nature of the concerns; e.g. how is the concern valued, how do concerns crosscut over the stakeholders. In the example we illustrated that, it is not always possible to make concerns –that influence decision-making process during the development of software– explicit during the design of software. Valuing concerns and relating them seems therefore important in giving design support for applying ASoC. A point of research is how to value different concerns that are modelled differently and from there give design support for applying ASoC.

– Are a number of concerns and their dominance applicable on forehand in projects? For instance, in case of the cost and evolution concern this seems to be true. A (relatively obvious) example of the dominance order could be as follows:
  – for parts of software that are technological dependent, do not invest a lot of time in designing flexible design constructs
  – for parts of the software that should be reusable and capable of evolving, do invest a lost of time in designing flexible design constructs
– A new modelling technique or direction means adjustment of existing processes or the definition of a new process. Since, at this moment, we do not know what kind of design support is necessary for applying ASoC, the best approach is to integrate the design support and its guidelines in existing processes. When there is enough experience with design support for applying ASoC, new processes can be defined, or existing ones be adjusted. For possible directions and connection points, we can use work already done in this area; such as for example the PREview system; a method for separation of concerns at requirements definition level.
– A more formal foundation for giving design support is one of the directions that were mentioned in the discussion group as a possible direction for expressing guidelines for design support for applying ASoC. The reason for formalising guidelines is the following: large complex systems will have numerous concerns and the value system how concerns are related can become very complex. Automation support can be very helpful in giving an overall view of the problems and the reasons why certain design decisions were taken. Set-theory is one of the formal theories that can be used here.

3.4 Requirements on ASoC Models

Group Members: Adeline Capouillez, Bart De Win, Eduardo Kessler Piveta, Mira Mezini, Mark Skipper, Bedir Tekinerdogan
Issues: Type of requirements for ASoC models; examples of requirements for ASoC models; technologies to support ASoC requirements

Problem Overview. In order to consider requirements on advanced separation of concerns, it is first necessary to consider why "advanced" ways to separate concerns are needed. The root of the software problem being solved by ASoC mechanisms is that many software concerns *crosscut* each other, and are therefore difficult to modularise. Two concerns, C1 and C2, are crosscutting if the following holds:

– There is a clear, modular description of both C1 and C2, in the decomposition scheme most appropriate for them.
– If we consider one of the concerns (e.g., C1) to be the reference decomposition scheme, we may be obliged to scatter at least one concept of C2 into at least one concept in C1

Object co-ordination according to the publisher-subscriber pattern and basic object decomposition are examples of crosscutting concerns. This discussion group focused on the need for flexible specification of crosscutting concerns, with their subsequent composition, as the key requirements on ASoC models.

Describing Crosscutting Concerns. This section describes some features an ASoC model should have to support the specification of a crosscutting concern. First, it should be possible to express each concern in the most appropriate decomposition scheme for it. For example, for many concerns, the object-oriented paradigm may suit its specification adequately. However, for others (e.g., our concern that handles the co-ordination of objects from before), the object-oriented paradigm does not work well. An ASoC model should not be restrictive as to the kinds of paradigms that may be used to describe any individual concern,

Secondly, the model should support the description of a concern that does not anticipate the points of interdependencies with other concerns. Of course, during composition, one concern may intervene with another. However, for the description of an individual concern, it should be possible not to discuss those intervention points. This requirement is part of a higher-level requirement on ASoC models to support the flexible specification of crosscutting concerns with *or without* details of its interdependencies. A range of possibilities is needed (Fig. 5).

Fig. 5. Range of valid concern descriptions

Finally, concern providers should be able to declare concern properties relevant for future deployments of the system. However, these properties should not include interdependencies. For example, a valid property is to say that the concern has some hard, real-time constraints. However, an assertion that "authentication should be executed before access control" is not valid since it is an inter-concern property.

Of course, inter-concern properties are important. It should be possible to describe and define these properties separately from the individual concerns. These would serve as input to the composition process, together with the relevant concerns. Thus it may be possible to express the "authentication before access control" constraint from above in some abstract way that is separate from the descriptions of concerns involved.

Composition. In any ASoC model, where concerns have been separated, they must be subsequently joined in order to achieve all required tasks. This section lists requirements on the composition element of ASoC models. The following requirements have been identified:

– A powerful means to express join points is required
– Powerful adaptation mechanisms for changing the behaviour of individual concerns at join points are very important
– It should be possible to use the result of a concern composition as a concern for the next higher level composition

– Composition specification can be a first-class entity – i.e., the composition may be performed at runtime.

3.5 Characteristics and Design Decisions on ASoC Models

Group Members: Pierre Crescenzo, Krystof Czarnecki, Kris De Volder, Erik Ernst, Robert Filman, Erik Hilsdale, David Lorentz, Harold Ossher

Issues: Design decisions required for advanced separation of concerns; issues and trade-offs required for making these decisions; interactions among design decisions; requirements on solution approaches; scenarios that highlight issues in making different design decisions.

Problem Overview. Although the complete set of issues and requirements on approaches to advanced separation of concerns is not yet known, there are a number of requirements on, and features of, ASoC approaches and mechanisms that are now considered "standard" (e.g. separation of crosscutting behaviour, composition of separately specified behaviours). There exists a design space of the features and properties of ASoC approaches. Each point of the design space is characterised by both positive and negative effects. In previous workshops, many design dimensions have been discussed for ASoC systems. This workshop focused on four of these: the interaction between genericity and aspects, ternary and binary representations, symmetry, and obliviousness.

Genericity vs. Aspects. Generics are the ability to parameterise a class (or module or procedure, etc.) with respect to elements such as types, functions and constants. Generics are seen in Ada generics, C++ templates, and the emerging Java generics package. The group concluded that some of the goals of AOP can be realised with generics, but that generics differ from AOP in that generics are an explicit parameterisation mechanism (the original programmer is parameterising the program with respect to something) while aspects support implicit, post hoc program parameterisation. The group also concluded that the relationship between generics and aspects, and how they may be integrated, is a good topic for further research.

Ternary vs. Binary Representations. The ternary vs binary issue asks the question: Where does the text (the specification) that ties the aspects to the code reside? Binary systems incorporate the specification in the code; ternary systems have a separate "file" for the specification. With binary systems, tangling the specification language with the rest of the program requires the programmer to think about it through the entire process. In order to debug the system, the programmer has to be aware of the compositions that are being done. The group also discussed possible reuse difficulties associated with tangling the composition/weaving specification with aspect code.

Symmetry. Symmetry is the issue of whether there is an identifiable base code on which aspects are applied, or if all elements are created equal, where there is some composition mechanism for building composites from elements and composites. The group concluded that the key issue is that aspect systems support closure (that is, that the "apply aspect" operation can be applied to the result of the "apply aspect" operation, and that the "apply aspect" operation can be applied to aspects).

Obliviousness. Obliviousness is the issue of the extent to which a component has knowledge of other components. An obliviousness spectrum was identified: (1) direct (named) call; (2) "Implicit invocation" [28] – it is known that something will happen, but not what. This is seen in both OO method dispatch and event mechanisms; and (3) aspects. The critical elements are what knowledge is exported. With direct, named calls and with implicit invocation, knowledge is exported explicitly by the program. With aspects, the AOP system defines what is exported. The obliviousness spectrum highlights issues associated with whether the programmer should have the ability to seal certain parts of the program from aspects (the aspect parallel to Java "private"). Possibilities (and benefits) here include giving the programmer the ability to restrict who can add aspects (for example, the development team may but customers may not). Another possibility relates to allowing the programmer to specify sections that may be "critical" – i.e., that adding some kinds of aspects to this section may be too "dangerous" (have a negative impact), but some other kinds may not negatively impact the section.

3.6   Conventional Solutions and Counter Examples

Group Members: Pascal Constanza, Lidia Fuentes, Juan Hernãndez, Gregor Kiczales, Klaus Ostermann.
Issues: Available conventional solutions to use to implement ASoC technologies, trade-offs advantages and disadvantages of conventional and ASoC approaches, the use of patterns

There were three main goals that for this focus group.

– Firstly, to identify what sort of current reuse approaches that do not use aspect-oriented techniques could be benefited from or implemented using aspect-oriented technologies. In case of the existence of such ASoC technology, the focus group tried to identify the trade-off's, advantages and disadvantages of the distinct approaches.
– And finally, to categorise which of the identified ASoC technology is best for some common scenarios/problems.

The discussion was focused on reuse technologies at different levels of abstraction because aspects and concerns can be expressed at different abstraction levels (see the summary of Feature Interaction discussion group). Consequently, the focus group considered reuse technologies not only at implementation level but also at design and architectural level.

Figure 6 summarises the conclusions regarding the goals mentioned above. Whereas the upper half of the figure depicts different aspect-oriented technologies, the bottom half shows the conventional software engineering reuse techniques, and they are explained in the following subsections.

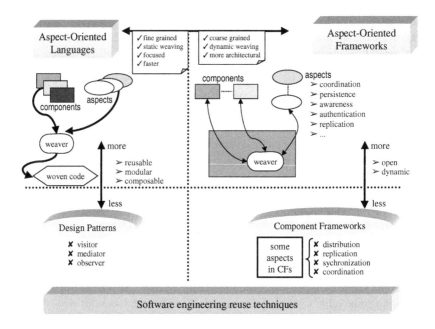

Fig. 6. Conventional solutions vs ASoC Technologies

Conventional Reuse Techniques. Frameworks and patterns facilitate reuse at different levels. Whereas the former focus on reuse of concrete designs, algorithms and their implementations in a particular language, the latter focus on reuse of abstract design and software architectures. Moreover, patterns are language independent [25].

Design Patterns. Design patterns provide a customisable solution to a concrete design problem as a set of few related classes that interact in a particular way [27]. The application of design patterns concerns the design phase of the software life cycle. Patterns may be applicable to the internal design of a component framework because they represent recurring solutions to given and known problems within a particular context. However and from the reuse point of view, design patterns show some drawbacks (position paper 16):

- First, design patterns are solutions driven by the user. Consequently, the application of design patterns to a concrete problem relies on users, so different users may produce different resulting systems.
- Besides, once a pattern is selected to provide a solution to a particular problem, it must be implemented in a given programming language. Patterns provide design reuse but not implementation code reuse. Consequently, a pattern has to be (re-)implemented every time it is applied.
- And finally, the implementation of some patterns using general purpose language like java leads to tangled code. This is the case of the observer, visitor and mediator pattern because of the invasive nature of them. Figure 7 intuitively depicts this

scenario, where the application of any of the mentioned patterns leads to code that cut across several components.

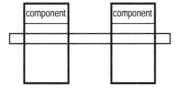

Fig. 7. Crosscutting components

Component Frameworks. During the last years, framework technology as consolidated as a suitable technology for the design and implementation of complex distributed systems. A component framework encapsulates a reusable, customisable software architecture as a collection of collaborating and extensible components [25].

Component frameworks offer a wide number of varying features, such as component interaction, distributed support and platform support among others. However, framework technology by itself is not enough to manage the complexity of middleware applications, because it does not provide the separation of concerns needed to implement the basic functionality of the components and the properties that cut across them as different entities. There are other features that are well-known aspects in the AO community that cut across functional components. This is the case of distribution, replication, synchronisation and co-ordination aspects. Aspect-oriented frameworks is a recent ASoC technology that tries to cope with these issues.

Aspect-Oriented Technologies. The previous reuse techniques may benefit from current ASoC technologies in order to solve the reusability problems mentioned in the previous section (see Fig. 6). On one hand, aspect-oriented languages such as AspectJ [29] may be used instead of general purpose programming languages for implementing patterns, producing thus components that are more reusable, modular and composable. On the other hand, the combination of aspect technologies with a framework approach leads to Aspect-Oriented Frameworks (position papers 5,16,22), which are more open and dynamic than component frameworks.

Aspect-Oriented Frameworks offer a more architectural perspective than AO languages. They are also coarse grained but they provide dynamic weaving instead of static weaving that it is present at AO languages such as AspectJ. Static weaving offers better performance than dynamic weaving. These are the trade-offs between both ASoC technologies; performance versus flexibility. It is necessary to weigh up.

AO Frameworks: Current aspect-oriented programming approaches model components and aspects as two separate entities, which are automatically weaved to produce the overall system. The resultant code is highly optimised but it is not flexible. In addition to these two entities, an aspect-oriented framework has a third entity that dynamically establishes the connections between components and aspects (see Fig. 6 and motivating papers **??**).

Having some architectural information, AO Frameworks allow the attachment of any sort of aspects to components of the specific domain. In aspect-oriented frameworks, components and aspects are developed in the same general purpose language and are composed dynamically at runtime through a middleware layer. The main goals of aspect-oriented frameworks are making explicit application architecture definition, loose coupling between components and aspects, and the possibility of COTS integration. In the approach presented by Lidia Fuentes in position paper 16, components and aspects are independent first order entities from the application domain that are weaved at run time. Aspects such as co-ordination, persistence, awareness, authentication or multiple views have been found in the collaborative virtual environment domain presented in paper 16. The framework detaches components and aspects interfaces from the final implementation classes, and they may evolve independently. Components have no knowledge about the aspects they are affected by and the number and type of aspects that are applicable to a component can change dynamically. The middleware layer is in charge of applying aspects to components though some composition information given by the software architect who specify how certain aspects must be applied to concrete components and the order in which they have to be applied.

Summarising, aspect-oriented frameworks offer the advantages of modularity, reusability, extensibility, configurability and adaptability already found in component frameworks plus separation of crosscutting concerns adopted by aspect-oriented technologies.

Aspect-Orientation and UML: Taking into consideration that crosscutting can occur in all phases of the software life cycle, we briefly discussed whether or not UML design could benefit from some ASoC technology.

Crosscutting is explicit in UML interaction diagrams. The main reason is that UML allows object-oriented system design but not aspect-oriented system modelling. Currently, there are works that extend the semantic of UML with:

- composition patterns that are used to separate the design of crosscutting requirements [24].
- new stereotypes to design well-known aspects such as synchronisation, distribution or replication, allowing thus aspect modelling at the design phase [26].

Having such designs, it is possible to automatically generate code for distinct aspect-oriented languages. With no doubt, this is an interesting and open research issue.

Acknowledgements. We would like to thank the participants of the workshop for their contributions: the position papers before the workshop, the presentations, group work and discussions during the workshop and the written reports of group work after the workshop:

Mehmet Aksit, Marie Beurton-Aimar, Adeline Capouillez, Constantinos Constantinides, Pascal Costanza, Pierre Crescenzo, Erik Ernst, Johan Fabry, Huan Fernandez, Robert Filman, Lidia Fuentes, Maurice Glandrup, Erik Hilsdale, Eduardo Kessler Piveta, Gregor Kiczales, Guenter Kniesel, Mira Mezini, Olivier Motelet, Amparo Navasa Martinez, Harold Ossher, Klaus Ostermann, Awais Rashid, Mark Skipper, Peri Tarr, Bedir Tekinerdogan, Soren Top, Eddy Truyen, Kris De Volder, Bart De Win and John Zinky,

List of Position Papers

1. Mehmet Aksit, Bedir Tekinerdogan and Lodewijk Bergmans, *The Six Concerns for Separation of Concerns*
2. Noury Bouraqadi-Saadani and Thomas Ledoux, *How to Weave*
3. Adeline Capouillez, Pierre Crescenzo and Philippe Lahire, *Separation of Concerns in OFL*
4. Yvonne Coady, Alex Brodsky, Dima Brodsky, Jody Pomkoski, Stephan Gudmundson, Joon Suan Ong and Gregor Kiczales, *Can AOP Support Extensibility in Client-Server Architectures?*
5. Constantinos Constantinides, Therapon Skotiniotis and Tzilla Elrad, *Providing Dynamic Adaptability in an Aspect-Oriented Framework*
6. Pascal Costanza, Gunter Kniesel and Michael Austermann, *Independent Extensibility for Aspect-Oriented Systems*
7. Kris De Volder, *Code Reuse, an Essential Concern in the Design of Aspect Languages?*
8. Remi Douence, Olivier Motelet and Mario Sudholt, *Sophisticated crosscuts for e-commerce*
9. Erik Ernst, *Loosely Coupled Class Families*
10. Johan Fabry, Johan Brichau and Tom Mens, *Moving Code*
11. Robert Filman, *What is Aspect-Oriented Programming, Revisited*
12. Stephan Gudmundson and Gregor Kiczales, *Addressing Practical Software Development Issues in AspectJ with a Pointcut*
13. Amparo Navasa, Miguel Perez and Juan Murillo, *Developing Component Based Systems using AOP Concepts*
14. Harold Ossher and Peri Tarr, *Some Micro-Reuse Challenges*
15. Klaus Ostermann and Mira Mezini, *Object-Oriented Composition is Tangled*
16. M. Pinto, M. Amor, L. Fuentes and J.M. Troya, *Run-time coordination of components: design patterns vs. component-aspect based platforms*
17. Eduardo Kessler Piveta and Luiz Carlos Zancanella,, *Aurelia: aspect oriented programming using a reflective approach*
18. Awais Rashid and Gerald Kotonya, *Risk Management in Component-based Development: A Separation of Concerns Perspective*
19. Mark Skipper, *Semantics of an object-oriented language with aspects and advice*
20. Soren Top, Bo Jorgensen, Claus Thybo and Peter Thusgaard, *Meta-level Architectures for Fault Tolerant Control (FTC) in Embedded Software Systems*
21. Eddy Truyen, Wouter Joosen, Bart VanHaute, Pierre Verbaeten and Bo Norregaard Jorgensen, *Customization of On-line Services with Simultaneous Client-Specific Views*
22. Bart Vanhaute, Bart De Win, Bart De Decker, *Building Frameworks in AspectJ*
23. John Zinky, Richard Shapiro, Joe Loyall, Partha Pal and Michael Atighetchi, *Separation of Concerns for Reuse of Systemic Adaptation in QuO 3.0*

References

24. S. Clarke and R. Walker. *Composition Patterns: An Approach to Designing Reusable Aspects*, In Proceedings of the 23rd International Conference on Software Engineering (Toronto, Canada; 12–19 May), pp. 5–14, 2001.
25. M. Fayad and D. Schmidt, *Object-Oriented Application Frameworks*, Communications of the ACM, 1997, 40, 10, October
26. J. L. Herrero and M. Sänchez and F. Sänchez, *Changing UML metamodel in order to represent separation of concerns*, Workshop on Defining Precise Semantics for UML at ECOOP'2001 (position paper), Budapest, Hungary, June, 2001

27. E. Gamma and R. Helm and R. Johnson and J. Vlissides, *Design patterns: Elements of Reusable Object-Oriented Software*, Addison-Wesley, 1995

28. David Garlan and David Notkin. Formalizing Design Spaces: Implicit Invocation Mechanisms. VDM '91: Formal Software Development Methods, pp. 31—44 (October 1991). Apears as Springer-Verlag Lecture Notes in Computer Science 551.

29. Gregor Kiczales and Erik Hilsdale and Jim Hugunin and Mik Kersten and Jeffrey Palm and William G. Griswold, 2001, *An Overview of AspectJ*, ECOOP'2001 Object-Oriented Programming, LNCS, 2072, Springer-Verlag

30. P. Tarr, M. D'Hondt, L. Bergmans & C. Lopes (eds.), *Workshop on Aspects and Dimensions of Concern: Requirements on, and Challenge Problems For, Advanced Separation Of Concerns*, to be published in the ECOOP2000 workshop proceedings, LNCS series, Springer-Verlag, 2000

Multiparadigm Programming with OO Languages

Kei Davis[1], Yannis Smaragdakis[2], and Jörg Striegnitz[3]

[1] Los Alamos National Laboratory, MS B256, Los Alamos, NM, USA
kei@lanl.gov
http://www.c3.lanl.gov/~{}kei/
[2] College of Computing, Georgia Institute of Technology, USA
yannis@cc.gatech.edu
http://www.cc.gatech.edu/~{}yannis/
[3] John von Neumann Institute for Computing, Research Center Juelich, Germany
J.Striegnitz@fz-juelich.de

Abstract. While OO has become ubiquitous for design, implementation, and even conceptualization, many practitioners recognize the need for other programming paradigms, according to problem domain. We seek answers to the question of how to address the need for other programming paradigms in the general context of OO languages. Can OO programming languages effectively support other programming paradigms? The tentative answer seems to be affirmative, at least for some paradigms; for example, significant progress has been made for the case of functional programming in C++. Additionally, several efforts have been made to integrate support for other paradigms as a front-end for OO languages (the Pizza language, extending Java, is a prominent example). This workshop seeks to bring together practitioners and researchers in this developing field to 'compare notes' on their work–that is, to describe techniques, idioms, methodologies, language extensions, software, or supporting theoretical work for expressing non-OO paradigms in OO languages. Work-in-progress descriptions are welcome, as are experience papers if they present a lesson to be learned.

1 Introduction

This event was something of an experiment: a few practitioners and proponents of multi-paradigm programming sought to determine whether there existed any other similarly-minded individuals, and if so if there were sufficient number and interest to comprise a 'critical mass' to justify similar future activities.

A workshop seemed the best forum for such an exploratory activity; since OO has a large and disparate following, and any practice worthy of being labeled 'multi-paradigm' is nearly certain of incorporating OO, holding such a workshop as an adjunct to a major OO conference seemed appropriate. ECOOP was chosen over its American counterpart OOPSLA because it has a wider scope.

The organizers had their own challenge to overcome, namely reaching a consensus about what we meant by 'multi-paradigm programming.' From the outset we agreed that this meant programming with multiple paradigms within a *single* programming language and not using separate languages to express parts of a larger whole (though we later relaxed this restriction to allow language cross-binding). Initially this was our only clearly

Á. Frohner (Ed.): ECOOP 2001 Workshops, LNCS 2323, pp. 131–134, 2002.

common understanding. To narrow the potential field we chose to use OO languages as the base languages for expressing multiple paradigms; this immediately led to the question of the eligibility of language extensions, pre-processing, meta-programming, and other supra- and extra-lingual facilities. We particularly sought theoretical considerations of multi-paradigm programming. Ultimately we settled on the following non-exclusive topics.

- Non-OO programming with OO languages;
- Merging functional/logic/OO/other programs (language crossbinding);
- Non-OO programming at the meta level (e.g. template metaprogramming);
- Module systems vs. object systems;
- OO design patterns and their relation to functional patterns;
- Type system relationships across languages.

Response to the call for papers was good but not overwhelming. Much more encouraging was the degree of enthusiasm expressed at the workshop, to be elaborated later.

The workshop was conducted as sequences of 2-3 presentations spaced with discussion sessions, with a final overall discussion. There was a consensus on a number of general points regarding multi-paradigm programming: *it is viable as an ongoing focus by practicioners, it is a practical means of solving real-world programming problems,* and *it should be taught early in a computing science curriculum.* Submissions were of sufficiently high quality that independent publication in full was warranted; they appear as a collection in *Multiparadigm Programming with Object-Oriented Languages (MPOOL 2001)*, NIC Series Volume 7, John von Neumann Institute for Computing, ISBN 3-00-007968-8. Enthusiasm was sufficiently great to warrant a permanent WWW site for technical material, topics of general interest, calls for papers and other announcements, etc.; see http://www.multiparadigm.org.

Participation and numbers of participants were judged by all to warrant the continuation of similar meetings in venues to be determined. There was also considerable optimism that with the increasingly sophisticated nature of computing that multi-paradigm programming has come of age as a legitimate topic in its own right.

2 Comparison

The position papers were diverse and do not admit to a coarse taxonomy. Nonetheless classification has been attempted, yielding the following: language design, new programming paradigms, language implementation, paradigm expression (in existing languages), language cross-binding, novel uses of multiple paradigms, and promulgation of multiparadigm programming. Following are very brief overviews of each paper. Complete papers may be obtained on-line at
http://www.fz-juelich.de/nic-series.

2.1 Language Design

Baumgartner, Jansche, and Peisert [1] describe Brew, a programming language being designed as a successor to Java, and so fundamentally object-based. In recognition of certain advantages of functional programming, support for functional programming is being incorporated into the design. The particular features to be incorporated are *closure objects* and an appropriate syntax for function types and function definitions.

2.2 New Programming Paradigms

Blažević and Budimac describe the programming language GENS [2]. GENS is based on a new paradigm called *environment-based programming* (formally based on an extended lambda calculus); stateful computations are encapulated in *environments*. Thus, rather than capture state by e.g. monads in a pure functional language (based on a typed lambda calculus), the mechanism for statefulness is built in.

2.3 Language Implementation

Zenger and Oderski [8] attack the problem of implementing programming languages in such a manner that arbitrary and unforeseen language entensions may be implemented (by a compiler) without modifying existing compiler code. In essesse they present some fundamental techniques for implementing *extensible* compilers in an object-oriented language. Their proof of concept exists as an implementation of an extensible Java compiler.

2.4 Paradigm Expression

Obtaining pure functional language-like behaviour in C++ has provided a number of interesting challenges for numerous researchers and practicioners. Järvi and Powell [4] address one such issue: the control of side effects when implementing partial functional application in C++.

Dijkstra and Swierstra [3] investigate the implementation in Java of a favorite functional programming idiom—lazy functional parser combinators. Their demonstration is three-faceted, comprising a Java library, a Haskell library, and a combining of the two.

2.5 Language Cross-Binding

Rashid [5] described a practical application of the use of multiple paradigms via language cross-binding. The specific context was the implementation of SADES, an object database evolution system built on top of Jasmine, a commercial object database management system. Three OO languages were employed: Java, C++, and ODQL (Object Database Query Language).

2.6 Novel Uses of Multiple Paradigms

Here we paraphrase from Wuyts and Ducasse' *Symbiotic Reflection between an Object-Oriented and a Logic Programming Language* [7]. They define *meta-programming* as using one system or language to reason about another one, and *reflection* as describing systems that have access to and change a causally connected representation of themselves, hence leading to *self-extensible* systems. Their claim is that to date most of the reflective language (pairs) have been implemented in the same paradigm. They propose *symbiotic reflection* as a way to integrate a meta-programming language with the object-oriented language it reasons about and is implemented in. New to their approach is that any element of the implementation language can be reasoned about and acted upon (not only the self representation), and that the languages are of different paradigms.

2.7   Promulgation of Multi-paradigm Programming

Van Roy and Haridi [6] presented highlights from their upcoming book *Concepts, Techniques, and Models of Computer Programming* (`http://www.info.ucl.ac.be/~pvr/book.pdf`).
The book provided an excellent opportunity for thorough discussion of many issues related to multi-paradigm programming and education. Van Roy proved to be a spirited speaker who sparked discussion and offered thoughtful insights. In this sense, the book presentation became something of an anchor or centerpiece of the workshop. The book and accompanying programming system (Mozart) aspire to be a logical successor in sophistication (in that they encompass several more paradigms) to Abelson and Sussman's *Structure and Interpretation of Computer Programs* and the programming language Scheme.

List of Position Papers

1. G. Baumgartner and M. Jansche and C. Peisert (Ohio State University, USA), *Support for Functional Programming in Brew.*
2. M. Blažević and Z. Budimac (University of Novi Sad, Yugoslavia), *An Environment-based Multiparadigm Language.*
3. A. Dijkstra and D. Swierstra (Utrecht University, The Netherlands) *Lazy Functional Parser Combinators in Java.*
4. J. Järvi and G. Powell (University of Turku, Finland, and Sierra Online Ltd., USA), *Side Effects and Partial Function Application in C++.*
5. A. Rashid (Lancaster University, UK), *Multi-Paradigm Implementation of an Object Database Evolution System.*
6. P. Van Roy and S. Haridi (Université Catholique de Louvain, Belgium, and Royal Institute of Technology, Sweden), *Extracts from the Upcoming Book "Concepts, Techniques, and Models of Computer Programming.*
7. R. Wuyts and S. Ducasse (Universität Bern, Switzerland), *Symbiotic Freflection between an Object-Oriented and a Logic Programming Language.*
8. M. Zenger and M. Oderski (Swiss Federal Institute of Technology, Switzerland), *Implementing Extensible Compilers.*

Generative Programming

Barbara Barth[1], Greg Butler[2], Krzysztof Czarnecki[3], and Ulrich Eisenecker[1]

[1] University of Applied Sciences Kaiserslautern, Zweibrücken, Germany
barth@informatik.fh-kl.de, ulrich.eisenecker@t-online.de
[2] Concordia University, Canada
gregb@cs.concordia.ca
[3] DaimlerChrysler Research and Technology, Germany
czarnecki@acm.org

Abstract. This report describes the results of a one-day workshop on Generative Programming (GP) at ECOOP'01. The goal of the workshop was to discuss the state-of-the-art of generative programming, share experience, consolidate successful techniques, discuss the relation of GP to object-oriented programming and other emerging approaches such as Aspect-Oriented Programming or Multidimensional Decomposition, and identify open issues for future work. This report gives a summary of the workshop contributions, debates, and the identified future directions.

1 Introduction and Overview

The Workshop on Generative Programming was held on June 19, 2001, at the ECOOP'01 conference in Budapest, and it was the first ECOOP workshop on this topic. The goal of the workshop was to discuss the state-of-the-art of generative programming, share experience, consolidate successful techniques, discuss the relation of GP to object-oriented programming and other emerging approaches such as Aspect-Oriented Programming or Multidimensional Decomposition, and identify open issues for future work. The workshop was attended by the total of 21 participants, including the organizers, presenters of 7 accepted paper contributions, and other ECOOP attendees. The call for participation, the contributions, and the workshop results can be accessed at http://www.generative-programming.org/ecoop-workshop.html.

The remaining part of this report is organized as follows. Section 2 gives an introduction to GP. The goals, topics, and the format of the workshop are outlined in Section 3. Section 4 gives a brief summary of each contribution including the debates. Section 5 gives an account of the identified future directions. The reports ends with the list of participants, related bibliography and resources, and position papers.

2 What Is Generative Programming?

In [3], generative programming is defined as "a software development paradigm based on modeling software system families such that, given a particular requirements specification, a highly customized and optimized intermediate or end-product can be automatically manufactured on demand from elementary, reusable implementation components by means of configuration knowledge."

Á. Frohner (Ed.): ECOOP 2001 Workshops, LNCS 2323, pp. 135–149, 2002.
© Springer-Verlag Berlin Heidelberg 2002

GP is about manufacturing software products out of components in an automated way (and within economic constraints), i.e. the way other industries have been producing mechanical, electronic, and other goods for decades. The transition to automated manufacturing in software requires two steps. First, we need to move our focus from engineering single systems to engineering families of systems-this will allow us to come up with the "right" implementation components. Second, we need to automate the assembly of the implementation components using generative technologies, such as program generators or dynamic reflection.

The key to automating the manufacture of software systems is a generative domain model, which consists of a problem space, a solution space, and the configuration knowledge mapping between them (see Fig. 1). The solution space consists of the implementation components with their possible combinations defined by a common generic architecture. Ideally, the implementation components are designed to

- maximize their combinability (i.e., ability to combine them in as many ways as possible),
- minimize redundancy (i.e., minimize code duplication), and
- maximize reuse.

The problem space, on the other hand, consists of the application-oriented concepts and features that application programmers would like to use to express their needs. The problem space gives rise to a domain-specific language (DSL).

The configuration knowledge specifies

- illegal feature combinations (certain combinations of features may be not allowed),
- default settings (if the application does not specify certain features, some reasonable defaults are assumed),
- default dependencies (some defaults may be computed based on some other features),
- construction rules (combinations of certain features translate into certain combinations of implementation components), and
- optimization rules.

The different elements of a generative domain model can be implemented using different technologies. Examples of technologies for implementing reusable components include generic programming (such as demonstrated by the C++ Standard Template Library), component models (e.g., Java Beans or ActiveX), distributed component platforms and architectures, (e.g., EJB, COM, or CORBA), domain-specific frameworks, and aspect-oriented approaches (e.g., AspectJ or HyperJ). Configuration knowledge can be implemented using preprocessors, static or dynamic metaprogramming capabilities built into a programming language (e.g., template metaprogramming in C++ or the reflective facilities in Smalltalk), or modularly extendible compilers and programming environments. Finally, DSLs can be implemented using new textual or graphical languages, programming language-specific features (e.g., by encoding features as enumeration constants in a language programming), or interactive GUI-based specification wizards.

GP requires a domain engineering process to come up with and to implement the generative domain model. This process starts with domain analysis consisting of domain

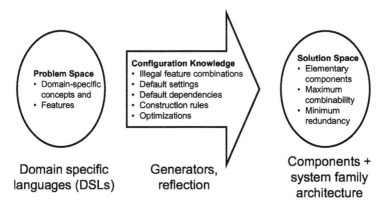

Fig. 1. Generative domain model

scoping, modeling common and variable features and their dependencies, and modeling domain concepts. It is followed by domain design, the result of which is a common architecture for the system family. Finally, the reusable assets such as reusable components, domain-specific languages, and configuration generators, are implemented. These assets are used in the separate process of application engineering to produce concrete systems.

GP is related to several areas of software engineering that are also the topic of other ECOOP workshops. The relationship can be characterized by analyzing which elements of a generative domain model are addressed by a given area (see Fig. 2). Components, architectures, and generic programming are primarily related to the solution space. Aspect-oriented programming provides more powerful encapsulation mechanisms than traditional component technologies. In particular, it allows us to replace many "little, scattered components" (such as those needed for logging or synchronization) and the configuration knowledge related to these components by well encapsulated aspectual modules. However, we still need to configure aspects and other components to implement abstract features such as performance properties. Therefore, aspect-oriented programming covers the solution space and only a part of the configuration knowledge. The problem space and the front part of the configuration knowledge are addressed by areas such as domain-specific languages, feature modeling, and feature interactions. Finally, system family and product line engineering span across the entire generative domain model because they provide the overall structure of the generative development process (including domain and application engineering).

The adjective "generative" in "generative programming" does not necessarily imply code generation, but it is rather used in its general meaning. For example, the American Heritage Dictionary[1] defines the term "generative" as "having the ability to originate, produce, or procreate," as opposed to the term "generic" which is defined as "relating to or descriptive of an entire group or class." In our context, "generative" implies not only

---

[1] American Heritage Dictionary of the English Language, 3rd Edition, Houghton Mifflin Company, 1996

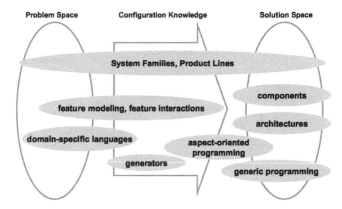

Fig. 2. Fields related to GP

encoding the elementary building blocks for a family of systems, but also automating the production process of systems from specifications.

It is important to note that GP can be applied at different levels, including the level of functions, classes, larger components, or even entire applications. Furthermore, GP is not limited to creating application code, GUIs, and testing code. The generated products may also include non-code artifacts, such as documentation, system installation, user training, maintenance and troubleshooting guidelines, etc.

3   Workshop Goals, Topics, and Format

As stated in the call for participation, the workshop aimed to bring together practitioners, researchers, academics, and students to discuss the state-of-the-art of GP, its relation to object-oriented programming and to other emerging approaches such as aspect-oriented programming or multidimensional decomposition, and its role in software-engineering in general. The goal was to share experience, consolidate successful techniques, analyze the relations between the various approaches, and identify open issues for future work.

Potential participants were asked to submit a two-page (or longer) position paper detailing their experience with GP, their perspective on the relation of GP and other emerging approaches, and their planned contribution to the workshop. Possible topics included

- synergy between object-oriented technology, components and generative techniques
- styles of generators (application generators, generators based on XML technologies, template languages (e.g., JSP), template metaprogramming, transformational systems, intentional languages, aspects, subjects, etc.), particularly their uses and limitations;
- generation of code artifacts, such as application logic, UIs, database schemas, and middleware integration;
- generation of non-code artifacts such as test cases, documentation, tutorials, and help systems;

- capturing configuration knowledge, for example, in DSLs, and extensible languages;
- influence on software architecture (e.g., building and customizing frameworks and applying patterns);
- testing generic and generative models; and
- industrial applications of generative technology.

The format of the workshop was designed to foster discussion and interaction rather than presentations. The workshop schedule consisted of two short presentation sessions in the morning, and one pro-and-contra session and one discussion session in the afternoon. The workshop started with a few words of explanation about the format and a short introductory talk on GP, with the contents outlined in Section 2. The short presentation sessions consisted of 10-minute talks by the authors of accepted paper contributions, followed by 5 minutes for answering questions. The questions were only to clarify any unclear points in the presentations. Any further discussions were postponed to the afternoon sessions. The presenters were asked to prepare their short talks with the goal of demonstrating some benefit of GP, ideally by giving an application example.

The short presentation sessions were followed by a pro-and-contra session (which was inspired by a famous television show in Germany), where each presentation was discussed according to the following questions:

Does the paper demonstrate an advantage of GP? Was there a benefit to apply GP? The pro-and-contra session consisted of a 10 minute pro-and-contra discussion for each paper. The idea was to have two volunteers for each paper, one being pro and defending the paper in the context of the above questions and one trying to come up with counterarguments. Within the 10 minutes the pro and the contra volunteer were asked to make 2-minute initial statements and then to exchange their arguments. They were also allowed to ask the audience for additional arguments, if they needed. The pro-and-contra session inspired lively debates and turned out to be a very efficient format to discuss the advantages and disadvantages of the different approaches and the relationships among them. The workshop was closed by a final open discussion, in which we identified and summarized open issues and topics for future work.

4   A Summary of the Contributions and the Debates

The paper contributions to this workshop can be classified into three categories

- *GP technologies*: logic metaprogramming [pos1], partial evaluation [pos7], and syntactic unit trees [pos4];
- *applications of GP*: encoding design patterns knowledge [pos6], architectural tunneling [pos2], and applying GP in projects [pos3];
- *generation of non-code artifacts*: generation of performance models [pos5]

The following subsections give a short summary of the contributions and the workshop debates.

4.1   Generative Programming Technologies

Logic Metaprogramming. In [pos1], Kris De Volder proposes the idea of using logic metaprogramming (LMP) as a technology for GP. The main idea of LMP is to

1. use logic facts as a DSL syntax to specify requested systems or components
2. use logic rules and constraints to characterize valid configurations
3. use logic rules to map a client's request (problem space) onto a concrete build plan (solution space); the execution of the build plan generates implementation code for the requested systems or components.

The position paper demonstrates this idea using the example of generating different kinds of counters, e.g., counters with different value types, with or without manual or automatic reset, with fixed or variable increment, etc. A concrete counter can be specified by a set of logic facts, e.g.:

```
specifycomponent(MyCounter,Counter).
increment(MyCounter,fixed<10>).
valueType(MyCounter,int).
autoReset(MyCounter,1000).
manualReset(MyCounter).
```

The configuration knowledge about the family of counters consists of valid configuration rules and rules mapping the request onto the solution space. The valid configuration rules check whether a given specification is valid. Whenever a such rule is violated, an error message can be printed by the system. For example, the following rule expresses the constraint that a counter specification must specify either a fixed or variable increment (but not both).

```
constraintMustHold(incrementDefinedFor(?Counter))  :-
   specifycomponent(?Counter,  Counter).
incrementDefinedFor(?Counter)  :-
   ( increment(?Counter,fixed<?aValue>);
     increment(?Counter,variable) ),
   NOT(increment(?Counter,fixed<?aValue>);
        increment(?Counter,variable) ).
```

The other kinds of rules are the one used to assemble components from primitive parts such as method and variable declarations and even individual statements or expressions. Some pre-planning rules may be useful to translate the user's specification into a more low-level set of features which can be mapped directly onto the solution space.

Some experience with LMP as a powerful code-generation paradigm was already made by applying it in the area of aspect-oriented programming [5].

Summary of the Debate. The most important advantage of LMP stressed during the workshop debate was the ability to express configuration knowledge in a declarative way. Also, there is an existing well-defined formalism this approach builds upon. A point that was criticized is the verbosity of specifying a system using logic facts. Another shortcoming of the current implementation compared to the technologies described in the following two sections is that the logic rules generate code by assembling any kind of text fragments (i.e., there is no typing of the implementation components).

Object-Oriented Program Specialization. The paper [pos7] by Ulrik Schultz proposes the use of object-oriented program specialization as a technology for GP. Automatic program specialization is a software engineering technique that configures a program fragment by generating an implementation dedicated to a specific usage context. Given a generic component that solves a whole family of problems and that is implemented in a standard programming language, program specialization can automatically configure this component by generating a specialized implementation. The paper considers automatic program specialization implemented using partial evaluation, which performs aggressive interprocedural constant propagation of all data types, and performs constant folding and control-flow simplifications based on the usage context [8]. The paper specifically concentrates on the automatic program specialization of object-oriented programs. It builds on recent work on JSpec [9], an automatic program specializer for Java.

JSpec uses specialization classes [12] to control the specialization of a program. A specialization class provides specialization information about a class in the program, by indicating what information is known and what methods to specialize. Specialization classes are non-intrusive in that they are separate from the main program. A collection of specialization classes that together specify a complete specialization scenario (i.e., all configuration parameters of a program component) can be considered a declarative aspect that extends the program with configuration information.

As an example, the paper gives an implementation of the Java class `Power`, which computes the power function (method `raise()`), and the specialization class `Cube`, which specifies that an optimized version of the method `raise()` is to be generated for an exponent of 3:

```
class Power {
  int exp;
  Power(int e) { exp=e; }
  int raise(int base) {
    int res=1, e=exp;
    while(e-- > 0) res*=base;
    return res;
  }
}

specclass Cube specializes Power {
  exp==3;
  int raise(int base);
}
```

Based on the code given above, JSpec generates an optimized version of the method `raise()`, which gets introduced into the original class using the introduction mechanisms of AspectJ. That is, the specializer generates the following AspectJ code:

```
aspect Cube {              // lists methods to
  introduction Power { // introduce into Power
    int raise_3(int base) { return 1*base*base*base; }
  }
}
```

The paper also mentions C++ template metaprogramming as a form of partial evaluation, an idea discussed in [11]. The main property of template metaprogramming as a partial evaluation technique is the need to code different versions of a component for different combinations of static and dynamic data. For example, we would need three versions of the power functions, one for the case where both the exponent and the base are static, one where the exponent is static and the base is dynamic, and one where both the exponent and the base are dynamic (see Section 10.14 in [3] for the complete code).

Ulrich Schultz compares both approaches and states that automatic partial specialization such as in the case of JSpec has the advantage of not requiring multiple versions of a program. On the other hand, the program to be specialized by JSpec needs to be written with partial specialization in mind. The programmer has to have the extensive knowledge of how JSpec works in order to ensure that the program gets specialized. Without that knowledge, it is hard to predict whether and how a given program will be specialized. In template metaprogramming, on the other hand, the specialization is explicitly encoded into the source program, and as a result, the specialization outcome is completely predictable. He concludes the ideal solution would be a hybrid approach that mixes detailed configuration information represented using aspects with a concise explicit syntax for indicating how certain program key points should be specialized. However, this is a topic for future work.

Summary of the Debate. The biggest advantage of this approach is provided by the homogeneous nature of metaprogramming and the automatic binding analysis. Homogeneous nature of JSpec means that there is no separate metalanguage and a base language as in the case of C++, where the metalanguage corresponds to the static level of C++ (e.g., templates, types, and static data) executed by the compiler and the base language corresponds to the dynamic level that gets executed at runtime. Automatic binding analysis allows for a flexible decision which variabilities of the generic code should be eliminated because this decision is not hardcoded into the program. The decision is made separately by providing specialization classes. Abstractly, we can think of this approach as turning binding time into a parameter. As already indicated in the position paper, the main disadvantage is the unpredictability of the specialization. Finding solutions to this problem represents the most important direction for future research.

Syntactic Unit Trees. The paper [pos4] by Marek Majkut introduces Syntactic Unit Trees (SUT), a technology for the representation of commonalities and variabilities in software product lines at the source code level. In this approach, the source code of one product in a product line is represented by a tree of code fragments. A tree structure without the code fragments assigned to it is called a frame. The idea of syntactic units trees is to reuse frames and code fragments to represent the different products in a product line.

Each node of a tree frame contains at most one reference to a source code fragment. Source code fragments have variation points used to insert other fragments positioned lower in the tree hierarchy to generate the source code of a complete system. Merging of source code fragments delivers complete source code for a product.

Syntactic unit trees have a type system of syntactic types that prevents creation of syntactically incorrect final source codes. This type system is based on the context free grammars of the programming languages the code fragments are written in. Source code fragments are typed by non-terminal symbols of a grammar. A source code fragment has a type represented by a non-terminal grammar symbol if it can be reduced to this non-terminal symbol. The variation points of a source code fragments are treated as non-terminal symbols during reduction. Source code fragments reducible to non-terminal symbols are called syntactic units and they can contain zero or more variation points. The following is an example of a syntactic unit that represents a Java syntactic unit of the type `ClassOrInterfaceDeclaration` (according to the grammar defined in [7], Chapter 8):

```
public class SomeClass {
  // comment within a class
  protected <#inst_var_1_type:Type#> instanceVar1;
  protected <#inst_var_2_type:Type#> instanceVar2;
  /**
   * Java-Doc comment
   */
  <#method_modifs:ModifiersOpt#>
    <#result_type:ResultType#>
    someMethod(<#method_arg_type:Type#> someArg) {
      checkArgument(someArg);
      return <#return_exp:Expression#>;
  }
}
```

This syntactic unit has six variation points denoted by declarators of the form `<#name:type#>`, where name is a name of the syntactic unit and type is its type name (i.e., the name of the non-terminal symbol).

A syntactic unit tree (SUT) consists of a tree frame and syntactic units assigned to its nodes. One syntactic unit can be shared among an arbitrary number of nodes. SUTs can be assembled and explored using a tool resembling the look-and-feel of a file system browser, where the left subwindow of the tool represents the tree structure and right subwindow shows the corresponding code fragments or the completely merged code. Finally, scripting facilities can be provided on top of the SUT model in order to allow the automatic assembly of syntactic units.

The SUT technology has some similarity to the Frame Technology of Bassett [2]. Tree layers in the SUT technology are similar to Bassett's frames. However, Bassett's frames do not contain any type system and allow the creation of illegal source code fragments.

Summary of the Debate. The biggest advantage of this technology is its simplicity, which also makes it well-suited for existing development processes in the industry. Compared to logic metaprogramming from Section 4.1, the SUT technology provides a simple mechanism for typing the code fragments being assembled. This typing has a syntactic character, which is weaker than what partial evaluation (Section 4.1) provides. The current approach supports only manual assembly, but it can be extended with scripting in the future. Furthermore, it has the strongest focus on handling static variabilities compared to the other two approaches. A concern that was raised during the discussion was how to find the appropriate granularity for the code fragments and avoid the proliferation of small code fragments that would impede maintenance. These concern could be addressed by an appropriate methodology accompanying the SUT toolkit.

4.2 Applications of Generative Programming

A Generative Approach to Expressing and Using Object-Oriented Design Patterns.
In [pos6], Vojislav D. Radonjic and Jean-Pierre Corriveau propose to use GP methods and techniques to represent design patterns as first class entities in the software development process, in order to make them more usable by designers, architects and any other stakeholders. In particular, their goal is to use domain analysis and modeling to make the relationship between forces and design variants explicit and to create generative representation of design patterns embodying the mapping from variant choices to pattern implementations. Representing the initial stage of the PhD work by Vojislav Radonjic, the position paper describes the problem, the initial idea, and benefits, although the approach still needs to be developed and validated.

This work is motivated by the authors' five year experience in industrial training of developers on the use of object-oriented design patterns. As a result, they have identified a number of critical issues limiting the effectiveness of pattern use in software development. In particular, the questions asked by participants of reading workshops on a selection of patterns from [6] lead the authors to suspect that the particular pattern document does not clearly communicate either the variants embodied in the design idea, or the forces that would lead one to select that variant. In the "GOF" format [6], discussion of forces are not localized to one section, but are distributed over several sections. Further, relationships between forces and variants are left largely to the imagination of the reader.

The intent of this work is to apply GP methods and techniques to make design patterns first-class abstractions in the design process. Ideally, they should be represented in a free-standing, unbounded form as opposed to being bound to frameworks or libraries. Furthermore, free-standing criterions should allow designers to select the best-fit pattern based on forces acting upon the particular design problem. The forces to be considered will be determined based on issues such as

- user-level features captured in a feature model,
- design flexibility, evolvability, maintainability, testability, and other abilities,
- optimizations, and
- implementation platform.

Feature modeling is proposed as a possible technique to explicitly represent the design space embodied in design patterns.

Summary of the Debate. The workshop debate has shown that this research direction is worth pursuing. There was some concern about the ability to capture the human side of design patterns and those aspects that are hard to formalize. On the other hand, efforts such as the Boost community (www.boost.org) and the work by Alexandrescu [1] have already demonstrated the potential of exploring the design space of design patterns and capturing it in libraries using generative methods and techniques, at least for C++.

Architectural Tunneling, Aspects, and GP for C++. Lutz Dominick reports in [pos2] on efforts at Siemens Corporate Technology to determine and realize the benefits of AOP and GP in the context of industrial software development projects. In particular, he proposes the concept of "architectural tunneling" as a metaphor capturing some of the benefits of applying these paradigms. Traditionally, handling variable requirements and evolution requires a generic architecture with preplanned variation points. One of the benefits of aspect-oriented programming is the ability to add new features to an existing piece of software, even if the software does not provide predesigned variation points for this feature. "Architectural tunneling" expresses the idea that, to some extent, it is possible to avoid the need for a generic architecture. Aspect technology allows one to add aspectual code to an application directly without the need of a generic architectural framework, and thus bypass the high up-front investment for such a framework. The term "tunneling" was borrowed from quantum physics. GP is used to control the configuration of features and how aspects get injected into the application code.

The current work at Siemens Corporate Technology concentrates on exploring the mechanisms and the benefits of AOP and GP techniques in C++. In particular, the question being investigated is how far one can go without language extensions or extra tools and by just applying the standard programming facilities of C++ such as templates and namespaces. The paper reports some encouraging results.

Summary of the Debate. The workshop debate confirmed the need for crisp metaphors to enable the effective marketing of new programming concepts, particularly in the industrial context. Architectural tunneling does convey an important benefit of aspect-oriented programming. On the other hand, this metaphor should not be misunderstood as to implying the elimination of generic architectures altogether. Only some parts of the generic architecture can be eliminated using aspects, i.e., some of the parts implementing the "hooks" for aspectual code. Also, adding more and more features to an application using AOP mechanisms without any restructuring will most probably lead to maintenance problems in the long run. In other words, AOP does not eliminate the need for refactoring and architectural design. The work on supporting AOP in C++ by standard C++ programming technques was considered usuful and encouraging. Even though this approach has limitations, the use of standard C++ and no need for extra tools is quite attractive in an industrial setting. Another argument for pursuing this approach is the difficulty to build C++ extensions (because of the high complexity of C++).

Position of Metabit Software. In [pos3], Robert Figura and Johannes Wilkes share their experience in deploying generative technologies at Metabit Software and their thoughts on future development in the area. Their application of generative technologies was motivated by the need to deal more effectively with incompatibilities between languages, libraries, and operating systems in the area of heterogeneous distributed programming for internet applications.

They report a 40 percent reduction in development cost due to the application of generative technologies. Encouraged by this success, they propose the development of a general purpose platform for GP. Some ideas about how such a platform could be structured could be gained from the Microsoft's Intentional Programming System ([10], also see Chapter 11 in [3] for a detailed description of the system). Ideally, the platform should be available for free, allowing access for low-budget developers, open source projects, and students. This would be important for its future acceptance and application. The platform itself could also be developed as an open-source effort.

Summary of the Debate. The discussion at the workshop confirmed the need for more industrial success stories on the application of generative technologies being documented. However, one problem that has to be addressed in this context is coming up with better ways of quantifying the benefits. There need to be some transparent ways to quantify the reduction in cost development or time to market.

The idea of an open source platform for GP found a wide acceptance within the workshop participants. There was the consensus that such a large effort can only be effectively undertaken by a whole community in an open-source style rather than by individuals. However, there was no agreement to what extent the necessary foundational theory for this kind of endeavor exists to guarantee its success.

4.3 Generating Non-code Artifacts

As already discussed, GP does not only concern the generation of code, but also generation of non-code artifacts such as documentation, system installation, user training, maintenance and troubleshooting guidelines, etc. The only workshop contribution that falls into this category was [pos5] by Dorin Petriu and Murray Woodside. This work proposes a technique to generate performance models from system specifications expressed using use case maps. The paper describes the necessary concepts as well as a toolset capable of generating the models (specifically so-called layered queuing networks) and simulating them or solving them analytically. The application of this technology is being explored in the domain of distributed systems.

Summary of the Debate. The workshop debate showed that, from the viewpoint of GP, not the generation of layered queuing networks from use case maps per se but the potential of applying performance modeling in product lines is the interesting issue. In particular, given a set of components and an architecture, performance modeling can be viewed as an important part of the domain configuration knowledge. This idea was considered as an interesting direction for future research. Furthermore, there was the consensus that more work in the area of generating non-code artifacts, especially in the area of testing, is needed.

5 Concluding Discussion

The workshop ended with an open discussion on the future direction in research, industrial application, and education of GP. The identified research directions include language issues such as exploiting partial evaluation in GP, language support for metaprogramming, modularly extendible languages, and language composition. Other research directions are paradigms and formalism for the representation and elicitation of configuration knowledge and testing generative models. The need for initiating an open-source development of a platform for GP was strongly expressed. Such an effort would allow exploring ideas and would greatly advance the research. The requests from industrial participants included the need to integrate the new developments with existing technologies, tools, and processes. Strategies for the introduction of generative technologies and methods in an organization still need to be developed. There is also need for documented case studies of industrial use as an evidence of industrial applicability. Finally, although a few universities already offer courses in GP, the educational efforts in this field in both universities and industry need to be intensified.

Participants

Barbara Barth (University of Applied Sciences Kaiserslautern, Zweibrücken, Germany; barth@informatik.fh-kl.de),

Marie Beurton-Aimar (University Bordeaux, France; aimar@u-bordeaux2.fr),

Greg Butler (Concordia University, Canada; gregb@cs.concordia.ca),

Krzysztof Czarnecki (DaimlerChrysler Research and Technology, Germany; czarnecki@acm.org),

Kris de Volder (University of British Columbia, Canada; kdvolder@cs.ubc.ca),

Maja D'Hondt (Vrije Universiteit Brussel, Belgium; mjdhondt@vub.ac.be),

Lutz Dominick (Siemens Munich, Germany; lutz.dominick@mchp.siemens.de),

Atze Dijkstra (Universiteit Utrecht, The Netherlands; atze@cs.uu.nl),

Robert Figura (Metabit Software, Germany; rfigura@metabit.com),

Jaakko Järvi (University of Turku, Finland; jaakko.jarvi@cs.utu.fi),

Richárd Jónás (University of Debrecen; Hungary; jonasr@math.klte.hu),

Marek Majkut (Intershop Research, Germany; m.majkut@intershop.com),

David Naumann (Stevens Institute of Technology, New York, USA; naumann@cs.stevens-tech.edu),

Dorin Petriu (Carleton University, Canada; dorin@sce.carleton.ca),

Vojislav D. Radonjic (Carleton University, Canada; radonjic@scs.carleton.ca),

Awais Rashid (Lancaster University, United Kingdom; awais@comp.lancs.ac.uk),

Ulrik P. Schultz (University of Aarhus, Denmark; ups@daimi.au.dk),

Yannis Smaragdakis (Georgia Tech, USA; yannis@cc.gatech.edu)

Jörg Striegnitz (Research Center Jülich, Germany; joerg@striegnitz.net),

Ragnhild Van Der Straeten (Vrije Universiteit Brussel, Belgium; rvdstrae@vub.ac.be),

Kristian Verelb (University of Debrecen, Hungary; sparrow@math.klte.hu),

Tim Walkenhorst (University of Applied Sciences Wedel, Germany; tim.walkenhorst@gmx.de)

Bibliography

Online resources on generative programming (including an online bibliography and freely downloadable tools such as for feature modeling) are available from the webpage of the "Gesellschaft für Informatik" Working Group on Generative and Component-Based Software Engineering at

    http://www.prakinf.tu-ilmenau.de/~czarn/generate/engl.html,
    http://www.generative-programming.org,
    http://craigc.com/,
    http://www.cs.utexas.edu/users/schwartz/.

Recent books on generative programming include [3], [1], and [4]. Two previous related workshops on "Generative Techniques for Product Lines" were held in 2000 at the First International Software Product Lines Conference (SPCL1) in Denver and in 2001 at the International Conference on Software Engineering (ICSE'01) in Toronto; see

`http://www.cs.concordia.ca/~faculty/gregb/splc-workshop/` and
`http://www.cs.concordia.ca/~faculty/gregb/icse-workshop/`.

Two meetings related to generative programming are the International Conference on Generative and Component-Based Software Engineering (GCSE) and the International Workshop on Semantics, Applications, and Implementation of Program Generation (SAIG). The GCSE'99, GCSE'00, and GCSE'01 proceedings were published by Springer-Verlag as LNCS 1799, LNCS 2177, and LNCS 2186. SAIG'00 and SAIG'01 proceedings were also published by Springer-Verlag as LNCS 1924 and LNCS 2196.

List of Position Papers

1. Kris De Volder (University of British Columbia, Canada),
   Generative Logic Meta-Programming
2. Lutz Dominick (Siemens Corporate Research, Germany),
   Tunneling, Aspects and GP for C++
3. Robert Figura and Johannes Wilkes (Metabit Software, Germany),
   Position of Metabit Software
4. Marek Majkut (Intershop Research),
   Syntactic Unit Trees for the Implementation of Software Product Lines
5. Dorin Petriu and Murray Woodside (Carleton University, Canada),
   Incorporating Performance Analysis in the Early Stages of Software Development Using Generative Programming Principles
6. Vojislav D. Radonjic and Jean-Pierre Corriveau (Carleton University, Canada),
   A Generative Approach to Expressing and Using Object-Oriented Design Patterns
7. Ulrik P. Schultz (University of Aarhus, Denmark),
   Object-Oriented Program Specialization: Aspect Into Aspects - Or Maybe Not?

References

1. A. Alexandrescu. *Modern C++ Design*. In: IEEE Transactions on Software Engineering. Addison-Wesley, Boston, MA, 2000
2. Paul G. Bassett. *Framing Software Reuse: Lessons form the Real World*. Prentice-Hall, 1997
3. K. Czarnecki and U. Eisenecker. *Generative Programming: Methods, Tools, and Applications*. Addison-Wesley, Boston, MA, 2000
4. J. C. Cleaveland. *Program Generators with XML and Java*. Prentice-Hall, XML Book Series, 2001
5. K. De Volder. Aspect-Oriented Logic Meta Programming. In *Meta-Level Architectures and Reflection*, P. Cointe (Ed.), LNCS 1616, Springer-Verlag, 1999, pp. 250-272
6. E. Gamma, R. Helm, R. Johnson, and J. Vlissides. *Design Patterns: Elements of Reusable Object-Oriented Software*. Addison-Wesley, Reading, MA, 1994
7. J. Gosling, B. Joy, G. Steele, and G. Bracha. *The Java (TM) Language Specification, Second Edition*. Addison-Wesley, 2000
8. N. Jones, C. Gomard, and P. Sestoft. *Partial Evaluation and Automatic Program Generation*. Prentice-Hall, 1993
9. U. Schultz. Object-Oriented Software Engineering Using Partial Evaluation. PhD thesis, University of Rennes I, Dec. 2000
10. C. Simonyi. The Death of Computer Languages, The Birth of Intentional Programming. Technical Report MSR-TR-95-52, Microsoft Research, 1995

11. T. Veldhuizen. C++ templates as partial evaluation. In *ACM SIGPLAN Workshop on Partial Evaluation and Semantics-Based Program Manipulation (PEPM'98)*, ACM Press, 1999, pp. 13-18,

12. E. Volanschi, C. Consel, G. Muller, and C. Cowan. Declarative specialization of object-oriented programs. In *OOPSLA'97 Conference Proceedings*, ACM Press, 1997, pp. 286-300

4th Workshop on Object-Oriented Architectural Evolution

Tom Mens[1] and Galal Hassan Galal[2]

[1] Postdoctoral Fellow of the Fund for Scientific Research - Flanders
Programming Technology Lab, Vrije Universiteit Brussel
Pleinlaan 2, B-1050 Brussel, Belgium
tom.mens@vub.ac.be
[2] School of Informatics and Multimedia Technology, University of North London
166-220 Holloway Road, London N7 8DB, United Kingdom
galal@acm.org

Abstract. The aim of the fourth workshop on Object-Oriented Architectural Evolution was to discuss into more detail a number of important issues raised during the previous workshop: the relationship between domain analysis and software architecture, the importance of architectural views and layering techniques, and the applicability of existing object-oriented principles and evolution techniques. This paper summarises the results of the debates held about these issues, reports on convergences of view taken place during the workshop, and suggests some research topics that are worthwhile to pursue in the future.

1 Introduction

The workshop on *Object-Oriented Architectural Evolution* was co-located with the 15th *European Conference on Object-Oriented Programming* (ECOOP 2001), which took place at the Eötvös Loránd University in Budapest, Hungary, June 2001. This workshop was the fourth in a series of consecutive ECOOP workshops in the area of software architecture and its evolution [1,2,3]. Previous workshops have proved very successful and stimulating, culminating in reports that contained novel and exciting views on what software architecture is, or should be, and how architectural issues may be approached from fresh perspectives. Past workshops also incorporated relevant experience reports and suggestions for future research in the area of evolving software architectures, especially object-oriented ones.

One full day was allocated for the workshop (Monday, June 18, 2001). In preparation to the workshop, participants were requested to provide partial answers to a list of questions that were suggested by the organisers as likely candidates to stimulate discussion.

In total, 11 submissions were received, 10 of which were accepted for workshop participation [16]. A total of 12 people (including the organisers and representatives of 8 submissions) actually attended the workshop. The workshop participants came from research institutes in 8 different countries: Belgium, Brazil, Denmark, Finland, France, Germany, Latvia and United Kingdom.

A. Frohner (Ed.): ECOOP 2001 Workshops, LNCS 2323, pp. 150–164, 2002.

2 Workshop Preparation

2.1 Q & A-Style

The nature of the workshop was intended to be incremental, building further on the results of the last three years. To ensure an active collaboration between the participants, the call for participation was built up in a Q & A-style. After a briefing of the results of the previous workshop [3], a number of tentative open questions was suggested to which participants needed to provide an answer before the workshop.

We are convinced that this way of soliciting submissions greatly contributed to the success of the workshop. The process of asking questions is a well-known hermeneutic cognitive process in philosophy. It made it much easier to compare points of divergence between participants' opinions, and enabled us to detect points of agreement on particular topics. Therefore, we believe that a Q & A-style would be an interesting alternative for other workshops as well.

2.2 Categories of Questions

Since the previous workshop [3] emphasised the need for *domain analysis*, as well as the importance of *architectural views* in combination with a *layering mechanism*, we decided to raise specific questions with the aim to explore these issues in more detail. The questions were subdivided into 5 categories:

1. Domain analysis
    a) What is the precise relationship between domain modelling and architectural design/modelling?
    b) How can domain analysis be used to derive a better (i.e. less change-sensitive) software architecture?
    c) Can we predict certain types of architectural evolution based on a given domain analysis? Which ones? How?
2. The use of multiple architectural views
    a) Should there be a predefined set of architectural views, or do the kinds of views depend on the problem domain?
    b) Is there a relationship between the different architectural views? Should we allow for explicit constraints between the views? How? Why (not)?
    c) Is there a correspondence between the architectural views and the architectural styles that can be used in those views?
3. Layered approach
    a) How should the different architectural layers be related? Should we put explicit constraints between them? How?
    b) Should there be a limited set of layers depending on the architectural view taken, or can there be an unlimited number of layers?
    c) How can layering ease the transition from a software architecture to the (object-oriented) software implementation?
    d) (How) can architectural styles other than a layered one be used to (i) facilitate evolution; (ii) ease the transition to the software implementation?

4. Impact of multi-layered view approach on architectural evolution
   a) How can views be used to guide/constrain/facilitate changes to the architecture and the implementation?
   b) Does it make sense to distinguish inter-view, intra-view, inter-layer and intra-layer evolution? What is the meaning of this?
   c) Is a multi-layered-view approach beneficial for checking or enforcing the conformance of a software implementation to its architecture? Does it become simpler to synchronise an architecture and its corresponding implementation?
5. Applicability of existing techniques
   a) Where do existing evolution approaches like reverse engineering, architectural recovery, restructuring, refactoring, architectural reconfiguration fit in? Can they be used in the above approach? How can they benefit from the ideas introduced above?
   b) Can object-oriented software engineering principles such as design patterns, frameworks and inheritance be used to facilitate evolution, or to ease the transition from a software architecture to a software implementation?
   c) How can one determine whether (part of) a given software architecture is stable?

3   Contributions

3.1   Additional Questions and Workshop Topics

Besides the questions mentioned above, several contributions proposed additional questions and topics to be discussed during the workshop:

The need for *separation of concerns* was addressed by various authors.

Harald Störrle, *Janis Osis* and *Stephen Cook* addressed the need for formalisms in the context of architectural evolution. This gave rise to a variety of questions. How formal does an architectural specification need to be? Does greater formality make evolvability easier to achieve? Should a domain analysis be formal?

Stephen Cook asked whether it is possible to assess the evolvability of alternative architectures objectively? Are existing design concepts such as cohesion and coupling relevant to architecture evolvability? If so, how should they be measured?

Christian Wege proposed to look at the software development process from an architecture point of view. More precisely, he posed the following questions. How do you identify those areas within an architecture which need special support by the development process? Which hints/guidelines for building the architecture can the architect derive from the used software development process? What could a round-trip between these two aspects look like? E.g., how should the development process be adapted to meet the needs of the architecture?

Albertina Lourenci emphasised the use of semiotic, hermeneutic and autopoietic reasoning and domain modelling to build more expressive and evolutive software architectures [12].

3.2   Controversial Statements

With the aim to stimulate discussions, some participants deliberately made some controversial statements in their contributions. For example, *Serge Demeyer* postulated the following challenging assumptions:

- A software architecture is something that fits on a single page.
- There is no such thing as architectural drift (erosion).
- Architectural recovery is not a viable research topic.

3.3   Clusters of Interest

All received submissions [16] were double reviewed by the organisers. By compiling all contributions in a so-called *contribution matrix* (see Table 1), and comparing the addressed topics, the organisers were able to divide the contributions into three major clusters of interest. The first relates to the possible links between the original problem domain and the software architecture(s) that can be related to it. The second addresses the range of available architectural views and layering techniques, and their relevant merits and contribution to the evolvability issue. The third relates to the applicability of existing object-oriented principles and evolution techniques for improving architectural object-oriented software evolution.

Table 1. Contribution matrix

Question	Respondent 1	Respondent 2	Respondent 3	Respondent 4	Respondent 5
1. Domain Analysis					
1.(a)	Osis				Lourenci et al.
1.(b)		Andrade et al.	Wege		Cook et al.
1.(c)		Osis			Cook et al.
2. Use of multiple architectural views					
2.(a)	Demeyer	Nowack et al.	Störrle	Maccari	
2.(b)			Störrle	Maccari	
2.(c)			Störrle	Maccari	
3. Layered Approach					
3.(a)		Andrade et al.			
3.(b)		Andrade et al.			
3.(c)				Maccari	
3.(d)	Demeyer	Briot et al.			
4. Impact of multi-layered view approach on architectural evolution					
4.(a)			Wege	Nowack et al.	
4.(b)		Andrade et al.			
4.(c)	Demeyer	Briot et al.			
5. Applicability of existing techniques					
5.(a)	Demeyer	Andrade et al.	Wege	Nowack et al.	Cook et al.
5.(b)	Briot et al.	Andrade et al.	Störrle	Maccari	Lourenci et al.
5.(c)	Osis				Cook et al.

4 Warm-Up Presentations

In the morning, after a general introduction and getting acquainted, two warm-up presentations were given. The topics were chosen according to the bias of the organisers, with the aim of stimulating discussions.

4.1 Designing for Architecture Evolvability

The first talk, presented by *Stephen Cook* based on joint work with Rachel Harrison and Brian Ritchie, was entitled "Designing for Architecture Evolvability: Some Conclusions from a Management Information System Case Study". During this presentation, a number of interesting ideas and guidelines were suggested:

It is important to look at evolvability as a viewpoint. Software designers' way of thinking changes significantly once they are encouraged to think about the evolvability of their designs, in terms of the aspects of change that are likely to affect their designs. This says something about the nature of training that needs to be provided to software designers. This idea of consciously thinking about evolvability is useful for all stakeholders involved in the software engineering process, including business analysts, domain experts, software developers and even project managers.

Patterns might be useful to localise evolution and improve evolvability of architectures.

Established software engineering principles (such as separation of concerns, abstraction, refinement) are useful to solve architectural problems. In order to achieve this, there is a need for an architectural language that explicitly incorporates these principles. Such an explicit language or formalism is also needed during domain analysis.

4.2 Reflecting on Architectural Evolution

The second talk, presented by *Palle Nowack* based on joint work with Lars Bendix, was entitled "Reflecting on Architectural Evolution: Questions from Change Management and Conceptual Modelling". Among others, he raised the following issues:

- A software architecture should essentially remain stable. We only have architectural evolution if a software system evolves in a discontinuous way.
- Changes to the software architecture can come from a variety of different sources: from changes in the problem domain, application domain, solution domain (e.g., changes in technology and infrastructure) and development domain.
- Instead of layering, separation of concerns and the associated principles of coupling and cohesion should be used, because they constitute commonly accepted architectural principles.
- Techniques from software configuration management [7,17,6,15,8] can be used to enhance tool support for architectural evolution. For example, one should try to identify the right units (operators and operands) for describing architecture operations. While these concepts are well-understood for configuration management, this is not the case for architectural change.

5   Summary of the Debate

This section summarises the discussions that were held during the remainder of the day. Section 5.1 summarises the debate held on the first cluster of interest identified in Sect. 3.3, namely the relationship between domain modelling and software architectures. Section 5.2 addresses the second cluster of interest, namely the use of architectural views and architectural layering. The third cluster of interest was only discussed very briefly, but instead a discussion ensued about the importance of the software process. This is summarised in Sect. 5.3.

5.1   Domain Analysis and Software Architecture

The first cluster of interest focused on the relationship between domain analysis/modelling and the derivation of a software architecture from it. This issue basically boils down to how to map elements of the domain to elements of a certain software architecture in a way that enhances the latter with respect to certain agreed priorities or quality attributes.

Domain Analysis. First we looked in more detail at the domain analysis, and brainstormed about what should be included in the domain model. As a very general guideline, *the domain model contains only those things or constraints that are imposed on the technical design from the outside.* Things that require an explicit decision from the software engineer (software architect, software designer or software developer) reside at a lower level and should be excluded from the domain model.

More precisely, the domain model can include the following information, although the exact content will vary enormously from organisation to organisation, and even from software system to software system:

– Business and organisational issues, organisational patterns, organisational structures, social structure, company culture
– Processes (interactional processes, design processes, planning processes, ...)
– IT infrastructure, in as far as this cannot be freely chosen (hardware configuration, network infrastructure, operating system, development environment)
– Stakeholders (includes users, domain experts, software engineers, designers, developers, managers, ...)
– Change scenarios (including design alternatives and quality attributes)
– The architecture of the domain: as a separate concept that needs some deliberation as to the optimal way of mapping into the architecture of the software artefact. The domain architecture is the set of domain concepts that describe it at a relatively high level of abstraction and their organisation. The assumption being that a mapping between the domain and the software artefact will enable the latter to change in tune with the domain more easily.
– Various relevant concepts that do not belong to any of the heading above

Note that the information contained in the domain model should not be restricted to a fixed moment in time. *The domain model should contain all relevant information from past activities, as well as future scenarios.* Indeed, it is important to introspect past activities to reflect upon future activities with the purpose of establishing the degree of variability of various elements of the domain and the architectures that support it. This also became apparent from Stephen Cook's presentation. When thinking about future evolvability, people start making different decisions.

Software Architecture. As a second part of the discussion, we addressed the question of what is an architecture and what should we do with it? The discussion started by statement of Serge Demeyer that "architecture is in the eyes of the beholder", which he linked to his controversial requirement that "a software architecture should fit on a single sheet of paper" (see Sect. 3.2). The discussion then went to approve that the nature of software architecture depends on the purpose behind having an architecture in the first place. Since there are typically many stakeholders involved, with each stakeholder having a specific purpose in mind, it then becomes vital to make an architectural representation explicit so as to enable sharing it amongst interested parties.

It is also important to develop a shared representation of such an architecture and to maintain it over time, so that changes are reflected in the representation and so that stakeholders can inspect the change against conflicts with their own purposes. Nokia, for example, has an architecture team with a variety of experts. A meeting-point document on architecture is regularly produced.

From Domain Model to Software Architecture. As a third part of the discussion, we tried to identify how the information contained in the domain model can help us to build a suitable software architecture. To this extent, we needed to address several questions. Which concepts in the domain model correspond to which parts of the software architecture? How do we determine which architectural style to use? How do we decide which views to take and what to include in each view?

It was mentioned that an architecture does not have to 'fix' everything specified by the domain model. The skill of the architect is to select from a large amount of data the elements that can or should be mapped onto the architecture.

5.2 Architectural Views and Layering Techniques

The second cluster of interest focused on architectural views and layering techniques.

Architectural Views. The workshop participants agreed that architectural views are necessary, although the number of views should be kept small. This necessity of views is also acknowledged by the recent IEEE 1471 standard on architecture descriptions [10,14]. It states that a view is a collection of models that represent one aspect of an entire system. A view applies to only one system, not to generalizations across many systems. The standard introduces the concept of viewpoints to capture common descriptive frameworks across many systems. Viewpoints are the vehicles for writing reusable, domain-specific architecture description standards. They establish the languages or notations used to create a view, the conventions for interpreting it, and any associated analytic techniques that might be used with the view. An architecture description must define the viewpoint for each view it contains.

Kruchten [11] proposes a 4+1 view model of software architectures using five concurrent views that each address a specific set of concerns of interest to different stakeholders in the system. The *logical view* supports the functional requirements, i.e., the services the system should provide to its end users. The *development view* describes the software's static organisation in its development environment. The *process view* describes concurrency and synchronisation aspects. The *physical view* describes the mapping of the software onto the hardware. Finally, the *"+1" view* illustrates architectural decisions using use cases or scenarios.

Allesandro Maccari expanded this into the following set of views used within Nokia. The *logical view* comprises the major logical components (expressed as subject areas or top-level areas) and their interactions. The *implementation view* corresponds to the development view of [11]. Additionally, there are 4 views that are not available in [11]. The *dynamic view* is a domain-specific view that deals with feature interaction, a very important issue in the domain of telecommunication software [13]. The *task view* allocates components into tasks. The *organisational view* maps the software architecture into the developing organization. Finally, the *conceptual view* represents the core layer of the architecture, which is impossible to change without rebuilding the entire software system. It contains the architectural rules and architecturally significant interaction patterns that need to be adhered to by the software system.

One important question is: *how detailed should each of these views be relative to each other?* Maccari mentioned *Conway's Law* [5], essentially stating that the architecture of the artefact mirrors the architecture of the team that developed it (and, more generally, the structure of a system tends to mirror the structure of the group producing it). The same comment was also made as regards the structure of the client organisation: quite often, the architecture of telecommunications software reflects the billing structure! The role of the chief architect is to balance the work organisation, and the architecture of the artefact.

In the context of architectural evolution, another important question was raised: *which views give you the most information about how the software will change?* The answer to this question was the conceptual, logical and dynamic view. The conceptual view acts as a boundary on design decisions to ensure, among many things, economic development, outside which you lose control over design decisions. The logical view maps the features of the system (as viewed by the user or the marketing department) to a high-level view of software areas. The dynamic view deals with feature interaction, and is also useful to use scenario-based software architecture assessment to compare and evaluate architectural proposals.

Next, the discussion focused on the question: *which information should be contained in the core layer of a software architecture?* In other words, what are the hard parts in the architecture we are contemplating? We expect the answer to be embedded in some way in a comprehensive understanding of the problem domain.

A representation of the core layer (i.e., the conceptual view) was suggested by Maccari: it is basically a set of constraints that act as a boundary. Within the boundary, software evolution remains manageable. Once the boundary has been crossed, the situation becomes unknown, and evolution of the software may become very difficult, if not impossible. Hence, the core layer of an architecture defines what shouldn't be changed, while it enables other kinds of change. Note that what is considered to be architectural and what is not changes with time, and according to the priorities and policies of the software development organisation.

Obviously, it is a difficult problem do decide which constraints should be included in the core layer, because the number and nature of constraints varies with the nature of the domain under consideration as well as the various technological offerings. Therefore, *each constraint in the core layer should be accompanied by a careful justification, possibly in the form of a concrete change scenario.* These change scenarios can be defined based on the domain model, and correspond to decisions one cannot afford to change because they are prohibitively expensive. Obviously, these decisions can vary dramatically from organisation to organisation, or even from system to system, which largely stresses the importance of a comprehensive understanding of the problem domain.

At Nokia, resources required for testing (primarily testing time) are a major driver of the choice of constraints and rules in the conceptual view to achieve a degree of predictability of integration testing resource requirements.

Layering. There was some disagreement about what it means to have a layered architecture, or even whether the notion of layering is beneficial from an architectural point of view. A number of alternative techniques were suggested: coupling and cohesion, composition and decomposition, clustering, and separation of concerns. One participant argued that the point of having an architecture is to think explicitly about the areas of high variability and isolate them into layers or areas that need to be loosely coupled from the rest of the architecture.

A potentially useful layering mechanism could be achieved by categorising the architectural elements in *collections that share the same likelihood of change*. This corresponds to the revolutionary definition of software architecture that was agreed upon during last year's workshop [3].

An advantage of this kind of layering mechanism is that, with normal evolution, changes would be limited to a single layer, causing ripple effects to only adjacent layers, with the architecting aim being isolating such effect to the relevant layer as far as possible. This facilitates the natural evolution of a system. Nevertheless, in his contribution, Serge Demeyer presented a counter example where numerous designers spent the best of their talents to devise a layered architecture. Unfortunately, when the actual software system was constructed it turned out that the neat arrangement of layers did not work out in practice because ripple effects always caused changes in at least two layers.

The Architectonic View. Galal presented a diagram that he used in the first workshop of this series to illustrate his architectonic view of software architecture. This view focuses on the adaptability and maintainability of software through an architectural emphasis. The view is based on Brand's ideas about how buildings learn and adapt over time [4]. Brand's *shearing* layers perspective of buildings refers to the layers of change that comprise buildings. Brand identifies 6 layers in a building that change at different rates. From the slowest to the fastest these are: Site, Structure, Skin, Services, Space Plan, and Stuff (meaning things like furniture, decorations, light fixtures and appliances). This view is fundamentally *normative*, i.e., it is based on a study of the types of changes that typically affect buildings, after construction and delivery to clients, as a result of adaptations by their users. Buildings that gracefully accommodate such changes are the ones that please their users most and remain useful for longer. Such buildings are capable of accommodation of unforeseen uses because the layers that make them up are loosely coupled. These layers *slip past* each other: changes to one layer do not necessitate changes to others. Note here that the low coupling is not at the level of individual bricks or other individual constructional elements: rather, the decoupling referred to is at the level of categories, or layers, of such elements. The constructional elements are categorised according to the degree of susceptibility to, or speed of, change that they share. The categorisation also relates to the degree in which each layer constrains others, and to the scale of disruption that the change of each entails.

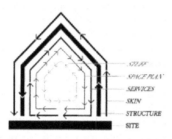

Another view congenial with Brand's is that of the architectural theorist and critic Kenneth Frampton [9]. He uses the term *architectonic attributes* to refer to the *light* versus *heavy* characteristics of constructional elements. He uses vernacular examples, such as the Greek temple, to show how the architectonic attributes of various construction technologies have been used to retain certain values that are germane to certain *cultures*. Frampton observes how the architectonic role of constructional material can be reversed from one culture to another: the relative lightness or heaviness of constructional elements is a function of the culture, its particular condition, and the expressions that it tries to achieve. So again, we encounter another view of architecture that demarcates categories of building blocks according to their relative stability characteristic, this time with the role of *cultural specificity* and variances spelled out. This position reflects that which was articulated by Maccari on how Nokia's software architecture reflected things such as the organisation of the development team, and the billing structure of mobile communications; also how the constraints implied by the architecture are these that the software development organisation wished to preserve as far as practicable.

The point that was made here is that the way in which architecture constrains an artefact of any sort is very much dependent on the culture that spawns it. What is *heavy* and stable is more constraining than what is *light*. The choice lies with the culture tradition that uses or indeed develops the building, or in our case, software. There is therefore a need to investigate these cultural and organisational choices, as well as the way in which they allow or constrain certain types of software evolution. For example, the conceptual architecture view that we reported is also a cultural and business choice, which leads to certain allowances to and certain constraints on how the software can be feasibly evolved. In the Nokia example therefore, the conceptual architecture is more akin to the "site" or "structure" layer in the figure.

We submit at this juncture that there is substantial validity to the view that software architecture should be less concerned with structural elements and more with categories of software system's components, in the large-grain. Stratifying such categories according to their relative rigidity, scale and speed, of change can help our architecting effort by making the *architectonic* nature of the software object as whole clearer and thus shareable by other stakeholders. This clarity means that the impact of various architectural decisions can be studied more carefully, and in conjunction with the relevant stakeholders. The aim is also to support the understanding and consequent design of systems, so that adaptability properties are maximised, but with respect to the particular situation (read culture) that we refer to. This view of systems was referred to as the architectonic view of software architecture.

5.3 Process Considerations

Much of current practice tends to add architecture at the end of the software design process if at all. This practice is not recommended as the designers' motivation to do a proper architecting job will be weak (since architecture, as an after thought will be produced mostly to satisfy a documentation standard, without being allowed to affect other design considerations). An architecture description should be the culmination of a process, not as something that we start with, and neither as something to be added later (this goes somewhat against the ethos of the software patterns movement, which tends to place the architecture up front). Architectural thinking and consideration should permeate the whole software design process, where iterations lead to the refinement of architecture against a selected set of purposes, or quality attributes.

There was also an analogy to be drawn between process and art. The traditional way of software engineering is like classical music, with strict rules of composition and tightly planned and directed performance. On the other hand, eXtreme Programming (XP) can be likened to improvised Jazz, where musicians create new tunes and idioms on the fly in response to fellow Jazz musicians. Palle Nowack pointed out, however, that even for Jazz improvisation, there are broad compositional rules that must be followed so that the result is indeed improvised Jazz that is pleasant to hear. This can be regarded as a kind of compositional architecture.

This brings us to problems with operationalising a sound architecting process: how do you get to software architecture? The issue of stakeholders comes up again here, as the utility of architecture to various stakeholders needs to be evident, so that the stakeholders are motivated to participate fully in the architecting process. This begs the question of who should the architects be exactly?

Since a large number of architectures are usually computationally equivalent, it is non-functional requirements (such as evolvability, reusability, scalability, flexibility) that drive the major part of software architecture. Wege (who is a proponent of XP [18]) reminded the group that XP states that designers should not think ahead, and focus on satisfying the immediately evident required functionality instead.

The group agreed that not all aspects of architecture are relevant to all types of software and that we must not generalise: the architectural implications for embedded systems are different from business systems. It was also stressed that architecting process issues are critical to getting from analyses of the domain to software architecture. From the viewpoint of operationalising the architecting process, the importance of representation formalisms was highlighted. Appropriate representational formalisms and primitives that cover a wide range of issues, but that also remain accessible to the variety of stakeholders present, need to be established and monitored.

6   Conclusions and Recommendations

This section summarises the convergences of views that have taken place during the workshop, and clearly shows that our worskhop series has made considerable progress.

6.1   Requirements for a Domain Model

All participants agreed that a domain model should not be overly complex, in that it should only contain constraints that are imposed on the software engineer from the outside, and that do not require any decision from the software engineer. There was also a consensus that a domain model should contain relevant information from past activities, as well as future scenarios.

6.2   Communicative Role of a Software Architecture

The communicative role of a software architecture was considered to be essential by all participants. The architecture document (which should be small) plays a vital role in the communication and resolution of views and enabling debate about architecture. A software architecture is a means to share information between the various stakeholders (not only software developers, but also the users, business analysts and project managers).

6.3   Evolutive Role of a Software Architecture

It is also important to *share a software architecture over time*, so that changes are reflected in the representation and so that stakeholders can inspect the change against conflicts with their own purposes. In this light of architectural evolution, it is absolutely essential that *a software architecture needs to be specified explicitly*. Whether this is best achieved informally, using natural language or a freehand drawing, or formally, using an architectural description language or modelling notation, remains an open issue.

Note that the need to take evolution of an architecture into account is also acknowlededged by the IEEE 1471 standard [10,14]. It defines architecture as "the fundamental organization of a system embodied in its components, their relationships to each other and to the environment, and the principles guiding its design and evolution."

6.4   The Constraining Role of Software Architecture

The tentative definition of software architecture that was proposed during the previous workshop [3] was reconsidered. Since it is very important that a software architecture should be robust towards evolution and change as little as possible, this definition focused on the quality requirement of robustness towards changes: *A software architecture is a collection of categories of elements that share the same likelihood of change. Each category contains software elements that exhibit shared stability characteristics.* Obviously, this definition focuses on an evolution viewpoint for software architectures. For other stakeholders, that have another viewpoint (e.g., security), a different definition might be more appropriate.

All participants of this year's workshop agreed with this definition, and amended it with an extra requirement: *A software architecture always contains a core layer that represents the hardest layer of change. It identifies those features that cannot be changed without rebuilding the entire software system.* To determine precisely what are the hard layers in the architecture that we are contemplating, a comprehensive understanding of the original problem domain is essential.

Although the core layer can be specified in a variety of ways, a specific representation was suggested : *The core layer of an architecture is basically a set of constraints.* This set acts as a boundary, within which software evolution remains manageable. Note that the architectural constraints are also subject to evolution due to changes in the domain or technology, so this boundary may change over time. Therefore, each constraint must be carefully justified in the form of a concrete change scenario that illustrates why a certain kind of change may be prohibitively expensive.

6.5   Need for a Formal Architecting Process

The group stressed that architecting process issues are critical to go from domain analysis to software architecture. From the viewpoint of operationalising the architecting process, the importance of representation formalisms was highlighted. These formalisms should cover a wide range of issues, but should also remain accessible to the variety of stakeholders present.

7   Future Plans

Obviously, there are still many outstanding questions that could not adequately be addressed during this workshop due to time constraints. The following questions were considered important by the participants, and might be the topics of next year's workshop.

What can we learn from real-world industrial case studies about managing software evolution? Concrete examples from practice are needed, including process issues, documentation and methodology.

Is architectural evolution essentially different from ordinary software evolution? How can we ease the transition from a software architecture to a software implementation?

Where do formalisms fit in? Which aspects of domain analysis and software architecture can/should be formalised? Which aspects are better left informal? Does greater formality make evolvability easier to achieve?

What existing techniques and tools can/should we use to support architectural evolution? This includes established object-oriented software engineering techniques (such as separation of concerns, refinement, abstraction and composition) as well as established evolution techniques (such as software configuration management).

How do proceed from the technical architecture to refactoring of the architecture?

8   List of Participants

Workshop Organizers. *Galal Hassan Galal* (University of North London, UK); *Tom Mens* (Vrije Universiteit Brussel, Belgium).

Authors of a Workshop Submission That Actually Attended the Workshop. *Jean-Pierre Briot* (Université Pierre et Marie Curie, Paris, France); *Stephen Cook* (University of Reading, UK); *Serge Demeyer* (Universiteit Antwerpen, Belgium); *Albertina Lourenci* (University of São Paulo, Brazil); *Allesandro Maccari* (Nokia Research Center, Finland); *Palle Nowack* (Aalborg University and University of Southern Denmark, Denmark); *Janis Osis* (Riga Technical University, Latvia); *Christian Wege* (University of Tubingen and DaimlerChrysler AG, Germany).

Last-Minute Workshop Attendees without a Submission. *Claudia Pons* (Universidad Nacional de La Plata, Argentina); *Pascale Rapicault* (Université de Nice Sophia Antipolis, France).

Co-authors of a Workshop Submission That Did Not Attend the Workshop. *Luis Andrade, João Gouveia* and *Georgios Koutsoukos* (Oblog Software SA, Portugal); *Lars Bendix* (Aalborg University, Denmark); *José Luiz Fiadeiro* (Universidade de Lisboa, Portugal); *Rachel Harrison* (University of Reading, UK); *Frédéric Peschanski* (Université Pierre et Marie Curie, Paris, France); *Brian Ritchie* (CRC Rutherford Appleton Laboratory, UK); *Harald Störrle* (Ludwig-Maximilians-Universität München, Germany); *Michel Wermelinger* (Universidade Nova de Lisboa, Portugal); João Antonio Zuffo (University of São Paulo, Brazil).

Acknowledgements. We express our extreme gratitude to all workshop participants, whose interesting contributions and active discussions made the workshop a real success.

The workshop was supported by the *Scientific Research Network on Foundations of Software Evolution*. This is a research consortium coordinated by the Programming Technology Lab of the Vrije Universiteit Brussel (Belgium), and it involves 9 research institutes from universities in 5 different European countries (Belgium, Germany, Austria, Switzerland, and Portugal). The consortium is financed by the Fund for Scientific Research - Flanders (Belgium).

References

1. Borne, I., Brito e Abreu, F., De Meuter, W., Galal, G. H.: Techniques, tools and formalisms for capturing and assessing architectural quality in object-oriented software. In: Demeyer, S., Bosch, J. (eds.): ECOOP 1998 Workshop Reader. Lecture Notes in Computer Science, Vol. 1543. Springer-Verlag, Berlin Heidelberg New York (1998) 44–71
2. Borne, I., Demeyer S., Galal, G. H.: Workshop on Object-Oriented Architectural Evolution. In: Moreira, A., Demeyer, S. (eds.): ECOOP 1999 Workshop Reader. Lecture Notes in Computer Science, Vol. 1743. Springer-Verlag, Berlin Heidelberg New York (1999) 57–79
3. Borne, I., Galal, G. H., Evans, H., Andrade, L. F.: Workshop on Object-Oriented Architectural Evolution. In: Malenfant, J., Moisan, S., Moreira, A. (eds.): ECOOP 2000 Workshop Reader. Lecture Notes in Computer Science, Vol. 1964. Springer-Verlag, Berlin Heidelberg New York (2000) 138–149
4. Brand, S.: How buildings learn - What happens after they're built. 2nd edn. Phoenix Illustrated, London (1994)
5. Conway, M.: How do Committees Invent? Datamation Journal (April 1968) 28-31.
6. Conradi, R. (ed.): Software Configuration Management. Proc. Symp. SCM-7 (Boston, MA, USA). Lecture Notes in Computer Science, Vol. 1235. Springer-Verlag, Berlin Heidelberg New York (1997)
7. Estublier, J. (ed.): Software Configuration Management. Selected Papers Symp. SCM-4 and SCM-5. Lecture Notes in Computer Science, Vol. 1005. Springer-Verlag, Berlin Heidelberg New York (1995)
8. Estublier, J. (ed.): System Configuration Management. Proc. Symp. SCM-9 (Toulouse, France). Lecture Notes in Computer Science, Vol. 1675. Springer-Verlag, Berlin Heidelberg New York (1999)
9. Frampton, K., Cava, J.E.: Studies in Tectonic Culture - The Poetics of Construction in Nineteenth and Twentieth Century Architecture. MIT Press (1995)
10. IEEE Software Engineering Standard 1471: Recommended Practice for Architectural Description for Software Intensive Systems. IEEE Computer Society Press (October 2000).
11. Kruchten, P.: The 4+1 view model of architecture. IEEE Software **12(6)**, IEEE Computer Society Press (1995) 42–50
12. Lourenci, A.: An evolutive architecture reasons as a semiotic, hermeneutic and autopoietic entity. Proc. Int. Workshop on Principles of Software Evolution, Vienna (September 2001)
13. Maccari, A., Tuovinen, A-P.: System family architectures: current challenges at Nokia. In: van der Linden, F. (ed.): Software Architectures for Product Families, Proc. 7th Int. Workshop Database Programming Languages. Lecture Notes in Computer Science, Vol. 1951. Springer-Verlag, Berlin Heidelberg New York (1999) 107–
14. Maier, M.W., Emery, D.E., Hilliard, R.: Software Architecture: Introducing IEEE Standard 1471. IEEE Computer **34(4)**, IEEE Computer Society Press (April 2001) 107–109
15. Magnusson, B. (ed.): System Configuration Management. Proc. Symp. SCM-8 (Brussels, Belgium). Lecture Notes in Computer Science, Vol. 1439. Springer-Verlag, Berlin Heidelberg New York (1998)
16. Mens, T., Galal, G. H.: Submissions for the 4th ECOOP workshop on object-oriented architectural evolution. Technical Report, Programming Technology Lab, Vrije Universiteit Brussel (2001) http://prog.vub.ac.be/OOAE/ECOOP2001/ooaesubmissions.pdf
17. Sommerville, I. (ed.): Software Configuration Management. Proc. Symp. SCM-6 (Berlin, Germany). Lecture Notes in Computer Science, Vol. 1167. Springer-Verlag, Berlin Heidelberg New York (1997)
18. Wege, C., Lippert, M.: Diagnosing evolution in test-infected code. In: Succi, G., Marchesi, M. (eds.): Extreme Programming Examined, Proc. 2nd Int. Conf. eXtreme Programming and Flexible Processes in Software Engineering. Addison-Wesley (2001) 127-131

7th Workshop on Mobile Object Systems

Ciarán Bryce[1] and Alexander Romanovsky[2]

[1] University of Geneva, Switzerland
bryce@cui.unige.ch
[2] University of Newcastle upon Tyne, UK
alexander.romanovsky@newcastle.ac.uk

1 Background

The ECOOP Mobile Object Systems Workshop is now in its 7th year. The workshop deals with issues of object orientation, mobile objects, mobile code and mobile agents. The theme of this year's workshop was Development of Robust and High Confidence Agent Applications.

In recent years, there has been a surge of interest in autonomous mobile objects and mobile agent systems. Security and fault-tolerance are the two most significant challenges in the widespread deployment of mobile agent systems. With regards to security, the goal is to protect host resources from malicious agents, protect agent state and code from tampering and misuse by malicious agents, authenticate agent credentials and delegate privileges. The mobile agent paradigm raises several unique problems concerning error detection, containment and recovery for building fault-tolerant applications. Mechanisms are needed that allow both the application and the system levels to perform recovery from failures. Building high confidence systems requires addressing issues related to both fault-tolerance and security.

The main objective of this workshop was to bring together a group of active researchers in this field to develop a common understanding of the important research problems and recent results. We felt that it would be beneficial to examine the fault-tolerance and security issues together. The designs of the mechanisms and structuring techniques in one area can impact the other in a system design. A number of research projects have addressed security issues in mobile agent systems, but fault tolerance problems in mobile objects have not received adequate attention yet.

For the program committee, we chose experts from all areas of the mobile object systems domain, many of whom had already participated in previous editions of the workshop in some form. The program committee was: Bob Gray (Dartmouth College, USA), Jarle Hulaas (Geneva University, Switzerland), Doug Lea (OSWEGO, USA), Jochen Liedtke (Karlsruhe University, Germany), Rafik Molva (Eurecom, France), Chrislain Razafimahefa (Geneva University, Switzerland), Cecilia Rubira (UNICAMP, Brazil), Peter Sewell (Cambridge University, UK), Luis Silva (University of Coimbra, Portugal), Niranjan Suri (Florida University, USA), and Walter Binder (Technical University of Vienna, Austria).

We are very grateful to these researchers for reviewing papers, and for contributing to the workshop over the years. We would also like to thank Anand Tripathi for helping us to organise the workshop.

Á. Frohner (Ed.): ECOOP 2001 Workshops, LNCS 2323, pp. 165–168, 2002.
© Springer-Verlag Berlin Heidelberg 2002

The workshop was held on Monday June 18th – just prior to the ECOOP conference – at the site of the Department of Computer Science at the Budapest Institute of Informatics.

The format of the workshop differed greatly from the 6th edition of the workshop held in Cannes, France in 2000. At that workshop, there were over 50 attendees, which was a record for the workshop. We decided on a format of 15-minute talks followed by 15 minutes of discussion for each talk. The number of presentations – 13 in all – meant that the format of the workshop was becoming too much of a conference, with too little time being left for discussion.

For this reason, we decided upon a smaller and more intimate format for this year's edition. The morning session was dedicated to paper presentations and discussions. In the afternoon, we had an invited talk from Eric Jul of Aalborg University.

2   The Talks

The first talk was given was entitled "Using Mobile Agents for Analysing Intrusion in Computer Networks" by Jay Aslam, Daniela Rus, David Kotz and Marco Cremonini from Dartmouth College in the USA. Jay Aslam gave the talk. They presented an intrusion detection system based on a mobile agent system. The issue addressed is that detecting security attacks today requires processing huge logs from many different computer systems. The authors argue that this is a task best done by agents, because they can travel asynchronously to other sites and because they can carry logic that can be adapted to the processing of huge logs. The system is built using Serval – a distributed information retrieval service – which is itself built using the D'Agents mobile agent system.

The next talk was entitled "Reliability through Strong Migration" by Xiaojin Wang, Jason Hallstrom and Gerard Baumgartner of Ohio State University in the USA. Gerard Baumgartner gave the talk. The goal of their system is reliability, which is achieved by being able to move Java programs between sites. Migration is strong in the sense that a program's state is moved along with its data. Capturing a program state is done by simulating its execution state. This technique is implemented using code rewriting. The authors show how tricky issues like program synchronisation are dealt with in the model.

After this, we had a talk entitled "A Software Model With Dynamic Adaptability for Mobile Code Programs" by Noriko Amano and Takuo Watanabe. The paper tackles the issue of dynamically updating systems using mobile code. The authors have already designed a system called DAS as well as a description language called LEAD++ that describes the modifications to be integrated into the system. This talk underlined the safety aspects of software updating. The approach is based on the introduction of assertions into the system that verifies consistency constraints on the loaded code. The Safe DAS model also has an exception mechanism as well as an atomic update mechanism.

The next talk was "Supporting Disconnected Operation in a Mobile System" by Marco Valente, Roberto Bigonba, Mariza Bigonba and Antonio Loueiro of the Universities of Minas Gerais in Belo Horizonte, Brazil. Marco Valente gave the talk. This paper looked at the increasing importance of disconnected operation in mobile agent systems. A model is presented that partitions objects into groups called containers. Containers are mobile and, whenever an object of a container is moved, then all other objects of the container are migrated with it. Connections between containers can be "broken" so one container is unable to prevent another container from being moved. The advantage of this model is that object containers can be relocated in a network to tolerate disconnection. An implementation of the system in Java was presented.

Ian Welch of Newcastle-upon-Tyne University in the UK gave the final talk of the first session. The talk was entitled "The Glasshouse – A Reflective Container for Mobile Code". The emphasis of the paper is on the strong relationship between the component-container model and behavioural reflection. The former is used in several systems (e.g., applets, Enterprise Java Beans) as a framework for integrating foreign code into an application. The latter – it is argued – can be used as an implementation framework for this model, since reflection allows all communications to be controlled and reprogrammed if needed. An example of intrusion tolerant servers was taken. The reflection has been implemented in Java in a system called Kava.

3   Eric Jul's Invited Talk

The invited talk given by Eric Jul was more of an animated general discussion than of a formal talk; everyone in the audience was invited to participate! It was a very suitable format for the workshop and everyone in the audience appreciated.

Eric Jul was one of the designers of the Emerald programming language. This was the first object-based language to contain object mobility. Emerald originated from the Eden project, which was an operating systems project at Washington University. The unit of mobility in Eden was the process, which became too large a unit to use for migration. Further, Eden required a more semantic framework for mobility.

In the discussion, Eric argued that many of the basic design issues that face mobile agent system and language designers today were faced in the Emerald system. The most important of these issues is the treatment of distribution.

One of the reasons why it is important to distinguish a local object call from a method call on a remote object is performance. While a local call can execute in a few instructions, a remote call, obviously, requires considerable time. It is therefore essential that the application programmer have a measure of control on how objects are distributed throughout the system. One solution to this in Emerald is the *attach* object primitive. Object attachment is an asynchronous relation. When an object is attached to another, it means that whenever the latter object is migrated, then the former object is moved along with it. This means that the two objects are always located on the same site, so all method calls between the two objects use the local method call implementation technique.

Another example of controlling object migration are the *fix* and *unfix* primitives which respectively bind and decouple an object from a site. Yet another feature important for distribution are the concrete type objects that represent types. These contain an object's code, and a site ensures that it has a type for each object before proceeding with execution.

A big issue that can prevent the success of a mobile object system is security. Allowing code from the network to execute on one's site poses well-known risks. There are two questions that must be asked. First "Why should I allow remote mobile objects to execute on my site?" and second, "How can I estimate the risks involved?" It is accepted that treatment of the security issue is still far from mature, and the biggest challenge to the mobile agent community.

The risks involved depend on the goal of the mobile object applications. This question was covered at several points during the day's discussion. One of the talks – from Dartmouth – presented a direct application of mobile object or agent technology. This was the intrusion detection agent system where agents were used to gather information from system logs. It was also suggested that peer-to-peer computing could be an ideal application domain for mobile agents. The advantage of using agents here is that the search for items on the network can happen "off-line" – while the user is disconnected from the system. Further, agents can help with the fact that the search space in peer-to-peer is huge and currently very difficult to manage.

During the day, we also discussed specific issues of mobility in a wireless setting, the complexity of emerging applications, and wondered if Java – the standard programming language for agent systems – is really suitable. Apart from the applications of peer-to-peer and wireless systems, we considered computing grids (in the USA and Europe), search engines, resource discovery, anonymous communication, and the new meaning of neighbours in mobile systems (which can rely, for example, on nodes being in the same domain, having the same IP address, being close geographically, etc.). Different meanings/understandings of mobility existing in the community were outlined and several properties of the applications were discussed as the main characteristics requiring mobile solutions: large volumes of data that cannot be carried to a master or/and kept there to be processed, needs in fast reaction, needs to access devices locally, complexity of the centralised static solutions.

4   Conclusions

The consensus at the end of the workshop was that the mobile object systems domain is alive and well, and people will continue researching the domain over the next few years. There was still some concern expressed however that few applications have been developed by the community, but excitement at the prospect of peer-to-peer systems or applications like Serval.

Compared to previous years, it is interesting to note that many issues are still hot topics. Security for instance was mentioned at many points. Another issue that is not going away is the debate over strong and weak mobility, i.e., whether strong mobility is truly required in mobile agent systems (currently no system really implements this though there is much work that examines how it can be implemented).

At the same time it is clear that new topics are appearing in the mobile agent systems community. One is support for wireless systems. Given that mobile agents are supposed to be able to execute autonomously on remote sites, the possibility of disconnection – in wireless environments – will test this promise of agent systems to the limit.

The general feeling at the end of a long day was that the workshop had been productive, and that the workshop series should be continued until next year at least. We should lastly mention that all papers and presentations of this year's workshop and of all previous editions are available at our web site: http://cui.unige.ch/~ecoopws

The Next 700 Distributed Object Systems

Eric Jul[1], Andrew Black[2], Anne-Marie Kermarrec[3], Doug Lea[4], and Salah Sadou[5,*]

[1] DIKU, University of Copenhagen, Denmark eric@diku.dk
[2] Oregon Graduate Institute, USA black@cse.ogi.edu
[3] Microsoft Research, Cambridge, UK annemk@microsoft.com
[4] State University of New York at Oswego, NY, USA dl@cs.oswego.edu
[5] Université de Bretagne Sud, Valoria, France sadou@info.uqam.ca

Abstract. The primary goal of the ECOOP Workshop on The Next 700 Distributed Object Systems was to identify the essential characteristics of the next generation of distributed object systems. Among many other topics, participants explored issues surrounding Peer-to-Peer computing, Failure handling, Context.

1 Introduction

The ECOOP 2001 workshop on The Next 700 Distributed Object Systems was a follow-up to previous ECOOP Workshops on various topics in distributed object systems. This year, instead of using a standard miniconference format, the workshop was focussed on a simple yet ambitious goal: to identify the essence of distributed object systems; the core elements that are likely to play some part in each of the next 700 distributed object systems.

The workshop was structured to help identify these issues by splitting the day into three sessions:

- Short presentations, mainly on in-progress work, on different approaches to distributed computing.
- A chaotic session in which everyone contributed topics and ideas to dozens of posters, later summarizing on index cards.
- Dividing into three working groups, each focusing on a single topic.

This active workshop format worked just fine given that there were not too many participants (approximately 25). The participants enjoyed the extra time for discussions. And the subjects were interesting because the participants helped chose them.

2 Short Presentations

The first session consisted of brief (10-15 minute) presentations of selected works in progress by participants, aimed at illustrating the diversity of approaches to distributed systems. These included:

---

* The initial organizing committee also included Jochen Liedtke, who died unexpectedly on June 10, 2001.

Á. Frohner (Ed.): ECOOP 2001 Workshops, LNCS 2323, pp. 169–173, 2002.

Message Passing. Structuring systems using oneway messages arranged via pipe-based constructions.

Events. Filtering multicasted events.

Long-Running Transactions. Check-out/check-in support.

Guarded Communication. Distributed versions of high-level concurrent programming constructs.

Roles. Structuring applications by assigning objects to role-based interfaces.

Quality of Service. Annotating components and services with QoS requirements.

Ubiquity. Large ad-hoc networks of loosely coupled devices.

3   Cards and Posters

In the second session, all participants proposed major categories of issues facing distributed systems. These included: Heterogeneity, Quality of Service (QoS), Structuring applications, partitioning and repartitioning, versioning, Object models, transactions, security, synchronous vs. asynchronous messaging, global references and object IDs, virtual machines, debugging, profiling, web-based messaging, Configuration and management, and Scripting.

   We then summarized these into a few key observations:

– Mobility and ubiquity are now commonplace, but most old problems underlying them remain unsolved.
– Basic OO concepts such as references and synchronous calls are often more of a hindrance than a help for new applications.
– There are still many different ways of defining the basic abstractions. There is no reason to think they will be subsumed by any small set of universal primitives.
– People can deal with most aspects of network failure and other "sociological" aspects of networking better than software can.
– Adaptativeness is the most commonly desired, but least well understood aspect of distribution.

4   Working Groups

In the third session of the workshop, we broke into three working groups focusing on particular problem domains, and reported the results to others in the final session. The three problem domains choosen where determined by participants writing their name onto posters that contained each issue. This worked surprisingly well.

4.1   Peer-to-Peer Computing

From one perspective, Peer-to-Peer (P2P) systems are just classic distributed object systems where every node can be both a client and a server. However, P2P systems also contain a number of characteristic features: They must be decentralized, self-organized, and scalable.

   The main challenges identified for P2P computing are:

Security and Privacy. Intrinsic use of encryption and security policies in basic protocols.

Naming, Routing, Trading, Discovery. The need for robust, decentralized protocols and services.

]Quality of Service.] Negotiations to obtain best service with respect to multiple criteria.

Consistency. Reconciling inconsistent data.

4.2 Failure

Accommodation of failure is a defining property of distributed systems. Yet few languages and frameworks have even tried to make the basic abstractions involved with failure handling visible to programmers. The working group set out to expose the issues involved in doing so.

The first question is: what is the unit of failure? We believe that the only useful answer is a *Component*; a unit of functionality that may be larger than a single OO class, but that encapsulates all internal state necessary to perform its primary services. Thus, without explicit support for components, it will be difficult at best for distributed systems to provide first-class failure support.

The second question is: What kinds of failures may be handled? General categories include:

- Process failure: crashes.
- Process misbehavior: failure to meet specs, Byzantine failures.
- Communication failure: network partitions and disconnects
- Memory: transaction failure
- Insufficient Quality of Service: missing timing deadlines
- Security failures
- Version mismatches
- Overload and Denial of service.

The third question is: how can a system provide basic support for failure handling? Among the options are:

Monitoring. A language or framework can help automate construction of Observers that check the operation of components. In some cases these may be implemented as classic distributed failure-detectors; in others they may be lightweight interceptors. Upon failure, a Supervisor component may be triggered to take an appropriate action.

Recovery Blocks. Recovery blocks extend the Exception constructs found in most programming languages to support full transactionality. A recovery block includes a user-defined acceptance test to detect failure in a code sequence, as well as user-defined rollback code that should be invoked upon failure. In some languages and contexts, some aspects of both can be automated in common cases.

The final question addressed was: Are there ways that distributed languages and systems can encourage fault tolerance without requiring such mechanisms? One set of answers is to provide better support for immutability. An immutable object can never become inconsistent. Similarly, a stateless service (i.e., one whose behavior is solely a function of its arguments, not internal state) never needs recovery. These facts are known and exploited by every good distributed system programmer, yet very few systems intrinsically support these notions. Doing so would not only encourage good design, but would also allow better automated support.

4.3   Context

Context in distributed systems denotes the collection of physical resources (CPU, memory, bandwidth, IO, devices), available software services and components (and their current states), and the Location (both geographic and network) where a software component is executing.

Distributed and mobile code must increasingly be context-aware. Obvious cases include code running on devices such mobile phones, which may need to take evasive action when battery power becomes low or the unit it disconnected. However, even "ordinary" distributed code needs to be aware of contextual bindings such as the prevailing Time Zone.

From this perspective, it is surprising that neither research nor production distributed systems have provided anything beyond piecemeal support for context. A more general plan of attack is needed. While we did not propose a general framework, we established some basic questions that must be addressed by any approach, along with a few possible answers:

- How is context represented? Possible answers include directory structures (as found in LDAP and OS Registries), extensions of language scoping mechanisms, and others.
- How is context information made available? Candidates include queries and change-events. However, there may be a need to impose security policies for revealing some kinds of context information.
- How are contextual *requirements* of components represented and communicated? For example, components might specify minimum and maximum demands in a requires/provides framework.
- When and how does context change? Not every component can be allowed to change every contextual binding, implying the need for some sort of permission mechanism.
- How is context propagated? For example, how are contextual bindings merged across nodes of a distributed system? Some bindings will change across nodes, but others will stay the same.
- How do you categorize and control dynamics? Some contextual bindings are relatively static, and some may be almost constantly changing. Similarly, a component may be able to ignore some changes profiles requires/provides frameworks
- Can you find out about context of other components? Can you change it?
- How do components adapt to changes? Responses include ignoring changes, adapt to them, gracefully shutting down, and catastrophic failure.
- How does all this impact system design?

5 Conclusions

By design, this workshop generated many more questions than answers. The main goal of this workshop was to lay out some of the essential issues that will be faced by the next generation of distributed object systems. While we did not arrive at an exhaustive, definitive listing, we managed to bring to the forefront many of the issues that both practitioners and researchers will be grappling with over the coming years.

The workshop format was well received: the majority of the time was spent discussing issues that the participants themselves had helped flush out.

Quantitative Approaches in Object-Oriented Software Engineering

Fernando Brito e Abreu[1], Brian Henderson-Sellers[2], Mario Piattini[3], Geert Poels[4], and
Houari A. Sahraoui[5]

[1] Universidade Nova de Lisboa & INESC, Rua Alves Redol, 9, Apartado 13069,
1000 Lisboa, Portugal
`fba@di.fct.unl.pt – fba@inesc.pt`
[2] University of Technology Sidney, Faculty of Information Technology, PO Box 123,
Broadway NSW 2007, Australia
`brian@it.uts.edu.au`
[3] Universidad de Castilla-La Mancha, Ronda de Calatrava, 5, 13071, Ciudad Real, Spain
`mpiattini@inf-cr.uclm.es`
[4] Katholieke Universiteit Leuven & VLEKHO Business School, Koningsstraat 336,
1030 Brussels, Belgium
`geert.poels@econ.kuleuven.ac.be – gpoels@vlekho.wenk.be`
[5] Université de Montréal, CP 6128 succ Centre-Ville, Montréal QC H3C 3J7, Québec, Canada
`sahraouh@iro.umontreal.ca`

Abstract. This report summarizes the contributions and debates of the 5th International ECOOP Workshop on Quantitative Approaches in Object-Oriented Software Engineering (QAOOSE 2001), which was held in Budapest on 18–19 June, 2001. The objective of the QAOOSE workshop series is to present, discuss and encourage the use of quantitative methods in object-oriented software engineering research and practice. This year's workshop included the presentation of eight position papers and one tutorial in the areas of "software metrics definition", "software size, complexity and quality assessment", and "software quality prediction models". The discussion sessions focused on current problems and future research directions in QAOOSE.

1 Introduction

The 5th International ECOOP Workshop on Quantitative Approaches in Object-Oriented Software Engineering (QAOOSE 2001) was a direct continuation of four successful workshops, held at previous editions of ECOOP in Cannes (2000), Lisbon (1999), Brussels (1998) and Aarhus (1995).[1] Like in previous years, the workshop attracted participants from academia and industry that are involved or interested in the application of quantitative methods in object oriented (OO) software engineering research and practice. A list of this year's workshop participants, including their contact information, can be found at the end of this report.

---

[1] The main objectives, themes, and results of the QAOOSE'99 and QAOOSE 2000 workshops are summarized in reports that have been published in Springer-Verlag LNCS ECOOP workshop readers [1,2].

Á. Frohner (Ed.): ECOOP 2001 Workshops, LNCS 2323, pp. 174–183, 2002.
© Springer-Verlag Berlin Heidelberg 2002

Quantitative approaches in the OO field is a broad but active research area that aims at the development and evaluation of methods, techniques, tools and practical guidelines to improve the quality of software products and the efficiency and effectiveness of software processes. The relevant research topics are diverse, but always include a strong focus on applying a scientific methodology based on data collection (either by objective measurements or subjective assessments) and analysis (by statistical or artificial intelligence techniques). Like in previous years, submissions of position papers were invited, but not limited, to the areas of metrics collection, quality assessment, metrics validation, and process management.

The 2001 edition of the workshop aimed to shed some light on recent research results and to point out future research directions that might interest not only the academic community but also industry. Over the years the QAOOSE workshop series has built an active research community working towards special topics of interest that were identified as open issues during previous workshop editions. This year we explicitly solicited contributions of new research on (i) automatic support to share research hypotheses, data, and results, (ii) measures for non-functional requirements, (iii) measures for component models, (iv) meta-metrics, and (v) the application of quantitative methods in industrial software processes.

A concrete result of the workshop series is a forthcoming Addison-Wesley book (to appear in 2002), which will contain chapters authored by participants selected from all previous workshop editions. Another product of QAOOSE is a special issue of the journal L´Objet: Software, Databases, Networks on quantitative approaches in OO software design [3]. This issue includes six externally refereed papers which are thoroughly extended and revised versions of position papers presented at the QAOOSE 2000 workshop.

This report is organized as follows. In Sect. 2 we present a comparative summary of this year's workshop contributions, organized by workshop session and topic area. In section 3 a summary of the workshop debates is given. In section 4 we present the workshop conclusions and the open issues that were identified. This report ends with the complete list of contributions,[2] the contact data of the workshop participants, and some relevant references.

2   Summary of the Contributions

Usually, the application of quantitative methods in software engineering follows a logical path (i) from the construction or selection of measurement instruments, (ii) over the measurement-based assessment and evaluation of software product quality, software process efficiency, and software engineering productivity, (iii) to the development and use of prediction models, based on historical measurement data.

On June 18, our workshop followed this structure. The position papers that were presented this day were organized into three presentation sessions, called (i) Metrics

---

[2] All contributions accepted to the workshop were published in the workshop's proceedings [4]. To obtain a copy of the proceedings (ISBN 90-806472-1-7), contact the executive editor (Geert Poels – gpoels@vlekho.wenk.be). Electronic versions of the position papers and tutorial materials (all in PDF format) can also be downloaded from the workshop's web pages (URL: http://www.iro.umontreal.ca/~sahraouh/qaoose01/QAOOSE01_program.html).

Definition, (ii) Assessment Models, and (iii) Predictive Models. On June 19, the Metrics Definition session, and actually the workshop itself, was continued by a tutorial given by Fernando Brito e Abreu on the definition of OO software metrics using the Object Constraint Language (OCL). It was the first time that a QAOOSE workshop was extended to a one-and-a-half-day event.

During the presentation sessions each attendee was asked to summarize the new ideas and limitations of each position paper presented. Our experience with last year's workshop (QAOOSE 2000 in Cannes) learned us that this exercise greatly helped to stimulate the workshop discussions. That is why we decided to continue this tradition.

It was recognized that the distribution of position papers across the three sessions, each meant to cover a different topic area, was at times arbitrary. Therefore, and also in order to facilitate the comparison between the contributions, we decided to split this section into just two sub-sections. In a first sub-section we present, discuss, and compare the contributions that deal with meta-models for metrics definition, the proposal of new metrics suites, or any other proposal related to software measurement or assessment instruments. In a second sub-section we do the same for contributions that focus on the use of metrics in descriptive or predictive models, or the actual development of these models. The latter sub-section also includes contributions presenting an empirical validation of proposed metrics.

2.1   Metrics Definition

Many of this year's workshop contributions relate to the definition of new metrics suites or other types of assessment instruments, or include proposals to improve the state-of-the-art in OO software measurement and quality assurance.

Problems with the currently available measurement instruments for OO software artifacts have been identified and discussed in previous QAOOSE workshops (see [1,2]). One problem with many, if not most, of the OO metrics suites is their lack of precision in metrics definitions. The resulting ambiguity is a severe hindrance to the widespread acceptance and use of metrics (and quantitative approaches in general) in industry. Without clear and precise definitions, it is impossible to examine the theoretical validity of the metrics, to replicate experiments aimed at the empirical validation of the metrics, and to automate the metrics collection process. To guarantee precision in metrics definitions a formal language is needed. The language for the metrics definitions should be (consistent with) the language in terms of which the entities to be measured, their interrelationships, and their constraints are specified. Clearly, current metrics suites have not been defined with respect to a formal meta-model of their object(s) of measurement, i.e. the type(s) of OO software artifact for which they are intended.

Interestingly, this year's workshop participants witnessed the presentation of two related, but distinct proposals for metrics definition based on a formal meta-model of OO design. In one of the sessions, Ralf Reissing introduced his meta-model called Object-oriented DEsign Model (ODEM). ODEM is based on the UML meta-model, which is the "de facto" standard meta-model for OO design. As ODEM is intended for the definition of metrics for high-level design, it borrows only those parts of the UML meta-model that relate to class and package diagrams. However, as explained by Reissing, the model can easily be extended to include other model elements (e.g.

object behavior). The added value of ODEM is a layer of abstractions defined on top of the UML meta-model. This new layer contains formally defined sets, relationships and attributes in terms of which metric definitions can be stated. Reissing further delivered a proof of concept by defining some example class, package and system metrics, and by redefining existing metrics (all of Martin's Package metrics and some of Chidamber and Kemerer's metrics) in the language of ODEM.

The competing proposal came from one of the workshop organizers, Fernando Brito e Abreu, in his tutorial on the second day of the workshop. There are remarkable similarities in both works. The research motives are nearly the same, and both meta-model proposals use elements of the UML meta-model. However, the approaches taken by these researchers to define metrics are different. Brito e Abreu does not define an additional layer on top of the UML meta-model, but instead uses OCL to define metrics as meta-model operations. The applicability limitations of the metrics can then be defined with OCL preconditions; the metrics results with OCL postconditions.

An advantage of Brito e Abreu's approach, compared to Reissing's proposal, is the greater standardization that comes along with it. OCL, as part of UML, is becoming very fast a standard specification language for invariants and assertions in OO design. A disadvantage might be that it requires the user to learn and master OCL,[3] whereas the set theoretic concepts in ODEM seem to be more accessible for non-programmers and non-modelers. Interestingly, in his position paper, Reissing explicitly motivates his choice not to use OCL (see p. 75 in [4]): "It was tried to use the OCL as a specification language for design metrics, but it does not seem to be suited for this purpose. Some metrics were extremely hard to express in OCL, and most of the resulting metric definitions were hard to read".

Another advantage of Brito e Abreu's approach is its flexibility. In his technical report, accompanying the tutorial, Brito e Abreu first describes (and formalizes) the GOODLY (Generic Object Oriented Design Language? Yes!) language, previously used to define the MOOD metrics, using UML and OCL. Next, the definition of the metrics in his new version of the MOOD suite, i.e. MOOD2, is specified using OCL. The approach of Brito e Abreu is however not limited to GOODLY, or even UML. In his outlook to further work, he describes ongoing and planned work where metrics will be specified using OCL directly for the UML meta-model and for other emerging meta-models like the OPEN Modeling Language (OML).

Whereas the contributions of Ralf Reissing and Fernando Brito e Abreu mainly concerned the formalization of existing metrics suites, other contributions presented new metrics proposals. Michel Dao, Therese Libourel, and Cyril Roume described their work on a new metrics suite for the evaluation of factorization and generalization in class hierarchies. In total, 18 new metrics are proposed for four levels of granularity in OO software, i.e. features, generic features (which are sets of features), classes, and class

---

[3] A document containing the Object Constraint Language specification can be downloaded from the workshop's web pages. It is part of the tutorial materials on metrics definition using OCL (URL: http://www.iro.umontreal.ca/~sahraouh/qaoose01/QAOOSE01_program.html).

hierarchies. The purpose of these metrics is to assess how much feature factorization[4] there is in a hierarchy of classes. The goal of the work is to incorporate these metrics in the class hierarchy construction tools that these researchers are currently building. The main principle underlying such tools is that class hierarchies must be maximally factorized, while introducing as few classes as possible for feature factorization. The proposed metrics can be used to highlight design defects with respect to feature factorization, and help software engineers chose the most promising design amongst alternative solutions.

Another metrics suite proposal was done by Marcela Genero. She briefly presented a set of 10 structural complexity metrics for UML class diagrams. The bulk of her presentation however focused on validating these metrics as maintainability indicators (cf. Sect. 2.2).

In the position paper of Ram and Raju a new metric, called Method Points, is presented to estimate the size of a software design that is composed from design patterns. This metric is especially useful in the presence of alternative designs that result from the use of different patterns. Method Points are a relative measure of size, meaning that the common parts in alternative designs are not taken into account. As a consequence, an evaluation of alternative designs based on size can be carried out with minimal effort.

Although one of the previous QAOOSE workshops has questioned the proposal of new metrics suites [1], the contributions presented and discussed in this year's workshop show that there are still unfilled niches for research on OO metrics. One promising area of research is that of metrics for database schemata.

The contribution of Olaf Herden touches upon this subject. Herden presented a framework for conducting quality reviews of database schemata. This framework consists of a formal (UML) meta-model capturing the different elements of quality reviews, and a process model for working with this meta-model. Herden further instantiated the meta-model for quality criteria of conceptual OO database schemata. He also sketched the architecture of the tool infrastructure that is needed to automate and document the reviews. Part of this architecture has been realized.

The final contribution we wish to mention in this sub-section is the one of Hind Kabaili. She and her colleagues have extended a previous change impact model to take into account the ripple effect and regression testing. The model identifies the classes in a C++ system that are affected (i.e. they need correction) by a change in another class the system. The impacted classes depend on the type of change and their relationship with the changed class. The ripple effect extension takes indirect relationships between classes into account. The model that accommodates regression testing determines which classes to retest (even if they do not need correction).

2.2   Metrics Use

Five contributions dealt with what we categorized as the use of OO metrics. There was a considerable diversity in the metrics applications presented, going from typical metrics

---

[4] Feature factorization in a class hierarchy is maximal if there is only one class that declares the feature (for a formal definition see p. 86 in [4]). The technique of feature factorization is used in a generalization process that aims at (re-)designing OO software such that reusability and extensibility are improved.

validation studies, where a relationship with a variable of interest (e.g. maintainability) is established, to the actual building of descriptive or predictive models. Regarding the latter aspect, it is worth mentioning that some contributions used techniques from the Artificial Intelligence and Machine Learning fields; a novel approach that is observed across the whole software measurement and empirical software engineering field. One of the QAOOSE workshops organizers, Houari A. Sahraoui, is a mayor proponent of the use of Machine Learning techniques in software quality models, and his influence and example is strongly felt in the QAOOSE research community.

In one of the sessions, Marcela Genero presented a typical metrics validation study.[5] She reported on a controlled experiment that was set up to evaluate the correlation between 10 UML class diagram structural complexity metrics (cf. Sect. 2.1) and subjective ratings of three UML class diagram maintainability sub-characteristics, i.e. their understandability, analyzability, and modifiability. The subjects were 7 professors of the Department of Computer Science at the University of Castilla-La Mancha (Ciudad Real, Spain) and 10 students enrolled in the final year of Computer Science. All subjects had to rate the understandability, analyzability, and modifiability of 28 class diagrams using a 7-point Likert scale, ranging from "Extremely difficult to understand (analyze, modify)" to "Extremely easy to understand (analyze, modify)". Spearman's correlation coefficient was used to analyze the correlation between these ratings and the values of the 10 structural complexity metrics. The analysis showed that there exists a significant correlation between most of the metrics and the maintainability ratings, which provides empirical evidence of the hypothesized relationship.

The discussion of Genero's work focused mainly on fundamental questions such as the evaluation of a design representation (i.e. a UML class diagram) instead of the system itself, and the investigation of class diagram maintainability instead of software maintainability. It was noted that the ultimate goal of many metrics is to use them as early quality indicators, which is why the focus of much of the research in this field is on the measurement of the internal properties of OO designs (and recently also OO conceptual models). It was however acknowledged that to obtain really useful indicators, we must also establish a relationship with the external quality of the software system that is based on the design or conceptual model.

The issue of metrics validation has also been touched upon in the presentation of Hind Kabaili. She described a future experiment that will investigate the ability of well-known OO design metrics (e.g. Chidamber and Kemerer's metrics, the MOOD set of metrics) to be used as changeability indicators for OO software. This experiment will use the extended change impact model for C++ systems, developed by Kabaili and colleagues (cf. Sect. 2.1).

In two of the workshop's presentations, the development of metrics-based quality prediction models was discussed. Marcela Genero presented and explained a new technique, called Fuzzy Prototypical Knowledge Discovery (FPKD), that extends the traditional Knowledge Discovery in Databases (KDD) process with concepts derived from fuzzy set theory. This technique was used to build a model that can predict the under-

---

[5] A more complete validation, containing both theoretical and empirical parts, can be found in the Ph.D. dissertation of Marcela Genero [5].

standability, analyzability, and modifiability ratings of a UML class diagram based on its structural complexity metrics values.

The presentation of Houari Sahraoui focused on two problems with current methods to build software quality prediction models: the use and interpretation of precise threshold values for metrics, and the lack of decision support offered by "naive" models that do not explain the observed relationship between internal software properties and external software quality characteristics. The proposed solution of Sahraoui and colleagues is to map crisp threshold values into fuzzy ones, and to explicitly include domain knowledge into a prediction model. The former is done using a fuzzification technique based on the distribution of the metric values. Any metric value that is an input to a predictive model can then be replaced by the fuzzy label assigned to it (e.g. "small", "medium", "large"). For instance, if the predictive model consists of a set of rules, then the crisp preconditions of these rules can be replaced by fuzzy ones. Regarding the rules derivation itself, Sahraoui and colleagues propose breaking up rules that do not explain causality very well, into a set of intuitive and easier to validate sub-rules. This can be accomplished by including domain knowledge (e.g. domain heuristics) into the model.

The discussion of this highly original proposal focused mainly on the elaboration of the causal model. It was acknowledged that the derivation of the sub-rules, which formalize relationships between intermediate causes, is hard to automate, and their justification must be done on intuitive grounds. The existence of domain-specific public repositories of validated relationships between software attributes would be of great help to the model builder. It must be noted that the creation of such repositories was identified as an open issue during the QAOOSE 2000 workshop (see [2]). Again, the urgent need to share research hypotheses, data, and results, preferably with automatic support of some kind, was stressed.

To end this sub-section we report on two contributions that propose the use of metrics for evaluation purposes. In the position paper of Poels, Dedene, and Viaene, some simple complexity metrics for existence dependency graphs, i.e. a specific type of OO static conceptual model, have been applied to five reference models for organizing a front-office. The results of this exercise have been used to determine an optimal level of service customization. In their presentation, Michel Dao, Therese Libourel, and Cyril Roume have described some ongoing experiments related to the application of their feature factorization metrics (cf. Sect. 2.1) to several JAVA packages. Measurements have been taken at four levels of granularity (i.e. feature, generic feature, class, hierarchy) to assess how well these packages were factorized. The findings of these experiments confirmed many of the already sustained factorization problems in the packages under study.

3   Summary of the Debates

The QAOOSE 2001 workshop featured a separate discussion session at the end of the first day, and a shorter one on day two to close the workshop. We do not repeat the comments here that pertain to individual or related position papers presented during the workshop. These comments are included in the text of the previous section. We focus here on a couple of general remarks by the workshop attendees, that hold for all research presented, and in fact for the QAOOSE field as a whole.

It was noticed that there are problems with cohesion metrics for OO software artifacts. Most of the published cohesion metrics, like Chidamber and Kemerer's LCOM, lack a precise definition. As a consequence, it is not clear how to compute them. Interestingly, a same comment was made in previous QAOOSE workshops (see [1,2]). Hopefully, the metrics (definition) standardization proposals made during this workshop (see Sect. 2.1) can alleviate some of the problems with OO cohesion metrics. But, as shown by Hind Kabaili in last year's workshop, semantic aspects must also be taken into account for an effective assessment of cohesion. Software metrics are syntax-based and are probably not sufficient to evaluate this property. Michel Dao and colleagues reached about the same conclusion for their factorization metrics. In general, much of this year's workshop discussions related to issues of metrics definition like meta-metrics, meta-models for metrics, and the semantic aspects involved.

Another general remark is the lack of theoretical validation of metrics for OO software artifacts. Also this area of research needs further attention. We need to make sure that it is known what is measured by a metric. We cannot expect a wide adoption of metrics-based evaluation and prediction instruments in industry if this problem remains unsolved.

Related to the previous comment is the question what data analysis techniques are best to build descriptive and predictive software quality and effort models. A comparative analysis of different techniques, including Machine Learning techniques, is very much desired. Bayesian networks of several models might also provide part of the answer.

Once there is sufficient confidence in the validity of measurement instruments and in the usefulness and effectiveness of quality or effort models based on these instruments, there is the question how to integrate all of this in the software development, maintenance, and reengineering processes. Further research in this domain is wanted too.

Another question is whether metrics can be used to validate claims about design patterns. We would for instance like to see studies that investigate whether the use of patterns actually improves the quality of software systems. A quantitative approach to studying this research question seems appropriate.

Finally, the need for metrics for dynamic design diagrams and for OO patterns, components, and architectures was reiterated, as was the plea for more public repositories of software engineering data, metric values, thresholds, and benchmarks. Regarding this latter aspect, an international effort is required.

4   Conclusions

To conclude we can safely state that QAOOSE 2001 was a success. We saw some very innovative proposals and work-in-process. Especially, the research efforts towards metrics standardization (i.e. the topic of meta-metrics) and the omnipresent focus on measuring early OO artifacts, like UML class diagrams and OO conceptual database schemata, were very encouraging. Moreover, these topics were identified as open issues during previous editions of our workshop, which is somehow a proof of the significance and impact of the QAOOSE workshop series.

We, as workshop organizers, commit ourselves to continue this workshop series and improve it further. The issues raised in Sect. 3, offer food for thought for the coming

QAOOSE workshop edition(s). We invite researchers, both established researchers and Master or Ph.D. students, to work towards these topics, and share their findings with us on the next occassion.

5   List of Contributions

The following position papers were presented at the workshop:

- Extending Software Quality Predictive Models Using Domain Knowledge by Houari Sahraoui, Mohamed Adel Serhani, and Mounir Boukadoum
- Empirical Validation of Measures for Class Diagram Structural Complexity through Controlled Experiments by Marcela Genero and Mario Piattini
- A Change Impact Model Encompassing Ripple Effect and Regression Testing by Hind Kabaili, Rudolf K. Keller, and F. Lustman
- Measuring Quality of Database Schemas by Reviewing Concept, Criteria and Tools by Olaf Herden
- Towards a Model for Object-Oriented Design Measurement by Ralf Reissing
- Towards a Metrics Suite for Evaluating Factorization and Generalization in Class Hierarchies by M. Dao, M. Huchard, H. Leblanc, T. Libourel, and C. Roume Two position papers were accepted, but not presented at the workshop:
- Estimating Relative Size When Alternative Designs Exist by D. Janaki Ram and S.V.G.K. Raju
- A Quantitative Assessment of the Complexity of Static Conceptual Schemata for Reference Types of Front-Office by Geert Poels, Guido Dedene, and Stijn Viaene The tutorial was documented by a technical report:
- Using OCL to Formalize Object Oriented Metrics Definitions by Fernando Brito e Abreu

6   List of Participants

The workshop gathered 14 people from 6 different countries.
Their names, affiliations and e-mail addresses are:

- Brito e Abreu, Fernando (UNL & INESC, Portugal)
  fba@inesc.pt
- Dao, Michel (France Télécom R&D, France)
  michel.dao@francetelecom.com
- Genero, Marcela (University of Castilla-La Mancha, Spain)
  mgenero@inf-cr.uclm.es
- Herden, Olaf (OFFIS, Germany)
  olaf.herden@offis.de
- Josset, François Xavier (BOUYGUES, France)
  fxjosset@bouygyes.com
- Kabaili, Hind (University of Montreal, Canada)
  kabaili@iro.umontreal.ca

- Lahire, Philippe (University of Nice, France)
  philippe.lahire@unice.fr
- Libourel, Therese (LIRMM, France)
  libourel@lirmm.fr
- Piattini, Mario (University of Castilla-La Mancha, Spain)
  mpiattini@inf-cr.uclm.es
- Poels, Geert (VLEKHO Business School, Belgium)
  gpoels@vlekho.wenk.be
- Reissing, Ralf (University of Stuttgart, Germany)
  reissing@informatik.uni-stuttgart.de
- Roume, Cyril (LIRMM, France)
  roume@lirmm.fr
- Sahraoui, Houari (University of Montreal, Canada)
  sahraouh@iro.umontreal.ca
- Van Belle, Werner (Vrije Universiteit Brussel, Belgium)
  werner.van.belle@vub.ac.be

Acknowledgments. The authors wish to thank one of the workshop participants, Marcela Genero (University of Castilla-La Mancha), for her great help in compiling and reviewing this report.

References

1. Brito e Abreu, F., Zuse, H., Sahraoui, H.A., Melo, W.L.: Quantitative Approaches in Object-Oriented Software Engineering. In: Moreira, A.M.D., Demeyer, S. (eds.): Object-Oriented Technology, ECOOP'99 Workshop Reader, ECOOP'99 Workshops, Panels, and Posters, Lisbon, Portugal, June 14-18, 1999, Proceedings. Lecture Notes in Computer Science, Vol. 1743, Springer-Verlag, Berlin (1999) 326-337
2. Brito e Abreu, F., Poels, G., Sahraoui, H.A., Zuse, H.: Quantitative Approaches in Object-Oriented Software Engineering. In: Malenfant, J., Moisan, S., Moreira, A.M.D. (eds.): Object-Oriented Technology, ECOOP 2000 Worskhop Reader, ECOOP 2000 Workshops, Panels, and Posters, Sophia Antipolis and Cannes, France, June 12-16, 2000, Proceedings. Lecture Notes in Computer Science, Vol. 1964, Springer-Verlag, Berlin (2000) 93-103
3. Brito e Abreu, F., Poels, G., Sahraoui, H.A., Zuse, H. (eds.): Quantitative Approaches in Object-Oriented Software Design. Special issue of L'Objet: Software, Databases, Networks 7 (2001)
4. Brito e Abreu, F., Henderson-Sellers, B., Piattini, M., Poels, G., Sahraoui, H.A. (eds.): Proceedings of the 5th International ECOOP Workshop on Quantitative Approaches in Object-Oriented Software Engineering. Leuven (2001)
5. Genero, M., Defining and Validating Metrics for Conceptual Models. Ph.D. dissertation, Dept. of Computer Science, University of Castilla-La Mancha. Ciudad Real (2001).

Object-Oriented Business Solutions

Rafael Corchuelo[1], Antonio Ruiz[1], Jörg R. Mühlbacher[2], and
Jesús D. García-Consuegra[3]

[1] Universidad de Sevilla, Dpto. de Lenguajes y Sistemas Informáticos
Avda. de la Reina Mercedes, s/n. E-41012 Sevilla, Spain
{corchu, aruiz}@lsi.us.es; http://tdg.lsi.us.es
[2] Johannes Kepler Universität, Institut für Informationsverarbeitung und Mikroprozessortechnik
Altenbergerstraße, 69. A-4040 Linz, Austria
muehlbacher@fim.uni-linz.ac.at; http://www.fim.uni-linz.ac.at
[3] Universidad de Castilla-La Mancha, Dpto. de Informática
Campus Universitario, s/n. E-02071 Albacete, Spain
jdgarcia@info-ab.uclm.es; http://www.info-ab.uclm.es/gsid

Abstract. This report summarises the presentations, discussions, and main results
of the ECOOP'01 Workshop on Object-Oriented Business Solutions (WOOBS).
It was not a pure scientific meeting, but a mixed gathering where people from the
industry and the academia met to exchange ideas, experiences and build a network of relationships with others committed to the emergence of object-oriented
business solutions. WOOBS had an invited talk on quality of service, twelve presentations and lively discussions during and after them. The main conclusions
were on the importance of Multi-Organisational Web-Based Systems in today's
e-commerce world, which justifies the study of a new multidisciplinary paradigm
called Web-Oriented Programming.

Keywords. agents, aspect-orientation, coordination, databases, distribution, e-commerce, middlewares, transactions, web services, XML.

Workshop web site: http://tdg.lsi.us.es/woobs01

1 Introduction

E-commerce is gaining currency as the Internet settles as a medium for fruitful commercial transactions. Anyone with a credit card and an Internet-enabled device is a potential
customer, and this is the reason why no corporation can resist jumping on the e-commerce
bandwagon. To achieve this goal, web-based, attractive, technically robust applications
are a cornerstone.

The e-world currently amounts to million Euros, and the underlying software industry
is investing a lot of money in researching on new tools and development methods so
that these applications can be built at sensible costs. This has entailed adapting existing
methods and tools, which have usually been procedural, to the new resources and means
the Internet provides, but at such a pace that they do not have enough time to consolidate
before new proposals sprout out.

Object-orientation and component-based solutions seem to be promising and the
trend towards incorporating them seems to be settling at an appropriate pace. At the

Á. Frohner (Ed.): ECOOP 2001 Workshops, LNCS 2323, pp. 184–200, 2002.

same time, the complexity of these applications increases, and one of the reasons lies in the heterogeneous nature of the run-time and development-time aspects to be taken into account: architecture, security, attractiveness, quality of service, security, robustness, and so on.

The aim of the workshop was to discuss the research carried out in universities and industries to solve the problems related to the construction of e-commerce applications using object-oriented technology, focusing on real-world industrial experiences and innovative infrastructure for building e-commerce solutions (ECS). The main conclusions of the workshop can be summarised as follows: (i) quality-awareness is an essential cornerstone of ECS; (ii) semantic certification seems a promising tool whose benefits may be extrapolated from the traditional goods market; (iii) web services are going to be the next generation building blocks for ECS; (iv) traditional middlewares are fading away in the Internet arena; (v) aspect-orientation is the key to succeed in the management and development of the different concerns that interact in an ECS; (vi) agents play an important role because they are pro-active and autonomous.

WOOBS attracted a variety of researchers interested in applying their results to producing ECS. As a result, the workshop benefited from multiple points of view and different perspectives and approaches. Cutting down the programme to fewer presentations would have allowed more and deeper discussions, but we think that bringing together researchers from such different disciplines proved useful since the exchange of ideas and experiences was helpful in identifying a number of key topics and issues that need to be further researched and will probably help PhD students to identify a clear research topic in this area.

In this report, we go into details about the discussions and presentations and show how they relate to the above-mentioned conclusions. It is divided into five sections: Sect. 2 reports on the invited talk; Sect. 3 summarises the papers that were accepted; Sect. 4 reports on the colloquium that took place after the authors presented their papers; finally, Sect. 5 shows our main conclusions.

Next edition of WOOBS will be held in the framework of the fifth International Conference on Business Information Systems (BIS) in Poznań, Poland, during April 24–25, 2002 (http://bis.kie.ae.poznan.pl/). In this new edition, we will go into deeper details about the hottest topics we identified during this edition and will also report on the results obtained in the interim.

2   Invited Talk

Professor Doctor Kurt Geihs was the invited speaker of WOOBS. He is a professor of Computer Science at the Technical University of Berlin, and his research and teaching focus on distributed systems and operating systems. Current research projects focus on middleware and software component technology for open distributed systems, network and system management, agent-based systems, and infrastructures for Internet applications. He received a Diplom-Informatiker degree from the Technical University Darmstadt, Germany, a M.Sc. degree in Computer Science from the University of California, Los Angeles, USA, and a Ph.D. degree from the Technical University Aachen, Germany. He worked for the IBM European Networking Centre in Heidelberg, Germany, before joining the academia. He was a professor of Computer Science at the University of Frankfurt until June 2001.

During his lecture, professor Geihs talked to us about the importance of Quality of Service (QoS) in the development of next generation e-commerce applications. It constitutes one of their cornerstones and challenges the established middleware design principles because they usually provide naive abstractions of the underlying machinery that are quickly broken as soon as QoS issues such as bandwidth fluctuation or partial failures are taken into account.

He discussed how distributed object systems that rely on a standardised middleware layer, CORBA in this case, can be extended so as to deal with QoS requirements in an feasible but still abstract way. He focused on the results of two projects called MAQS and QCCS, and presented their approaches, goals and preliminary results. A short abstract of these projects follows.

A Management Architecture for Quality of Service (MAQS). A part of the invited talk focused on how the results of the MAQS project can be used to integrate QoS concerns into an object-oriented middleware such as CORBA. Usually, their most publicised feature is that they provide high-level abstractions of the underlying distributed computational machinery by means of which a programmer can work with his or her objects as if they resided on the same machine. However, such a level of transparency is quickly broken as soon as the programmer comes down to earth and has to deal with partial failures, bandwidth fluctuation, security concerns, transmission errors, and so on. All of these problems need to be addressed during the construction of an ECS, and, therefore, it would be desirable for a middleware to be able to deal with them in an elegant, robust, easy-to-use way.

The MAQS project addresses the integration of QoS concerns into ECS, or more generally, distributed systems in a broad sense, at both design/ implementation time and run time. At design/implementation time, QoS specifications have to be provided, and they must be in an adequate format so that negotiation, monitoring, and adaptation is possible and easy to map into programming languages such as C++ or Java. At run time, QoS-aware interaction can be further decomposed into three steps: Establishment of a connection, interaction itself, and shutting down. During the establishement of an interaction, both clients and servers negotiate the level of quality they require and can provide, respectively, which mainly depends on the availability of resources; during a QoS-aware interaction, monitoring is used to ensure the server provides its services at the QoS level it promised (renegotiation may be needed if it cannot achieve such a level); when a client finishes using a service, the interaction is closed and the resources it used are freed and charged if necessary.

Geihs's team has recently built a framework prototype for QoS integration based on the results of the MAQS project. It relies on MICO, a public domain CORBA 2.3 implementation initially developed by his team, and its core is an extension to CORBA IDL called QIDL that offers two new constructs for defining QoS interfaces and assigning them to service interfaces. A QoS interface defines a conceptual artefact that must be implemented to ensure a given component implements a certain quality level. Its definition consists of a number of QoS parameters that define the state of such artefacts or help define what a client requires and a server may provide, and a number of QoS operations that can be used to retrieve information or influence the behaviour of a QoS artefact.

To demonstrate the feasibility of this approach, Geihs's team have used the framework to build several QoS artefacts that include a simple multicast and group-membership protocol that can be used for voting and pooling, as well as a mechanism for streaming and load balancing. The results about load balancing are being applied in a joint project with a major German bank because they can help improve the response times of the investment banking applications it uses.

Current work focuses on completing the infrastructure they need to build real-world applications that need both monitoring, resource control, accounting, billing and charging. Their current negotiation component is also under hot improvement because it is only suitable for closed systems under the assumption that services do not optimise their profit using any knowledge about a client's preferences. Geihs's team is researching on strategies for open distributed systems where this assumption does not hold in general.

Quality-Controlled Component-Based Software Development. Another part of the invited talk focused on the QCCS project, which aims at researching a new approach for component-based software construction in which QoS concerns can be modelled independently from functionality. Professor Geihs thinks that quality is the only way to succeed in achieving a higher degree of reusability, adaptability and composability than traditional techniques.

QCCS deals with the following quality aspects: functional behaviour, structural properties, synchronisation properties, and use constraints. Components that have been designed according to the QCCS methodology will have proven properties which are specified in contracts and can thus be safely applied to build complex services from scratch by instantiating standardised frameworks.

Contracts are a core part of the QCCS methodology. They are the means a programmer can use to specify what his or her components can do and how good the results will be, or what they expect from other components. They can be classified into the following categories: (i) Basic contracts, which consist of the definition of a syntactic interface, (ii) synchronisation contracts, which specify how components residing on different nodes can collaborate synchronously, and (iii) QoS contracts, which describe issues such as performance or reliability.

Professor Geihs used the following example to explain further these concepts: consider, for instance, a database that stores replicated data on several nodes for the sake of robustness and fault-tolerance. Data cannot be replicated instantaneously, so the information at different nodes may be temporarily inconsistent due to network delays and bandwidth fluctuation. Using a QoS contract framework, a client can choose amongst several contracts the one that best suits its needs. A contract might ensure, for instance, that a query returns always the latest data (with a presumably high delay), whereas another might ensure a query returns the most up-to-date data found in less than, say, two seconds. Depending on the quality a client needs, a different contract may be selected dynamically at run time.

However, we are not likely to succeed in the ever-demanding component market unless we can deliver components that implement a given quality level in a short period of time. Thus, a technique in which QoS concerns are separated from functionality can significantly enhance maintenance and adaptation. This technique is popularly known as Aspect-Oriented Programming (AOP) and it allows to develop partial implementations that address particular aspects that can be woven into a single component later.

To merge contract-based design techniques and AOP, Geihs's team use the multiple view modelling capabilities of UML. The Object Constraint Language (OCL) is used to specify invariants, and pre- and post-conditions on the operations that constitute a contract. They have also defined several domain-specific stereotypes for dealing with quality concerns.

The methodology and tools are going to be validated using two real-world applications. The first one is a workflow system that aims at supporting business processes by providing tools that facilitate cooperation; the second one is a new Internet-based information system that helps users retrieve information about a certain geographical or administrative region.

3   Contributions

Over forty papers were submitted and peer-reviewed by two or three members of the programme committee. Only thirteen were finally accepted for presentation.

3.1   On Defining and Building Object-Oriented Views for Advanced Applications

R. Wrembel
Poznań University of Technology, Poland

Abstract. Contemporary information systems should allow to have access various sources of data maintained within a company/institution for the purpose of analysis. These data are often in different formats and have different complexity, e.g. relational, object-oriented, semistructured, HTML, spreadsheets, flat files. This data heterogeneity causes difficulties in accessing them. There are two approaches to the integration of heterogeneous data sources, namely, a virtual approach and a data warehouse approach. A very important mechanism applied in data integration is a view. For the integration of data having complex structure object-oriented views are very promising. In this paper we present: the concept of an object-oriented view for the application in object-relational data warehousing system, the issues concerning object-oriented view materialisation and maintenance, the prototype system that we have implemented, and some experimental results.

3.2   CBR-BDI Agents for an E-Commerce Environment

J.M. Corchado
University of Salamanca, Spain

Abstract. This paper shows how to build deliberative agents using case-based reasoning systems. Deliberative agents and Case-based Reasoning systems are presented. The advantages and disadvantages of deliberative agents are outlined and then it is shown how to solve some of their inconvenients, especially those related to their implementation and adaptation. The Internet has emerged as one of the most popular vehicles for disseminating and sharing information through computer networks. A multiagent-based system for e-business, in which CBR-BDI agents have been used, is also presented and evaluated in this paper.

3.3 Agentspace as a Middleware for E-Commerce Applications

S. Ambroszkiewicz and T. Nowak
Polish Academy of Sciences, Poland

Abstract. Agentspace is an emerging environment resulting from process automation in the Internet and Web. It is supposed that autonomous software (mobile) agents provide the automation. The agents realize the goals delegated to them by their human masters. Interoperability is crucial to assure meaningful interaction, communication and cooperation between heterogeneous agents and services. In order to realize the goals, the agents must create, manage and reconfigure complex workflows. Our research aims at extracting a minimum that is necessary and sufficient for providing transparency between users and services, i.e. for joining applications as services in agentspace on the one hand and for using them by heterogeneous agents (on behalf of their users) on the other hand.

3.4 Intelligent Agents and XML – A Method for Accessing Webportals in Both B2C and B2B E-Commerce

J.R. Mühlbacher, S. Reisinger, and M. Sonntag
Johannes Kepler Universität, Austria

Abstract. In E-Commerce today webportals are important and also intelligent agents grow in significance. Our approach is to combine them in designing webportals and interfaces for both users and agents. In this paper we discuss the problems in automatically accessing portals and possible solutions for them through using OOM methods. The solution selected by us, using an XML-based standard and dynamically reconfigurable protocols, is described afterwards and the methods used are shown. We also briefly present an example, a webportal for sports information to give an impression of a practical application.

3.5 Coordination Technologies for Business Strategy Support – A Case Study in StockTrading

G. Koutsoukos[1], T. Kotridis[2], L. Andrade[1,3], J.L. Fiadeiro[3,5], J. Gouveia[1], and M. Wermelinger[3,4]
[1] OBLOG Software, Portugal; [2] Accenture, UK; [3] ATX Software, Portugal; [4] Universidade Nova de Lisboa, Portugal; [5] Universidade de Lisboa, Portugal

Abstract. In today's global and highly competitive business environments, to the question of whether technology is forming business or vice-versa, organizations are replying by integrating their business and IT strategies, thus using technology to do business. On-line business and virtual organizations is the trend as e-commerce numbers are increasing and the emerging wireless data technologies are fuelling the creation of new business opportunities. Flexibility, innovation and change have become critical success factors for every business organization. Business strategies have now, more and more, a short-term time horizon and, for the first time, can be put in practice by in-formation systems alone (strategic information systems). As a consequence, there is an increasing pressure for building software systems that are dynamically reconfigurable and adaptive to changes imposed either by technology innovation or new business needs. Unfortunately, OO languages and the technologies associated with component-based frameworks have fallen short of re-dressing this situation, which may explain why software teams are still struggling to compete with the fast business and technology evolution and, as shown by numerous scientific studies on large-scale software systems, more than 80% of the total cost of software development is still devoted to software maintenance.

In this paper we show how a new semantic primitive (coordination contract) that we presented previously as an extension to OO modeling languages, together with the design patterns that support its implementation over component-based platforms, can be used in support for a new approach to Business Modeling based on the definition of "software strategic libraries" and (re)configuration mechanisms that will deliver "business reactive" information systems. We present our case on the basis of some simple, but real-life examples from the Stock-Trading industry. We discuss why OO techniques such as inheritance and clientship are too static and white-box in order to model and implement such volatile assets and we present how coordination contracts can provide a more dynamic modeling and implementation alternative. We, also, illustrate how contracts promote the idea of building systems using libraries of stable components and strategic evolving components, allowing organizations to cope with the volatility and turbulence of today's business environments.

3.6   A DPE Architecture Supporting the Deployment of Distributed Applications

T. Li, A. Hoffmann, M. Born, and I. Schieferdecker
GMD FOKUS, Germany

Abstract. With the unprecedented increase of the complexity of today's distributed appli-cations the deployment of such applications onto heterogeneous middleware platforms becomes more and more a challenge to the developer and administrator of such appli-cations. Deployment of distributed systems encompasses the distribution as well as the configuration of their components. The Eurescom project P924 targets concepts, meth-ods, and notations for the deployment of distributed component-based applications onto target middleware platforms. In this paper, we focus on this project's platform aspects. A DPE architecture to support the deployment of distributed application is elaborated.

3.7   Transaction Services for Business Objects Middleware

J. Nummenmaa[1] *and P. Thanisch*[2]
[1] *University of Tampere, Finland;* [2] *University of Edinburgh, Scotland*

Abstract. Transaction processing systems ensure that properties such as atomicity and isolation hold for transactions executing in a distributed, multi-user environment. It is now recognised that these transactional properties are useful for a much wider class of business object applications. However, it is notoriously difficult to develop robust software that provides such services in a failure-prone distributed environment. Consequently, do-it-yourself transactional facilities have been incorporated in the leading distributed objects middleware platforms. The use of such transactional facilities comes at a computational cost. Furthermore, some distributed objects applications are too complicated to benefit from these facilities. In view of this, we produce check-lists of criteria to determine whether a distributed business objects application can usefully exploit transactional services. We also discuss some potential problems.

3.8   Transparent Distribution in the Artavan Web Application Server

F. Sánchez, J.M. Murillo, R. Rodríguez, P. Bachiller, A. Gazo, A. Gómez, J.L. González, and M. Sánchez
University of Extremadura, Spain

Abstract. In this paper we present an experience using the Aspect Oriented Programming paradigm (AOP) to obtain a transparent and middleware independent object distribution in Artavan, a Web Application Server (WAS) developed in Teleserver, a Spanish company. The aim is allowing the programmers to serve applications using Corba or JavaRmi without mixing the distribution code with the functional one, promoting reusability and adaptability. This work is being developed under a contract between Teleserver and the University of Extremadura with the aim of doing applied research. This is only a part of the whole work where we are improving the WAS using other object oriented concepts.

3.9   A Performance Assessment Model for Web-Based CORBA Applications

J. Hosszú
Budapest University of Technology and Economics, Hungary

Abstract. This paper presents how discrete event simulation can be used for performance evaluation of distributed systems. general aspects of building the multi-layered object-oriented simulation model, sample application, and measurement results for various configurations are introduced.

The analysis focuses on scalability, throughput and latency of large scale distributed systems, which are critical performance issues in e-commerce applications. Using the method, performance of a system may be assessed without deploying it. However, the technology being considered rely on the Common Object-Request Broker Architecture, the model can be adopted to other distributed technologies as well.

3.10 On Dynamic Service Composition and Its Applicability to E-Business Software Systems

V. Tosic[1], D. Mennie[2], and B. Pagurek[1]
[1]*Carleton University, Canada;* [2]*The Bulldog Group Inc., Canada*

Abstract. This paper discusses dynamic service composition and its applicability to e-business software systems. It also presents the ICARIS architecture for dynamic service composition and its application to dynamic, on-demand establishment of security and trust relationships. Addition of security extensions to a B2C e-commerce system is used to illustrate dynamic service composition in ICARIS.

Dynamic service composition is the process of creating new services at run-time from a set of service components. Static (design-time or deployment-time) software composition is not flexible and agile enough to accommodate frequent runtime changes of requirements and/or operational circumstances that cannot be anticipated in advance. Dynamic service composition enables run-time construction of new, potentially unanticipated, services, while minimizing both human involvement and disruption of system operation. The potential benefits of greater system flexibility, agility, and availability are crucial in many e-business systems that have to cope with the constant change of technical and business circumstances and increased diversity and mobility of users, systems, and resources.

ICARIS is a general-purpose dynamic service composition architecture based on Jini, JavaBeans, and XML. As the research goal was to explore maximal reuse of existing technologies, the base technologies were not modified. However, the Jini Lookup Service was extended to support semantically rich XML service specifications and their advanced ("fuzzy") matching. In addition, ICARIS has built-in mechanisms for preventing failed compositions and unexpected runtime feature interactions. The ICARIS architecture supports three composition techniques: composite service interface, stand-alone composite service using the pipe-and-filter architecture style, and stand-alone composite service with the single body of code. ICARIS was successfully used in the Composable Security Application to introduce security services into applications that were not originally designed with security mechanisms. This experiment showed viability and feasibility of suggested concepts and demonstrated applicability of dynamic service composition in e-business systems.

3.11 An XML-Based E-Commerce Architecture Proposal

F.J. García, M.N. Moreno, and J.A. Hernández
University of Salamanca, Spain

Abstract. We present an e-commerce architecture proposal by means of which an organisation can easily jump on the virtual commerce bandwagon, expanding its marketspace to unexpected limits, whatever its size is. Aiming at easing the implementation, we propose the development of a software tool that allows the definition, publication and update of a catalogue of products, and the setting up of a web server architecture that allows clients to have access to it. To create a uniform environment, the architecture needs to focus on a well-defined business sector, easy to expand to others where businesses are based on product catalogues. An e-commerce server has to provide end-users with services such as searching for a product in any published catalogue, shopping cart management, selling certificates, navigation help, and so on through a uniform, intuitive interface. The whole system is built over a self-maintained platform, able to configure itself when changes are incorporated by the enterprise, with a minimum interaction with the web master. To facilitate the access to the information, a visual, intuitive tool is provided to enable the definition of business logic aspects such as catalogue of products for sale, full descriptions, selling policies, and so on. The communication between the tool and the server is implemented using XML over secure protocols. The server provides the tool with the definition pattern for the products, and it will be the tool in charge of the maintenance of the virtual enterprise by sending all necessary data in the same language.

3.12   Using the Aspect Moderator Framework For Evolving Business Requirements

F. Akkawi, M. Lee, A. Bader, and T. Elrad
Illinois Institute of Technology, USA

Abstract. While the cost and complexity of the enabling technologies for e-commerce applications decrease, the design and development of the e-commerce applications are becoming more expensive and complex. This is mainly due to the lack of a formal design methodology that stresses the separation of concerns. There are many diverse concerns that if intermixed will make the resulting software system hard to maintain and scale and consequently force re-engineering. The Aspect Moderator Framework (AMF) is an aspect-oriented approach that solves these problems. The AMF attempts to address design concerns like concurrency, security, scalability, and reliability in a way to maximize code reusability and minimize the impact of these concerns on the stability, maintainability and reconfigurability of the e-commerce applications.

3.13   BMD NTCS: From COBOL to OOP

M. Knasmüller
BMD Systemhaus Ges.m.b.H., Austria

Abstract. Introducing object-oriented programming to old-style programmers is a rather hard task. This paper presents some experiences from BMD Steyr, Austrians leading producer of accountancy software. We have more than 50 developers; most of them were maintaining a character-based COBOL-product, an integrated system supporting all business aspects. Now they are implementing the NTCS project, a complete reengineering of the product using OOP. In the first years there were two main tasks: Firstly, implementing the necessary Windows tools, secondly, updating the COBOL programmers. In a first step we chose a development environment: Delphi. Using it, we implemented our own class library, where we had a strong look on efficient input possibilities, on equal appearance of all parts and on implementing as much as possible in this library. Using this strategy the implementation of the accountancy software itself can be done in a short time. This not only because of the earlier release date, but also because of the reduction of the time in which the new software is developed and the old software must be maintained in parallel. Another important point is to turn the COBOL programmers to object-oriented programmers and there the best method is education, education, and once more education. We divide the necessary knowledge about object-oriented programming into three courses with weekly lectures and exercises. In the first part we learned all the necessary things that make a programmer excellent: type safety, procedures, pointers and most important data abstraction. Afterwards we introduced the terms classes, inheritance and dynamic binding. In the last part we explained the different classes of the class library. More information is available in the book "From COBOL to OOP", published by dpunkt.verlag. BMD NTCS is – in Austrian terms – a very large project with a duration of about five years and a budget of about ten million Euros. Now, we have already finished the implementation of two sub-projects, an archive of documents and a balance sheet program. We chose these parts of our software, because there the advantages of a Windows product are more important than a high optimised input possibility. Future work will concentrate on implementing all the other parts of our software system.

4   Colloquium

After presenting their papers, the authors engaged in discussion of some topics that were not covered previously. Dr. Corchuelo sparked off discussion and he pointed out that all of the discussion topics identified during previous sessions need to be addressed in the context of a new kind of systems he called Multi-Organisational Web-Based Systems, or MOWS for short.

Corchuelo – In recent years, the design of reference architectures for systems distributed on the Internet has attracted the attention of an increasing number of researchers and practitioners who have focused on platforms, languages, middlewares or interoperability concerns. The main reason for such a great interest is that this network has experienced a rapid shift from information and entertainment to electronic commerce, which has gained importance and grown exponentially. That is the reason why Multi-Organisational Web-Based Systems are becoming so usual and successful. They are composed of a relatively small number of coarse-grained web services provided and supported by different organisations that need to cooperate frequently. For instance: tourist agencies, banking systems, stock traders, virtual fishmarkets, and so on.

Ruiz – They are not new at all, but I agree in that traditional development techniques or methods for addressing the issues that arise in the context of ECS need a clearly identified context that is completely different from the traditional set. The Internet has overnight changed the way applications are developed and managed, so that it is necessary to have a clear description of this new scenario. I think that investing time, effort and money on studying these systems at an abstraction level that allows to have a good perspective over them is necessary.

Geihs – Can you, please, tell us about the main features of a MOWS and why you think they deserve special attention?

Corchuelo – I think the main features of a MOWS are the following: (i) They lack a middleware layer in the traditional sense because they are interconnected by means of the Internet, i.e., they use standard protocols such as HTTP or SOAP and languages such as HTML or XML to communicate; providing high-level services such as transactions, security, or persistence is far more difficult in this scenario than in traditional middle-wares. (ii) They must be economically optimal; in traditional applications this may be a complex problem, but it is even more difficult on the Internet because the availability of services and their quality may change all of a sudden. (iv) They are multi-coordinated, in the sense that most ECS cannot be easily decomposed into client/server or message passing patterns; instead, several entities on the net coordinate, exchange information and collaborate to obtain a result. (v) They must be quality-enabled and proactive, in the sense that quality (not only quantitative QoS, but also qualitative quality) is essential and needs to be achieved in a highly automated way.

Ruiz – One of the main aims of the software industry consists of producing high-quality applications at costs that should be as reduced as possible. Unfortunately, building such applications keeps on being quite a handmade activity that lacks standardised, consolidated enough automated production methods. Furthermore, the Internet has entailed a great revolution in this industry, and it is driving electronic commerce activities at an ever-increasing pace. This has implied adapting existing methods and tools to the new resources and means the Internet provides, but at such a pace that they do not have enough time to consolidate before new proposals sprout out. That is why I think that studying MOWS as a separate kind of systems may help identify key issues that will conduct the development of future methods and tools.

Attendees agreed on the necessity of studying such systems as a new paradigm and the importance of the features that make them unique. Some of them pointed then out that enabling technologies such as UMTS will, undoubtedly, play a fundamental role in next generation ECS and will surely change the way we conceive MOWS at present. However, what about the infrastructure software able to take advantage of such technology to build ECS?

Koutsoukos – MOWS are then ECS that will exploit the idea of web-services, and mobile phones will be the essential device to have access to them. I wonder why a new technology for delivering services. Was not enough with CORBA?

Corchuelo – Essentially, web-services are built on top of standard Internet protocols and languages, and that is the reason why they are becoming so successful. You do not have to buy an ORB, instead you use HTTP/SOAP as a transport protocol, XML as a data language and tools such as BizTalk to map a scheme into another if it does not suit your needs. Do not you think middlewares such as CORBA are fading away?

This question sparked off a vivid discussion. We are in no doubt that middlewares such as CORBA are widely used nowadays. However, they are more often used to build the internal part of an electronic service than to interface with others on the Internet. When such a middleware is used to interface with other systems, all of the organisations involved usually agree on using the implementation provided by the same vendor to avoid connectivity problems and performance penalties. Some attendees pointed out important industrial experiences in which CORBA was also used to interface with other systems, but many agreed in that CORBA will be mostly used as an internal infrastructure, whereas protocols and languages such as HTTP, SOAP or XML will surely rule the future "Internet middleware".

We then moved to the problem of combining different aspects into a single ECS.

Corchuelo – Let us, please, stop for a moment, and let us think about the many inter-related aspects that can influence an ECS. Just a middleware, call it CORBA or HTTP/SOAP, is not enough to engineer complex ECS.

Akkawi – Yes sure: persistence, synchronisation, security, reliability, robustness. . . there are so many aspects that are not functional but have an impact on how an ECS may behave that it is necessary to have tools to eject them out of the functional core to enhance modularity, maintainability, adaptation. . .

Corchuelo – Those aspects are very important and it is obviously necessary to deal with them independently from the functionality a web service has to implement. However, I would like to point out other interesting problems with which you can come up easily when designing an ECS. They are not usually dealt with using aspects, but I am sure they are also aspects, namely: information retrieval, high-level quality attributes such as portability or price, coordination, chiefly multiparty interaction, intelligence. . .

Reisinger – What do you mean by aspect-oriented information retrieval?

Corchuelo – Distribution, heterogeneity and rapid change are the key features of MOWS, because the Internet market changes with every passing minute. Never has it been so wide the spectrum of available information sources. Thus, to keep our MOWS economically optimal it is often necessary to change the web services on which they rely. The problem is that if our business rules depend on the exact primitives we need to use to retrieve information from such heterogeneous sources, we are then likely to spend a lot of time and effort every time they change. As Akkawi pointed out, the idea is to eject the code responsible for retrieving information out of the functional code, thus keeping it clean and independent from the actual information sources it uses.

We then turned to the important role of agents in such problems.

Nowak – Intelligent agents may help a lot in achieving such a goal.

Ruiz – Right, but there is an important problem to be addressed: how to bridge the gap between ontologies that have been developed independently on the Internet? I mean, how can an agent retrieve information from a new site whose ontology is new or does not exist at all, as is the usual case?

Reisinger – That is the problem of interoperability in a broad sense, and I think the solution consists of having ontology repositories in which we can store, update and manage ontologies in different application domains together with mappings that allow us to bridge the semantic gap between them, if possible. ebXML is a good example. It is a modular suite of specifications that enables enterprises to conduct business over the Internet because it provides them with a standard method to exchange business messages, conduct trading relationships, communicate data in common terms and define and register business processes.

Geihs – Having those ontologies is obviously a part of the problem, but I think that mobility is also necessary to achieve such goals in an efficient manner.

Akkawi – That is then a pretty complex aspect.

Wrembel – Yes, and homogenising views may help a lot.

Nowak – That justifies the need for agent platforms supporting the creation, management and reconfiguration of complex workflows. It is not enough with infrastructure services, but agents need more advanced platforms that bring them higher-level services that allow them to interoperate meaningfully. Introducing homogenising views is a good approach, by the way.

Mobile agents led to a new issue: semantic certification.

Tosic – Another interesting point is that of composing the services each agent provides. In this case, dynamic composition techniques are essential.

Corchuelo – Sure, and I think your paper on dynamic service composition is a valuable contribution in this sense because MOWS can be basically understood as "big" services composed of many building blocks that can be viewed as lower-level services. The problem is how can you assure a composition of services, being them provided by web artefacts or agents, performs the tasks it is supposed to perform and delivers its functionality at a given quality level.

Ruiz – The key here may be certification. Guaranteeing that a service implements a given functionality at a given quality level is, in my honest opinion, absolutely impossible unless we test it. There might be people who would call me heretic because I do not use a state-of-the-art theoretical method, but I think testing is the only method you can use to certify a service conforms to its specification. I think that certifying a component with regard to a syntactic, protocol, semantic, and quality interface is a good solution. In the future, there might be new companies specialised on certification. Thus, component assemblers might build applications from certified components and services, and thus interoperability checks would be easier. However, it is necessary a great deal of standardization to achieve this goal, i.e., we need standardised ontologies and maps between different versions of the same ontology, if possible.

Corchuelo – Remember that is the approach SETCO uses to certify a product implements the SET protocol.

Koutsoukos – It is an interesting idea to certify components in such a way. You might have a guarantee certificate as if you were buying a traditional good. However, I am not aware of any initiative that uses it, except for the SET case.

Nummenmaa – Certificates are also a good idea in the context of transactions because you can certify a system performs its task coherently and you have a guarantee certificate you can use to ask your providers for responsibilities.

Tosic – I think certification has a good potential in conjunction with a registry such as UDDI. This is the name of a group of web-based registries that expose information about web services different vendors have developed (or are developing). Including such certificates might influence how a programmer trusts a service, and I agree on guarantees being important in the software industry.

This raised many questions about quality concerns.

Ruiz – Thus, a certificate may be viewed as the description of a number of high-level quality attributes such as robustness, reliability, security and the like. I mean that all of these attributes are valuable and then must be an essential part of every component or web-service. Thus certificates must be in a form so that an ECS can seek for the web services it needs in a highly automated way.

Akkawi – Thus, you mean that they should be described by means of an aspect-language and woven to build components.

Corchuelo – It would be nice to be able to encapsulate those aspects into independent packages that can be woven. However, the problem here is not to implement them, but to expose information about quality features so that every time a web service needs to use another, it can decide which implementation to use according to how they maximise a number of quality criteria. It is, we need a language for implementing quality aspects and another language for "documenting" them and making them available to others. Professor Geihs told us about a proposal in this direction, although the quality aspects with which he works are relatively low-level with regard to quality attributes such as complexity, price, resolution, availability or such.

Akkawi – Which are, in your opinion, the key problems incorporating such "reflective information" about quality aspects may solve?

Corchuelo – (i) Automatisation, i.e., the ability of an ECS to seek for the web services it needs autonomously; (ii) conformance, i.e., its ability to select a set of services that fulfill the quality level they need so as to achieve the quality level they promise; (iii) and economic optimality, definitely.

Ruiz – Sure. However, you have forgotten several important issues that need to be addressed: (i) temporal awareness, because quality requirements may change depending on the day, hour or month; (ii) negotiation mechanisms, so that clients can weak or strength their requirements according to the offers of a server; (iii) multiparty awareness, because typical problems in the context of ECS usually involve several parties that need to agree and cooperate to achieve a goal.

5   Conclusions

During presentations and discussions we identified ECS as a special kind of so called Multi-Organisational Web-based Systems (MOWS). The increasing demand and complexity of ECS based on the Internet, the need for reducing development and running costs, and the new opportunities that web services offer are the main reasons behind the forecast popularity of MOWS. In such systems, several organisations offer end-user web services such as banking, booking or information retrieval, whose functionality relies on a number of back-end web services provided by other organisations. To achieve optimal MOWS, they must be open systems that must be able to search for the services on which they rely automatically and dynamically.

Summing up, the rapid evolution of the Internet demands an ever-increasing ability to adapt to a medium that is in continuous change and evolution, thus automatisation is the key to succeeding. Studying MOWS from an abstract point of view and adapting current methodologies and tools to the their specific features may help identifying key problems that are inherent to these systems.

Next, we summarise some of our conclusions, some of the problems we identified, and the solutions we sketched at WOOBS:

Infrastructure:
1. Traditional middlewares such as CORBA will keep playing a prominent role in the design of back-ends.
2. It seems that protocols such as HTTP or SOAP will replace traditional middlewares in the Internet arena.

Development:
1. Aspect-orientation is one of the keys in succeeding in the development of complex web-services in which many mutually-influencing aspects are merged and combined.
2. Agents may be viewed as an enabling technology to build ECS that can search for information on the Internet.
3. Information retrieval may be expressed as an independent aspect, and will help evolving software. However, it is necessary to adapt agent services to the Internet setting so that they can develop their full potential in ECS.
4. The semantic gap between the ontologies different data sources use is one of the main problems to be addressed. Banks of ontologies and mappings between them are necessary.
5. Multiparty coordination models are necessary, chiefly in ECS in which several parties need to negotiate and reach agreements on-line.

Certification:
1. It is necessary to guarantee a service implements what its specification states. Certification seems a promising tool.
2. Certification allow clients to use guarantee certificates as if they were buying traditional goods. This concept is novel in the software arena.

Quality:
1. Optimality and conformance seem to be the cornerstones of quality.
2. Quality documents must be formalised so that they allow automatic checking. Furthermore, quality documents must include both QoS clauses on attributes such as delays, jitting or mean time to fails, and higher-level clauses on attributes such as cost per connection, security level or binding policies.
3. It is necessary to extend current architectural description languages so that they can take quality requirements into account, and it is necessary to extend current distributed run-time platforms such as CORBA, COM+ or .NET so that quality documents are first-class elements.
4. It is necessary to include quality monitoring mechanisms so that it is possible to check if the provider of a web service fulfills the quality level agreement it reached with a customer.

The importance of MOWS in the current e-world sufficiently justifies the study of a new paradigm called WOP (*Web-Oriented Programming*). The goal is to provide software architects with a number of tools to solve critical problems such as *optimality* and *conformance*, which are both closely related to the automatic management and negotiation of quality requirements.

Resources

- BIZTALK. http://www.biztalk.org
- ebXML. http://www.ebxml.org
- MAQS project.
  http://www.vsb.informatik.uni-frankfurt.de/maqs/Project.html
- QCCS project. http://www.qccs.org
- SET (Secure Electronic Transaction). http://www.setco.org
- UDDI (Universal Description, Discovery and Integration of Business for the Web).
  http://www.uddi.org
- UMTS (Universal Mobile Telecommunications System).
  http://www.umts-forum.org
- Web services (by Microsoft).
  http://msdn.microsoft.com/msdnmag/issues/0900/WebPlatform/
  WebPlatform.asp
- Web services (by Sun). http://www.sun.com/software/sunone

Acknowledgements. First and foremost, the organisers of WOOBS would like to thank all of the participants of the workshop, including the members of the programme committee, for their hard work before, during and after the workshop; they are responsible for its great deal of success. We also thank the organisers of the ECOOP conference for their help and continuous support. If it had not been for them, WOOBS would not have been possible.

Finally, we would also like to thank Atef Bader, because we got inspiration for our evaluation form from a previous one he designed, Microsoft and Telvent (Abengoa Group) for their generous financial support, Fundación Dintel for their generous supply of material, Sadiel for their support in project GEOZOCO, and Ciber Sur for their coverage of the event.

4th Workshop on OO and Operating Systems

Darío Álvarez Gutiérrez[1], Francisco Ballesteros[2], and Paniti Netinant[3]

[1] Department of Informatics, Universidad de Oviedo, Asturias, Spain
darioa@correo.uniovi.es
[2] Universidad Rey Juan Carlos, Madrid, Spain
nemo@gsyc.escet.urjc.es
[3] Computer Science Department, University of Bangkok, Thailand
netipan@iit.edu

Abstract. The workshop aims to bring together researchers and developers working on object-oriented operating systems and to provide a platform for discussing problems arising from the application of object-orientation to operating systems and solutions for them. Suggested topics for position papers and discussions include, but are not restricted to: adaptable and adaptive OOOS, frameworks for OOOS, architecture of OOOS, distributed OOOS and middleware, aspect orientation and OOOS design, what are the penalties of OO in OS and how to avoid them, reflective OOOS, OOOS tools, reusability and interoperability of OOOS components, OOOS configurability, maintenance, tuning and optimization, OOOS for embedded systems, real-time OOOS.

1 Introduction

The first ECOOP Workshop on Object-Orientation and Operating Systems was held at ECOOP'97 in Jyväskylä, Finland [15]. It was organized by Frank Schubert, Lutz Wohlrab, and Henning Schmidt.

Since it provided a good forum for interesting discussions, the participants suggested that this workshop be periodically organized biannually. At ECOOP'98 (which did not have a OOOSWS) Francisco Ballesteros and Ashish Singhai joined the organizing team.

The second ECOOP Workshop on Object-Orientation and Operating Systems was held at ECOOP'99 in Lisbon, Portugal [16]. It was organized by Lutz Wohlrab, Francisco Ballesteros, Henning Schmidt, Frank Schubert, and Ashish Singhai. During ECOOP'99, participants decided to meet yearly and therefore organized ECOOP-OOOSWS'2000, which was held in Cannes, France [17], with Darío Álvarez and Reinhard Meyer joining as organizers.

The ECOOP-OOOSWS'2001 workshop is therefore the fourth in the workshop series, and took place in Budapest, Hungary, on June 19th, 2001.

In OOOSWS prospective participants submit a position paper. Submitted papers are reviewed by the organizers. Participation is by invitation only. The number of participants is limited to facilitate lively discussions.

A distinguished member of the OOOS community is asked to give an invited talk. For ECOOP-OOOSWS'2001 the invited talk was given by Alan Dearle.

Á. Frohner (Ed.): ECOOP 2001 Workshops, LNCS 2323, pp. 201–208, 2002.
© Springer-Verlag Berlin Heidelberg 2002

This year we had 7 position papers accepted. Authors of accepted position papers give a full talk and a discussion happens after each presentation and at the end of the workshop.

For the first time in the workshop series, we also had live demonstrations of working systems at the end of the workshop, hosted by their developers participating in the workshop.

The invited talk was given by Alan Dearle, from the School of Computer Science of the University of Saint Andrews, Scotland. Besides Alan's talk, ECOOP-OOOSWS'2001 had 7 talks and was attended by 15 participants from 9 different countries. The participants were:

- Álvarez Gutiérrez, Darío – University of Oviedo, Spain
- Beuche, Danilo – University of Magdeburg, Germany
- Breuness, Cees-Bart – University of Nijmegen, Netherlands
- Dearle, Alan – University of Saint Andrews, United Kingdom
- Elrad, Tzilla – Illinois Institute of Technology, U.S.A.
- Gal, Andreas – University of Magdeburg, Germany
- García Perez-Schofield, J. Baltasar - University of Vigo, Spain
- Gombas, Gabor – Eotvos Lorand University, Hungary
- Kiczales, Gregor – University of British Columbia, Canada
- Mahieu, Tom – K.U. Leuven, Belgium
- Michiels, Sam – K.U. Leuven, Belgium
- Netinant, Paniti – University of Bangkok, Thailand
- Ortín Soler, Francisco – University of Oviedo, Spain
- Schulthess, Peter – Ulm University, Germany
- Spinczyk, Olaf – University of Magdeburg, Germany

The paper presentations were structured into four sessions:

1. "Frameworks",
2. "Aspects",
3. "Reflection",
4. "Persistence", and
5. "Demos".

Before the sessions, we had the invited talk, and between and after the sessions we had discussion time.

2   Presentations and Discussions

We give here a report of the invited talk, the different presentations and the discussions that arose after each one.

Invited Talk

Alan Dearle gave the invited talk [8], disserting about Persistence, Operating Systems and current Trends in Computer Science. He started with a brief introduction of the principles of orthogonal persistence, introduced in 1978 by Atkinson and refined in 1982 by Atkinson and Morrison. During the 80s several languages were developed that supported orthogonal persistence notably PS-algol and Napier88. Also about this time Keedy and Rosenberg developed the Monads operating system, which supported some aspects of orthogonal persistence. The 1990s have seen a number of operating system initiatives to support orthogonal persistence including Keykos, L4, and Grasshopper and Charm where he was very involved.

Then he examined the requirements of orthogonal persistence, looking at the attempts to support it at both the language and operating system levels and examined how relevant these approaches are set against the current trends of Java, XML, the World Wide Web, ubiquitous computing and the like.

One of the controversial things that arose on the discussion was that Alan thought that nowadays it is better to implement memory management completely in software rather than using hardware memory management units. The reason was that the time taken by servicing page fault interrupts did not improve as much as for regular instructions, so it took less time doing it just with regular instrucions. However, Peter Schultess pointed that in his Plurix system (presented later [7]) they can process a very high number of page interrupts per second. Alan said that his personal experience was pointing on the other direction, but then it was just a matter of using whichever technique that was better suited at the moment.

Alan made another interested reflection about systems research, as he was now using a commercial microkernel (QNX) as a basis, developing his system above it. Some commercial systems are now stable and fast enough for his purposes. Some pointed that, however, for other kernel research (rather than more middleware-oriented) they are not an option.

Minisession: Frameworks

The first presentation of a position paper (Dynamic Protocol Stack Composition: Protocol Independent Addressing [1]) was given by Sam Michiels in the context of the minisession about frameworks. He presented a generic addressing framework (GAF) that enables the development of protocol stack independent applications. This framework has been developed in the context of dynamic protocol stack composition. Having a way to compose and build protocol stacks is not sufficient, as the protocol layers a stack is composed of have an impact on the addressing used inside the stack. Since addresses are used by applications, the impact of modifying the stack dynamically is not automatically transparent. The addressing framework he presented provides a generalised view on network communication to solve this addressing problem. They validated the GAF in a proof-of-concept prototype, which was demoed at the end of the workshop.

Session: Aspects

Gregor Kiczales opened the session devoted to aspects presenting the position paper (Exploring an Aspect-Oriented Approach to OS Code [2]). He pointed that operating system code is complex. But, while substantial complexity is inherent to this domain, he believed that other complexity is caused by modularity problems. In the paper, they explored aspect-oriented programming (using the AspectC language) as a means of making this kind of complexity unnecessary. They showed that simple linguistic constructs can be used to modularize prefetching for mapped files in FreeBSD 3.3, an aspect of the system that is otherwise unclear because its implementation is spread out in the code.

The second position paper about aspects was presented by Olaf Spinczyk (On Minimal Overhead Operating Systems and Aspect-Oriented Programming [3]). He works in the area of deeply embedded systems, which are forced to operate under extreme resource constraints in terms of memory, CPU time, and power consumption. They apply the program family concept in this domain (the PURE family of Operating Systems) to implement reusable and highly configurable operating systems. He focused then on their approach to use aspect-oriented programming to modify and optimize the inter-object relations and communication pathways in an object-oriented family of operating system. The aim of this approach is to produce stream-lined application-specific operating systems, minimizing the code size and runtime overhead.

Paniti Netinant presented the last position paper about aspects (Implementing Producers/Consumers Problem Using Aspect-Oriented Framework [4]). Coinciding with Gregor, he stated that For software systems such as operating systems, the interaction of their components becomes more complex. This interaction may limit reusability, adaptability, and make it difficult to validate the design and correctness of the system. As a result, re-engineering of these systems might be inevitable to meet future requirements. He argued that supporting separation of concerns in the design and implementation of operating systems can provide a number of benefits such as comprehension, reusability, extensibility and adaptability in both design and implementation. But then, in order to maximize these benefits, such a support is difficult to accomplish. System aspectual properties define as crosscutting concerns of many components of the system, for example synchronization, scheduling, performance, fault tolerance, etc. Aspect-Oriented Programming is a paradigm proposal that aims at separating components and aspects from the early stages of the software life cycle, and combines them together at the implementation phase. Instead of using a new language, he showed another approach, a C++ Aspect-Oriented Framework (ACL) that can be used for system software such as operating systems in order to apply Aspect-Oriented techniques to it, demonstrating it using the Producers/Consumers problem. He also showed how the separation of system aspectual properties from components, The framework, which is based on aspect-oriented technology as well as language and architecture independence, is a three-dimensional model consists of aspects, components, and layers.

During the discussions, some interesting points arose. For example, Gregor was primarily concerned in Software Engineering, and used the OS refactoring project to learn how AOP will perform with real, complex systems. Sometimes the aspects get tangled together, as his presentation showed, but he expects that this tangling is not important and AOP really makes an improvement for software development.

He tries to prove that aspects are good statically for configuring systems, and suggested that OS people worked on this, for example making systems that can load aspects dynamically. For instance, Paniti's C++ aspect framework could be used for implementing this kind of systems.

There was a bit of controversy about whether AOP could be applied without having a specific language or tool that can be used for different aspects or not. Gregor pointed that one could apply separation of concerns using a language (such as AspectC) or using a domain specific language for a given or given set of concerns (as the PURE people did).

Minisession: Reflection

The minisession about reflection was opened by Francisco Ortín Soler. In his presentation (Building a Completely Adaptable Reflective System [5]) he outlined his approach to build completely adaptable systems. Reflection is one of the main techniques used to develop adaptable systems and, currently, different kinds of reflective systems exist. Compile-time reflection systems provide the ability to customize their language but they are not adaptable at runtime. On the other hand, runtime reflection systems define meta-object protocols to customize the system semantics at runtime. However, these meta-object protocols restrict the way a system may be adapted before its execution, and they do not permit the customization of its language. His system implements a non-restrictive reflection mechanism over a virtual machine (called nitrO), in which every feature may be adapted at runtime. No meta-object protocol is used and, therefore, it is not needed to specify previously what may be reflected. With this reflective system, the programming language may be also customized at runtime.

One of the questions that were issued was about the problems emerging from the high degree of customization provided for the system. When one can customize even the language individually we could arrive to a situation similar to the proliferation of different C language flavors, for example. Francisco agreed that this is inevitable, as this is indeed the main goal: to build a system where everything is adaptable. However, you can always restrict the degree of adaption to suit your needs if diversity is not advisable, but the system does not impose this limitation.

Session: Persistence

J. Baltasar García Perez-Schofield presented the first position paper (Extending Containers to Address the Main Problems of Persistent Object-Oriented Operating Systems: Clustering, Memory Protection and Schema Evolution [6]) of the session about persistence. He discussed the three main problems that must be addressed when designing and implementing any persistent system: clustering, memory protection and schema evolution. Then he presented a novel approach using a model based on the concept of container, and compared this approach with the orthogonal persistence model. From the architecture of object-oriented operating systems, a container is a kind of cluster extended to the higher layers of the operating system. He showed how this model presents some valuable advantages when compared with other persistent systems. He also showed a successful implementation of this model in Barbados, a Persistent Programming Environment, in which initial performance tests supported his conclusions.

The last paper of the session and of the workshop (Architecture of an Object-Oriented Cluster Operating System [7]) was presented by Peter Schultess. He gave an overview of the Plurix project, that implements an object-oriented Operating System (OS) for

PC clusters. Network communication is implemented via the well-known Distributed Shared Memory (DSM) paradigm using restartable transactions and an optimistic synchronization scheme to guarantee memory consistency. He stated that they believed that using a DSM management for a general purpose OS offers interesting perspectives, e.g. for simplified development of distributed applications. The OS (including the kernel and drivers) is written in Java using his own Plurix Java Compiler (PJC) translating Java source texts directly into Intel machine instructions. PJC is an integral part of the language-based OS and tailor-made for compiling in their own persisten DSM environment. Furthermore, device-level programming is supported by some minor language extensions. He explained with more detail the architecture of the DSM kernel and integration aspects of PJC. He concluding showing early performance results and discussed experiences of using the Java language for OS development.

One topic not directly related to any presentation that was discussed was the shortage of Ph.D. students that want to work in the field of operating systems and systems programming. There was consensus on this, as it was noticed by many participants from different countries. One of the reasons might be that this kind of research takes much time and it is not fashionable, so students do not choose it or leave soon.

In fact, this shortage was one of the reasons why Peter used Java for the Plurix project, so that students were more attracted to work in the project as Java is more fashionable. He argued that the language is OK, but it has some drawbacks (heavier, slower, not single pass compiler and slower than Oberon, for example). However, his personal experience showed that Java can be used for systems programming (even for drivers).

Demos

There was also, for the first time in the workshop series, live demonstrations of systems.

Andreas Gal did a demo of the PURE system, showing the use of the configuration tools to generate a member of the family of operating systems that is minimal according to the funcionality selected by the user. Some very simple systems can be even 200 bytes in size. He showed a running embedded system with a 8K microcontroller, temperature and wind sensors, display and a monitoring application. The system also sent the data to a laptop through an USB connection, thus having a USB device driver and protocol implementation for the transmission of the data.

Tom Mahieu demoed the prototype implementation of the Generic Address Framework. He showed how two different protcol stacks were constructed for the same application. One was an UDP/IP/Ethernet stack, while the other was a UDP/Ethernet stack, eliminating the middle IP protocol. The application, worked with both stacks without needing changes.

List of Position Papers

1. Sam Michiels, Tom Mahieu, Frank Matthijs and Pierre Verbaeten (Distrinet, Department of Computer Science, K.U. Leuven, Belgium), *Dynamic Protocol Stack Composition: Protocol Independent Addressing*
2. Yvonne Coady, Gregor Kiczales, Michael Feeley, Norman Hutchinson, Joon Suan Ong and Stephan Gudmundson (University of British Columbia, Canada), *Exploring an Aspect-Oriented Approach to OS Code*

3. Andreas Gal, Wolfgang Schroder-Preikschat and Olaf Spinczyk (University of Magdeburg, Germany), *On Minimal Overhead Operating Systems and Aspect-Oriented Programming*
4. Paniti Netinant (University of Bangkok, Thailand), Tzilla Elrad (Computer Science Department, Illinois Institute of Technology, U.S.A.), *Implementing Producers/Consumers Problem Using Aspect-Oriented Framework*
5. Francisco Ortín Soler and Juan Manuel Cueva Lovelle (Department of Informatics, University of Oviedo, Spain), *Building a Completely Adaptable Reflective System*
6. J. Baltasar García Perez-Schofield (Department of Computer Science, University of Vigo, Spain), T.B. Cooper (Director of Smarts Pty Ltd., Sydney, Australia), E. García Roselló and M. Pérez Cota (Department of Computer Science, University of Vigo, Spain), *Extending Containers to Address the Main Problems of Persistent Object-Oriented Operating Systems: Clustering, Memory Protection and Schema Evolution*
7. O. Marquardt, M. Schoettner, M. Wende, and P. Schulthess (Department of Distributed Systems, University of Ulm, Germany), *Architecture of an Object-Oriented Cluster Operating System*
8. Alan Dearle (School of Computer Science, University of St Andrews, Scotland), *Persistence, Operating Systems and current trends in Computer Science*

Web References

9. The Charm Persistent Operating System,
   `http://www-os.dcs.st-and.ac.uk/Charm/`
10. PURE family of OS, development page,
    `http://ivs.cs.uni-magdeburg.de/~pure/`
11. Aspect-Oriented Frameworks,
    `http://www.iit.edu/~{}concur/lag/projects.html`
12. nitrO VM and the Computational Reflection Research Group of the University of Oviedo,
    `http://www.di.uniovi.es/reflection/lab/`
13. Container Model for persistence, `http://www.ei.uvigo.es/~jgarcia/imo/`
14. The Plurix project homepage, `http://www.plurix.de/`

References

15. Frank Schubert, Lutz Wohlrab, and Henning Schmidt. ECOOP Workshop on Object-Orientation and Operating Systems. In Jan Bosch and Stuart Mitchell, editors, *Object-Oriented Technology: ECOOP'97 Workshop Reader*, number 1357 in Lecture Notes in Computer Science, Jyväskylä, Finland. 1997. Springer Verlag.
16. Lutz Wohlrab, Frank Schubert, Francisco Ballesteros, Henning Schmidt, and Ashish Singhai. 2nd ECOOP Workshop on Object-Orientation and Operating Systems. In Ana Moreira and Serge Demeyer, editors, *Object-Oriented Technology: ECOOP'99 Workshop Reader*, number 1743 in Lecture Notes in Computer Science, Lisbon, Portugal. 1999. Springer Verlag.
17. Francisco Ballesteros, Frank Schubert, Asish Singhai, Darío Álvarez Gutiérrez, and Reinhard Meyer. 3rd ECOOP Workshop on Object-Orientation and Operating Systems. In J. Malefant, S. Moisan, and A. Moreira, editors, *Object-Oriented Technology: ECOOP'2000 Workshop Reader*, number 1964 in Lecture Notes in Computer Science, Cannes, France. 2000. Springer Verlag.

Panel: The Next 700 Distributed Object Systems

Eric Jul[1], Andrew Black[2], Doug Lea[3], Robert Filman[4], and Ian Welch[5]

[1] DIKU, University of Copenhagen, Denmark eric@diku.dk
[2] Oregon Graduate Institute, USA black@cse.ogi.edu
[3] State University of New York at Oswego, NY, USA dl@cs.oswego.edu
[4] NASA Ames Research Center, USA rfilman@arc.nasa.gov
[5] University of Newcastle, United Kingdom i.s.welch@ncl.ac.uk

Abstract. The primary goal of the ECOOP 2001 Panel on The Next 700 Distributed Object Systems was to present a number of the essential characteristics of the next generation of distributed object systems as identified by participants in the ECOOP 2001 Workshop on The Next 700 Distributed Object Systems. Among many other topics, participants explored issues surrounding Peer-to-Peer computing, Failure handling, Context.

1 Introduction

The idea of the panel was to leverage off of the forward looking workshop on The Next 700 Distributed Object Systems[1] by presenting some of the main ideas and discussions that came out of the workshop. This short summary of some of the ideas and issues presented by the panel was written by the Panel Moderator, Eric Jul.

The workshop was a follow-up to previous ECOOP Workshops on various topics in distributed object systems. This year, instead of using a standard miniconference format, the workshop was focussed on a simple yet ambitious goal: to identify the essence of distributed object systems; the core elements that are likely to play some part in each of the next 700 distributed object systems. There is a separate workshop summary in the ECOOP 2001 workshop reader.

The workshop was structured to help identify these issues by splitting the day into three sessions:

- Short presentations, mainly on in-progress work, on different approaches to distributed computing.
- A chaotic session in which everyone contributed topics and ideas to dozens of posters, later summarizing on index cards. A total of about 25 subjects were identified.
- Dividing into three working groups, each focusing on a single topic.

This active workshop format worked just fine given that there were not too many participants (approximately 25). The participants enjoyed the extra time for discussions. And the subjects were interesting because the participants helped chose them.

Four of the participants in the workshop went onto the panel which was moderated by the workshop chair, Eric Jul. The panelists were:

---

[1] http://www.diku.dk/users/eric/Next700.html

Á. Frohner (Ed.): ECOOP 2001 Workshops, LNCS 2323, pp. 208–212, 2002.
© Springer-Verlag Berlin Heidelberg 2002

Andrew Black Oregon Graduate Institute
Robert Filman NASA Ames Research Center
Doug Lea State University of New York at Oswego
Ian Welch University of Newcastle

2 Issues Presented

2.1 Immutability

The first issue presented concerned the concept of Immutability. Immutable objects have a number of nice properties:

No aliasing or identity problems
May be copied or shared
No coherence problems because copies cannot be updated.
No concurrency control problems
Fault-tolerance
No cache invalidation required

Problems with immutability:

Systems must know about immutability to obtain advantages
Immutability declarations needed
Immutability definition Several different definitions possible: shallow? deep?
Initialization needs to be defined Objects cannot be immutable *during* initialization.

2.2 Failure

There are a number of unsolved problems with failures. In a distributed environment failures are common and need to be handled as an integral part of most applications.

There needs to be appropriate boundary specifications, e.g., including timing properties, functional properties, etc.

An observation: People can deal with most aspects of network failure and other "sociological" aspects of networking better than software can.

There needs to be recovery mechanisms—tools rather than solutions. For example, acceptance tests, rollback, or transactions.

An intriguing question addressed was: Are there ways that distributed languages and systems can encourage fault tolerance without requiring such mechanisms? One set of answers is to provide better support for immutability. An immutable object can never become inconsistent. Similarly, a stateless service (i.e., one whose behavior is solely a function of its arguments, not internal state) never needs recovery. These facts are known and exploited by every good distributed system programmer, yet very few systems intrinsically support these notions. Doing so would not only encourage good design, but would also allow better automated support.

2.3 Peer-to-Peer Computing

From one perspective, Peer-to-Peer (P2P) systems are just classic distributed object systems where every node can be both a client and a server. However, P2P systems also contain a number of characteristic features: They must be decentralized, self-organized, and scalable.

The main challenges identified for P2P computing are:

Identifying the level at which to be aware

Security and privacy Intrinsic use of encryption and security policies in basic protocols.

Naming, routing, trading, discovery The need for robust, decentralized protocols and services.

Quality of service Negotiations to obtain best service with respect to multiple criteria.

Consistency Reconciliating inconsistent data.

2.4 Mobility

One interesting observation is that during the past many years we have seen a development from an emphasis on *portabilityh* then *persistence* then *mobility*–and is the next step then *ubiquity*?

Many of the problems underlying mobility and ubiquity are old calssic problems but good solutions are still to be found.

2.5 Components and Middleware

Component architectures will prevail for many years. And the development, unfortunately, is leading to more and more bloated systems–at some point there will be a need to move from "How to do it all" to "How to do it small, fast, scalable".

2.6 Quality of Service Challenges

There will be an increeasing pressure to provide QoS as systems become ubituitous and that the emphasis is on multimedia, graphic interfaces, etc., all requiring a high degree of processing power and—very important—low latencies. Our more traditional systems with often very high variances in QoS must change.

2.7 Context

Context in distributed systems denotes the collection of physical resources (CPU, memory, bandwidth, IO, devices), available software services and components (and their current states), and the Location (both geographic and network) where a software component is executing.

Distributed and mobile code must increasingly be context-aware. Obvious cases include code running on devices such mobile phones, which may need to take evasive action when battery power becomes low or the unit it disconnected. However, even "ordinary" distributed code needs to be aware of contextual bindings such as the prevailing Time Zone.

From this perspective, it is surprising that neither research nor production distributed systems have provided anything beyond piecemeal support for context. A more general plan of attack is needed. While we did not propose a general framework, we established some basic questions that must be addressed by any approach, along with a few possible answers:

- How is context represented? Possible answers include directory structures (as found in LDAP and OS Registries), extensions of language scoping mechanisms, and others.
- How is context information made available? Candidates include queries and change-events. However, there may be a need to impose security policies for revealing some kinds of context information.
- How are contextual *requirements* of components represented and communicated? For example, components might specify minimum and maximum demands in a requires/provides framework.
- When and how does context change? Not every component can be allowed to change every contextual binding, implying the need for some sort of permission mechanism.
- How is context propagated? For example, how are contextual bindings merged across nodes of a distributed system? Some bindings will change across nodes, but others will stay the same.
- How do you categorize and control dynamics? Some contextual bindings are relatively static, and some may be almost constantly changing. Similarly, a component may be able to ignore some changes profiles requires/provides frameworks
- Can you find out about context of other components? Can you change it?
- How do components adapt to changes? Responses include ignoring changes, adapt to them, gracefully shutting down, and catastrophic failure.
- How does all this impact system design?

3 Beyond Objects

The panel also had some observations concerning the future after objects:

Some examples include more components but also possibly objects plus support for providing information about objects.

Some of the thinking is:

- Richer communication mechanisms
- Conversational protocols
- Agents
- Agencies

4 Conclusions

As did the workshop, the panel seemed to generate more questions than answers. The main goal of this panel was to present and discuss issues that will be faced by the next generation of distributed object systems. While we did not arrive at an exhaustive, definitive listing, we managed to bring to the forefront many of the issues that both practitioners and researchers will be grappling with over the coming years.

Poster Session

Viktória Zsók[1] and István Juhász[2]

[1] Eötvös Loránd University, Budapest, Hungary
zsv@inf.elte.hu
[2] University of Debrecen, Hungary
pici@it.math.klte.hu

Introduction

Posters provide an easy and informal means for presenting ongoing research to the ECOOP audience. This report contains eight abstracts of the posters that were on display during the entire conference. They were presented by the authors having the opportunity for personal connections with the attendees. The topics cover the breadth of object-oriented technology from theory to experiences in applications.

1 Business Process Oriented Component Retrieval

Thorsten Teschke
Oldenburg Research and Development Institute for
Computer Science Tools and Systems (OFFIS)
Escherweg 2, 26121 Oldenburg, Germany
thorsten.teschke@offis.de

Component software promises the development of software systems by composing and configuring pre-fabricated software artefacts. Recently, a number of component markets have emerged which offer a multitude of components. These components conform to various component models and range from fine-grained GUI components to coarse-grained business application software modules. In our work, we employ an object-oriented abstraction from the underlying component models and focus on coarse-grained components which offer relevant functionality in the business domain (cf. [1]).

Among the advantages of component software are the improved possibility to tailor software solutions to an enterprise's requirements by making use of the variety of components available on component markets. Current component markets, however, offer only very limited means of searching and assessing components. They do not regard the fact that customers often have captured their requirements in comprehensive business process models, and consequently the use of business process knowledge for the retrieval of components has been largely neglected in the past. We believe that the development of component-based business application software that is tailored to an enterprise's requirements necessitates the use of business process knowledge for the retrieval of components. In our work we are therefore interested in the development of a component retrieval service which supports the business process oriented search and assessment of components on component markets.

The approach presented on our poster consists of three parts:

Á. Frohner (Ed.): ECOOP 2001 Workshops, LNCS 2323, pp. 213–223, 2002.

1. **Component Description Language:** A prerequisite to the use of business process knowledge for component retrieval is the presence of comprehensive, business logic oriented component descriptions. Such component descriptions are required to reflect the types of information that may be processed by a component, the information processing functionality provided by a component, and the interaction sequences supported by a component. We will present our *component description language CDL* [3] which we employ for the business process oriented description of components and component-based application software systems.

2. **Component Retrieval Using Behavioural Subtyping:** Component retrieval basically is a software reuse problem. In the object-oriented paradigm, the question of software reuse deals with the substitutability of classes respectively their instances. Substitutability is usually captured by the concept of subtyping [4]. The idea of *behavioural subtyping* is to regard the behaviour of classes / objects either through pre- and postconditions (cf. [5]) or interaction protocols (cf. [2]) in addition to their method signatures. On our poster we will illustrate how we intend to transfer the idea of behavioural subtyping to business process oriented component retrieval: a business process which is to be executed in an enterprise represents a requirement (and thus the supertype) which should be supported by some component (representing the subtype) through the provision of adequate functionality.

3. **Standardized Terminology:** Successful business process oriented component retrieval depends on matches of the terms used in a business process model and those used in component descriptions. In order to be able to make sound decisions regarding matches between requests and component descriptions instead of relying on occasional matches a standardized terminology is required. We will outline how we intend to support component retrieval by means of *standardized* and *domain-specific terminologies*.

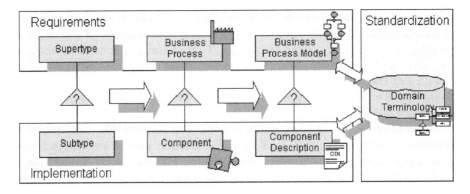

Fig. 1. Relationship between subtyping and business process oriented component retrieval

Figure 1 illustrates how we intend to transfer the idea of behavioural subtyping to business process oriented component retrieval using CDL component descriptions and standardized, domain-specific terminologies.

KOSOBAR Project Homepage:
`http://kosobar.offis.uni-oldenburg.de/`.

2 Access Graphs: Formalizing Static Access Control Mechanisms

Gilles Ardourel, Marianne Huchard
LIRMM, 161, rue Ada, 34392 Montpellier Cedex 5, France
{ardourel,huchard}@lirmm.fr

Encapsulation and modularity are supported by various access control mechanisms that manage implementation hiding and define interfaces adapted to different client profiles. Part of these access controls is *static*, which is an important feature, because many accesses are thus checked at compile time. Static access control mechanisms operate at different granularity levels (e.g. package, class, object) and rule different rights like accessing, inheriting or redefining a property (method or attribute), using, deriving or instantiating a class, and casting.

In spite of this significant place, there appears to be:

1. no consensual policy for static access control,
2. no language-independent formalism which would be general enough to represent any conceivable static access control mechanism,
3. many work to do in order to formally study static access control and propose useful handling tools.

Towards a Consensual General Policy

Concerning the first point, a study has shown that the main policies currently are the following:

- some languages (like Eiffel) explicitly mention admitted client classes for each property, while other languages (like C++, Java) associate predefined keywords (e.g. public, protected) to several elements (e.g. properties, classes, inheritance links),which determine categories of admitted clients (e.g all classes, subclasses),
- some languages (Eiffel, Smalltalk) consider differently an access from an instance to one of its own properties, and an access from an instance to a property of another instance, even if the two instances belong to the same class.

These policies influence important language features such as reusability or extensibility. One of our long-term objectives is to propose a simple and general policy which would ensure such features.

Formalizing Access Control

Concerning the second point, the diversity of mechanisms and syntactic structures relative to access control does not allow understanding and reasoning about access control mechanisms or access situations in a general way. To that end, we propose *access graphs*, a language-independent formalism. To describe roughly access graphs, vertices represent classes, and edges represent accesses allowed between instances. More precisely, an edge (c1,c2) is labelled by the set of properties of an instance of c2 that an instance of c1 can access (intra-instances and inter-instances accesses are differentiated).

Applications

Concerning the third point, the *access graph*-based formalism is useful to base theoretical work about access control mechanisms as well as software engineering tools. The intuitive aspect of access graphs is an help in understanding access controls for a program and in modelling access controls at the design step. Access graphs allowed us to formally characterize and discuss Java, Eiffel, Smalltalk and partly Ada95 and C++ mechanisms. Whether a programming language is fitted or not for implementing design decisions concerning access control can be determined thanks to such characterizations. Access graphs also help in reasoning about these languages (e.g. to know if they respect some rules as subtyping) and translating programs from a language to another. Our current work consists in defining several software engineering tools that help in editing, extracting from code or verifying access graphs and explicating access errors.

Additional information:
`http://www.lirmm.fr/~ardourel/Rech/RR-Lirmm01072.pdf`.

3   Specifying the Usage and Composition of Software Components

Pascal Rapicault
Laboratoire I3S (CNRS), 930, Route des Colles, B.P. 145,
06903 Sophia-Antipolis Cedex, France
Object Technology International, Inc., 1181 NC Amstelveen, The Netherlands
`pascal.rapicault@essi.fr`

Even the best designed components are complex to use and to compose.

Just by looking at a component, it is impossible to guess how to use the different methods making its interface, and especially to guess in which order those methods need to be called. Moreover some components require other components to work with. However, the relation binding components together, and the flow of messages between them is not clearly expressed (what calls what, which callback is expected, etc.). This vagueness makes component writing and assembling difficult. For example, when a program badly assembles components or simply misuses a component, it may by luck contains some compile time errors, but also runtime errors difficult to understand.

To minimize those problems, users need to have information about how to use components, and how they cooperate with others. Our proposal consists in adding (meta) information to a component. We call it **behavioral views**.

Behavioral views describe how components cooperate with others from a "client" and/or a "composition" perspective. They focus on messages send and how they flow between components. Behavioral views also allow to express multi-threaded behavior and exceptions.

The client point of view explains how to use a component from a user perspective. For a given component, it indicates in which order components methods must be invoked.

Each method comes with a list of messages it sends to other components. This view allows to see if a component requires other resources to work (in matter of component) and if so, to detail how it uses them (initialisation sequence, dependency during execution, . . .).

The composition point of view explains how a component makes use of another one. The methods appearing in this view belong to the component being used. All these methods come with a list of expected callbacks indicating which messages the used component is expected to call. This view puts requirements on a component used by the component containing this view.

To briefly sum up, given a component A using a component B and C behavioral views are:

- Component A has a client view, a composition view on B and one on C
- Component B has a client view,
- Component C has a client view

Points of views are represented by a StateCharts like graphical notation called Sync-Charts (Synchronous Charts)[6]. Its most important advantage is a precise semantics based on the Esterel programming language. Views can be integrated in any component model since they also have a textual form (an Esterel program [7], or a system of boolean equations).

Beyond the ability of documenting behavioral properties of a component and of highlighting interaction patterns between components, behavioral views allow to check and debug the use of a component [8], and the correctness of a group of collaborating components. Since Esterel model allows model checking, we are currently working on a usage of checkers to perform compile time checks.

4 GUIML – Creating Dynamic GUI Objects Using XML

Lajos Kollár
Department of Information Technology,
Institute of Mathematics and Informatics, University of Debrecen
P.O. Box 12, H-4010, Debrecen, Hungary
kollarl@it.math.klte.hu

Due to the world-wide expansion of interest in the Web in the past few years, a new strategy for application development has appeared in the IT world: Web modeling. This strategy covers the whole process of developing Web applications and places emphasis on designing user interfaces, as well. Web modeling uses XML as description language which is suitable for defining markup languages.

Nowadays, the majority of applications interact with the user by the help of Graphics User Interfaces (GUIs). Such an interface is a composition of windows, buttons, listboxes, textfields, etc. However, this composition is 'wired into' the text of program source which causes that applications become hardly customizable and they can be altered with a lot of difficulties.

An interface to a dynamic Web application can change from time to time (depending on users' needs) which infers the (relatively) frequent modification of the source code. However, if multiplatform environments are addressed, then this modification (and recompilation) should be made on all the supported platforms, even if different programming languages are used. This consumes both a lot of work and time unnecessarily.

The need has been arosen for finding a solution to uniform handling of the structure of application's information base and the user interfaces visualizing them. Pieces of information required to build up the presentation can be collected on the server side so that clients can access those data.

GUIML, stands for Graphics User Interface Markup Language, is a platform and programming language neutral way of describing user interfaces. A GUIML document contains the definition of an user interface. Since GUIML is an XML-based language it makes the internalization of user interfaces very easy, whereas it includes the possibility of sharing the user interface definition among developer teams. GUIML helps us avoid anomalies, reduces the time of building user interfaces, improves portability of application and, in addition, it fits well into the whole process of Web application development.

Description of GUIML:
http://www.klte.hu/~kollarl/ecoop/.

5   PACC – Predictable Assembly from Certifiable Components

Scott A. Hissam, Judith Stafford, Kurt Wallnau
Software Engineering Institute
Carnegie Mellon University
Pittsburgh, PA 15213 USA
shissam,jas,kcw@sei.cmu.edu

The use of software components in the assembly of larger systems is a clear and visible industry trend. More often than not, the practice of assembling systems from components is fraught with trial and error. This is due, in part, because the properties of a component are not well known to us during composition resulting in mismatch. PACC is developing a technology that supports composing systems from precompiled components in such a way that the quality of the system can be accurately predicted before acquiring/building its constituents.

Compositional reasoning requires more knowledge about the behavioral and extra-functional properties of components than has traditionally been provided in component interfaces. For instance, it is not possible to reason about maximum end-to-end latency in a system unless one knows something about the maximum end-to-end latency of input-output pathways in the constituent components. Our approach to predicting properties of component-based systems is to study three questions and their inter-dependencies:

1. What types of system quality attributes are developers interested in predicting during design?
2. What types of analysis techniques exist to support reasoning about these quality attributes?

3. What type of information must components supply about themselves in order to make this information available in support of these analysis techniques and how is that information measured?

These three questions form a feedback loop: the types of compositional reasoning that can be accomplished depend on the types of component properties that can be measured. Thus, in the end the types of quality attributes a developer can reason about depend on the types of analysis techniques that are available for both compositional reasoning and implementation property measurement. This feedback loop will provide a foundation for a sustainable and transitionable improvement in predicting the quality attributes of systems, and confidence in the software components that make up these systems.

Our session will present up to the minute, work in progress results from PACC in establishing a technical foundation for continuous improvement in our ability to characterize and reason about the qualities of an assembled system at design-time and our understanding of the component properties that contribute to these system qualities.

References:

http://www.sei.cmu.edu/pacc/.

6   JMangler – A Framework for Load-Time Transformation of Java Class Files

Günter Kniesel, Pascal Costanza
University of Bonn, Institute of Computer Science III,
Römerstr. 164, D-53117 Bonn, Germany
kniesel,costanza@cs.uni-bonn.de
Michael Austermann
SCOOP GmbH, Im Ahlefeld 23, D-53819 Neunkirchen-Seelscheid, Germany
maustermann@scoop-gmbh.de

6.1   Introduction

Tight development schedules and high quality expectations of customers create an ever increasing pressure for (re)use of readily available third-party components. At the same time, rapid changes in markets, legislation and enterprise strategies result in *unforeseen changes of requirements* that a software has to meet. The *inability to adapt* third-party components whose *source code is unavailable* to unforeseen changes of requirements effectively prevents software development teams from achieving the necessary degree of reuse.

The Java Class File Format is the first widely-used binary format that contains enough symbolic information to enable automated analysis and transformation. However, transformation of Java Class Files, is complicated by the fact that Java allows the name and contents of dynamically loaded classes to be determined at run-time, via reflection. Code that has been loaded already cannot be transformed anymore. So the only point where it is possible to determine *all* classes that are actually *used* by a program and adapt them as needed is the dynamic class loading process.

6.2   Class Loader and JVM Independence

Current proposals for load-time transformation of Java classes are either dependent on the use of a specific class loader or dependent on a specific JVM implementation. This is not due to an inadequacy of the Java platform but to a wrong choice of the level where to hook into the Java Class Loader Architecture. JMangler follows an approach that ensures both, class loader and JVM independence, by providing a modified version of the class ClassLoader. Because the modified behaviour is enforced for every subclass of *ClassLoader*, JMangler is activated whenever an application-specific class is loaded. Figure 2 illustrates this approach.

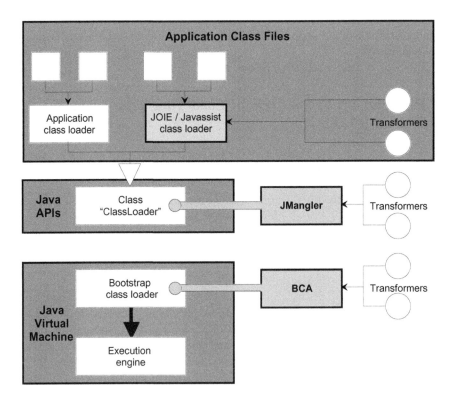

Fig. 2. Integration of JMangler into Java's class loader architecture, compared to previous approaches

6.3   Composition of Transformers

JMangler is the first load-time transformation tool that explicitly allows transformers to be treated as components. The main challenge in this respect is to enable unanticipated composition of independently developed transformers.

In general, there is no satisfactory means to safely combine transformers that have been developed independently, without being specifically designed for joint use. One problem of unanticipated composition is the possible occurrence of mutual dependencies among transformers or among transformed classes. Because the framework cannot determine whether a given set of transformers are mutually dependent it must always be prepared for the worst case. In the case of mutual dependencies, applying each transformation only once may result in potentially incomplete programs. Therefore transformations must be iterated until a fixed point is reached, that is until no transformer requests any further changes.

Unfortunately, iterating transformations that have been composed in different orders yields different fixpoints, in the general case. However, it can be shown that independent development and automatic combination, without human advice, is possible for a significant class of interface transformations.

The distinction between interface and code transformations is reflected in the transformation process, which is partitioned into two phases. In the first phase, each interface transformer analyzes the classes on target, decides which transformations are to be carried out and requests these transformations from JMangler. The framework checks the validity of requested transformations, chooses the order in which legal transformations are to be applied and performs the transformations. This process is repeated until no further interface modification requests are issued. In the second phase, only code transformers are activated. They are executed exactly in the order indicated in the transformer configuration file that is passed as a parameter to JMangler.

A detailed description of JMangler is given in [9]. Complete information on JMangler (papers, tutorial, download version, source code) can be found at `http://javalab.cs.uni-bonn.de/research/jmangler/`.

7   Image Objects in Object-Relational Database Management Systems

Krisztián Veréb
Department of Information Technology,
Institute of Mathematics and Informatics, University of Debrecen
P.O. Box 12, H-4010, Debrecen, Hungary
`sparrow@math.klte.hu`

Storing of image objects in databases cannot be considered a completely solved problem nowadays. The question is how image information can be modelled to be able to stored and queried very easily. The restriction of relational databases has to be exceeded to achieve these ideas and use object-oriented tools.

Every image is an object with attributes and behaviour irrespectively of its representation or its function. So the first task is to create the object model of images. We show how the image information can be modelled. The second one is to adopt this object model into an Object-Relational Database to co-operate with existing components. During this process a lot of problems could arise. How can the inheritance be modelled if the database management system does not support it? What kind of behaviour could be inherited? So the main goal is to adopt the object-oriented image model into an Object-Relational Database with inheritance to ease the queries and to create an object-oriented image data cartridge.

We use the Oracle interMedia as the base of the development and show how an Image Processing Tool (IPT) object hierarchy can be created to solve our problems. The object hierarchy is the most important part of our IPT cartridge. The IPT models the image representation techniques used in most cases such as chain coding, quadtree and bitmap matrix representations. A control object and a static control package is given as well to control the processing algorithms and ease the queries. The cartridge technology using object-oriented approaches is the most suitable way to implement such research results.

References:
`http://www.klte.hu/~verebk.`

8   From COBOL to OOP

Markus Knasmüller
BMD Systemhaus Ges.m.b.H. Steyr
Sierninger Str. 190, 4400 Steyr, Austria
`knasmueller@bmd.at`

Introducing object-oriented programming to old-style programmers is a rather hard task. This poster presents some experiences from BMD Steyr, Austrians leading producer of accountancy software. BMD Steyr has a software department with more than 40 developers; most of them were maintaining a character-based Cobol-product. This product – an integrated system supporting all business aspects – is used by more than 10000 customers including Austrians biggest tax consultants and some of Austrians biggest companies. Now they are implementing the NTCS project, a complete reengineering of the product using object-orientation.

The most important point at the beginning of such a project is to turn the COBOL programmers to object-oriented programmers and there the best method is education, education, and once more education.

We decided to divide the necessary knowledge about object-oriented programming into three parts and offered three courses with weekly lectures and exercises. The lectures were rather similar to those that the author was involved at the Johannes Kepler University of Linz (Prof. Mössenböck). But some things were changed. First, we removed some theoretical materials and all academic terms, like ontology. Furthermore we used Object-Pascal as the programming language instead of Oberon which was used at the university, because we had already decided that we would take Object-Pascal in our company. Since Oberon and Pascal are very similar languages, changing the examples was rather easy.

In the first part of our object-oriented programming course we learned all the necessary things that make a programmer excellent. We spoke about structured types, type safety, procedures, local variables, pointers and most important data abstraction. Of course all this was not really new for the participants, but their Cobol environment did not really support it.

Afterwards we introduced *classes*. Classes are rather similar to abstract data types, so we started by explaining the syntactical differences between an abstract data type and a class. Using this process we overcame the fear about the term "object-oriented programming". We showed a new syntax for the already known abstract data type and only afterwards the participants found out that they are now working with objects.

Later we introduced *inheritance* and *dynamic binding*. Inheritance was simply explained as type extension. A subclass is an extension of a base type, i.e. it *inherits* the fields and methods of the base type and may declare additional fields and methods for its own. The explanation of dynamic binding was hard work, but based on the explanation of inheritance, we could explain that the compatibility between a subclass and its base class makes it possible for a variable at run time to contain objects of various types that react differently to a message.

In the last part of the course we explained the different classes of the Delphi class library. Based on the already known facts about object-oriented programming, this was rather simple and could mostly be done by the participants themselves by reading the manual.

More information about the course is available in the book "From COBOL to OOP", published by the German dpunkt.verlag and at
`http://www.ssw.uni-linz.ac.at/Staff/MK.htm.`

References

1. P. Herzum, O. Sims: *Business Component Factory*, John Wiley and Sons, 2000.
2. O. Nierstrasz: *Regular Types for Active Objects*, in O. Nierstrasz, D. Tsichritzis (eds.): Object-Oriented Software Composition, Prentice Hall, 1995.
3. T. Teschke, J. Ritter: *Towards a Foundation of Component-Oriented Software Reference Models*, Proceedings of net.objectdays2000, Erfurt, Germany, 2000.
4. P. Wegner, B. Zdonik: *Inheritance as an Incremental Modification Mechanism or What Like Is and Isn't Like*, in S. Gjessing, K. Nygaard (eds.): Proceedings of ECOOP '88, Oslo, Springer-Verlag, Lecture Notes in Computer Science 322, 1988.
5. A. Zaremski, J. Wing: *Specification Matching of Software Components*, in: ACM Transactions on Software Engineering and Methodology, Volume 6, Issue 4, 1997.
6. André Charles: *Representation and analysis of reactive behaviors: a synchronous approach*, in CESA, pp. 19-29, 1996.
7. Frédéric Boussinot, Robert De Simone: *Another Look at Real Time Programming*, Proc. of the IEEE, vol. 79, pp 1293-1304, 1991.
8. Pascal Rapicault, Frédéric Mallet: *Behavioral specification of java component using synccharts*, in Workshop on pervasive component systems – ECOOP, 2000.
9. G. Kniesel, P. Costanza, M. Austermann: JMangler – A Framework for Load-Time Transformation of Java Class Files, *Proceedings of IEEE International Workshop on Source Code Analysis and Manipulation (SCAM 2001)*, Florence, Italy, November 2001. To be published by IEEE Computer Society Press, http://computer.org.

Author Index

Lecture Notes in Computer Science

For information about Vols. 1–2255
please contact your bookseller or Springer-Verlag